TRICKSTERS IN THE MADHOUSE

Tricksters in the Madhouse

Lakers vs. Globetrotters, 1948

JOHN CHRISTGAU

University of Nebraska Press
Lincoln & London

© 2004 by the Board of Regents
of the University of Nebraska
All rights reserved
Manufactured in the
United States of America

∞

Library of Congress
Cataloging-in-Publication Data
Christgau, John.
Tricksters in the Madhouse : Lakers vs. Globetrotters, 1948 / John Christgau.
p. cm.
Includes bibliographical references.
ISBN 0-8032-1526-6 (hardcover : alk. paper)
1. Minneapolis Lakers (Basketball team)—History. 2. Harlem
Globetrotters—History. 3. Sports rivalries—United States. I. Title.
GV885.42.M56C47 2004
796.323'09776'579—dc22 2004005102

Set in Janson by Bookcomp, Inc.
Designed by Roger Buchholz.
Printed by Thomson-Shore, Inc.

*The best band in the world
is the clown's band in the circus.*

Louis Armstrong

Contents

I. First Quarter

1. The Race   3
2. Ma Piersall   11
3. The Kangaroo Kid   20
4. Babe   29
5. Goose   37
6. Ermer   43
7. The Fastest Runner on Sixty-first Street   50

II. Second Quarter

8. Blackie   57
9. The King of Basketball   65
10. The Crisco Kid   72
11. Olson's Terrible Swedes   78
12. Sambo   86

III. Halftime

13. Johnny and Abe   95

IV. Third Quarter

14. Bucky   105
15. Pop   113
16. Marques   122

V. Fourth Quarter

17. Ted   135
18. The Wee Ice Mon   141
19. David and Goliath   148
20. The Father, the Son, the Holy Ghost   155
21. The Shot   162
22. Sweetwater   168

VI. Over Time

23. Shaq   177
24. Rigo   182

Notes   191
Sources and Acknowledgments   217

TRICKSTERS IN THE MADHOUSE

I

FIRST QUARTER

1

The Race

The floodlights over the floor of Chicago Stadium hang like tulip bells from long cords, and a blue fog of cigarette smoke swirls beneath the lights. From the third tier of seats, above the smoke and lights, the players gathered for the center jump appear as colorful as images drawn in crayon. The Minneapolis team wears the colors of the Swedish flag—royal blue piping on their shorts and the word "Lakers" in golden yellow across their jerseys. Their opponents wear shorts with broad red stripes. Their jerseys are deep blue, with gold stars sprinkled around the name "Harlem Globe Trotters."

The Lakers' center is George Mikan, a towering hulk who hardly seems to fit in a jump circle that from those high seats looks like a tiny bull's-eye on the court. There is little room left for the Globetrotters' Reece "Goose" Tatum, who is half a foot shorter than Mikan and standing beanpole stiff, his freakishly long arms pinned to his body as if he is being squeezed with Mikan in a phone booth. Goose's bizarre pose suggests he is about to launch into one of the jump ball antics for which he is famous. Perhaps he'll snatch the ball from the startled official, then go off at a flatfoot sprint for an easy basket. Perhaps he'll hold Mikan's pants so that he jumps out of them when the official throws up the ball. Perhaps he'll rearrange the Lakers on the court in a comic tableau guaranteed to lead to an easy basket for the Globetrotters.

But not tonight. Even though the Globetrotters have done their usual "Magic Circle" routine, with six players choreographing their passing and ball-juggling tricks to the whistled music of "Sweet Georgia Brown," tonight is serious basketball, and Goose crouches suddenly. He lifts one foot, plants it behind himself, then looks up and waits. Mikan crouches also. The official, whose coal black pants and black-and-white striped shirt seem like an incongruous center for the rest of the bright colors, crouches slightly himself and prepares for the throw. For a split second, everyone freezes.

It is an oddly static beginning for a game that can explode with furious action. It is also a far cry from those early days of basketball when teams were so warlike and ferocious in their play that to start the action officials tossed the ball from the safety of the sidelines to "cagers" inside a net cage.

Now, however, the official leans close to the two posed jumpers, rolls the ball so that one hand is on the bottom, the other on the side to steady it, then dips his body as he tosses the ball in perfectly straight upward flight between the two men.

Mikan and Goose jump together. For a moment it seems that Mikan's height advantage will mean just an easy tap to one of his teammates. But at the peak of its flight, the ball hangs as Goose rises higher and higher, as if he is floating up toward the lights, and his long arm stretches past Mikan's and tips the ball to husky forward Babe Pressley. Pressley dribbles awkwardly into the Globetrotters' frontcourt, as if any second he will lose control of the ball, as if the ball has a will of its own and he is stumbling after it, trying to capture it. It is hardly the ballet of slick ballhandling for which the Globetrotters are world renowned, and when Pressley finally has the ball in hand twenty-five feet from the basket, he has to pivot to avoid the two Lakers defenders who are chasing after him, hoping to steal the ball. He whirls a second time and finishes facing the basket. Still covered by two defenders, he cups the ball in one wrist and with a flair meant to reclaim his grace, he pumps his left knee like a drum major and flips a shovel pass directly behind him to his teammate, guard Ermer Robinson.

The huge crowd roars with pleasure. The slick pass is the realization of the antic promises of Goose Tatum's comic phone-booth stance in the jump circle. But Robinson appears not to hear the laughter. His face so stern it could be mistaken for mock seriousness, he poses with the ball just in front of his nose, drops his head slightly as he takes a bead on the basket, then steps with his right foot as he releases the long, one-hand shot.

It is too flat, skidding along beneath the smoky scud hanging over the floor. The shot glances off the front rim, caroms untouched onto

4

the floor between scrambling players, and then is snatched by the Lakers' Jim Pollard and Herm Schaefer. Pollard relinquishes the ball to Schaefer, then gallops downcourt after his teammates. Schaefer walks slowly up the court, banging the ball with a slow dribble that in the sudden quiet makes it clear that no matter how quickly the Harlem Globetrotters can set up and shoot, the Minneapolis Lakers will take their own sweet time.

The night before, a fiery meteor explosion lit up the night sky of the Midwest. It might have been taken as a cosmic bulletin for the game, and in the sudden warm spell that hit Chicago, fans had begun lining up for admission to Chicago Stadium at 3 a.m. By midafternoon, strong chilly winds off Lake Michigan made the flags along the roofline of Chicago Stadium crack like gunshots. Still, no one left the ticket line, and by game time, the stadium announcer reported that the standing-room-only crowd of 17,823 fans was the largest ever to watch a professional basketball game in Chicago.[1]

It wasn't just the standing-room-only crowd that was unusual. There were black fans everywhere now, and in that high third tier, the seats were filled with young black and white faces, some of whom had skipped school that Thursday to stand in line all day for cheap, seventy-five-cent tickets. Part of it was the appeal of the Globetrotters, whose "Harlem" designation on their jerseys didn't disguise the fact that they were really Chicago's team and drew huge crowds whenever they appeared there. But it was also the appeal of this particular game. The first-year Minneapolis Lakers were tearing up the National Basketball League (NBL) and were being touted as the best basketball team ever. Oh, there might have been teams in the past with one star or even five good players who ran motion offenses that turned like the gears of a clock. But few teams ever had two such powerful basketball figures as the Lakers' towering George Mikan, who had made his college reputation in Chicago, and leaping Jim Pollard, who was even better than Mikan, some insisted. Defending the two was like trying to plug the leaks in a pipeline. Whatever you did to stop one, baskets poured from the other.

There is no doubt that it is either Mikan or Pollard the Lakers will turn to immediately as Schaefer enters the frontcourt, then crosses to Pollard's left forward position, still walking the ball with a slow dribble. Schaefer's two-hand chest pass to Pollard is leisurely and deliberate.

Pollard receives the pass with two hands at his chest. He turns and faces Mikan, who is at the low post, using both arms as bars to keep Goose Tatum behind him. Pollard lifts the ball over his head, makes one jerk fake of the pass, pauses, waits for Mikan to bring his hands up, then snaps a high bullet pass. Mikan reaches for it with both hands, but it slips through his fingers and bangs the pipe standards that support the basket. The basket shivers, and the sudden groan from the fans reflects a disappointment so keen even the building seems to be quivering in distress.

Globetrotters' ball. No score.

Fay Young, sports editor for the *Chicago Defender*, the influential black newspaper whose masthead celebrated itself as the "World's Greatest Weekly," sat at the scorer's table beside a young intern. Young had been looking forward to the game for weeks, as a match-up between two great teams. But now he thought to deliver a few journalistic cautions to the intern about objectivity. "You don't care who wins," he said. "The contest is what counts, the drama of the battle."

The intern nodded. He wasn't about to contradict the veteran Fay Young, whose graying hair, square glasses, and smoldering pipe gave him the dignity of an incontrovertible sage.

But Young hadn't won his convictions easily, he confessed to the intern. And as the Globetrotters brought the ball up court after the Lakers' turnover, he recalled the time as a young reporter when he had given strong advice to a black football coach whose quarter-back had repeatedly called terrible plays.

"That bonehead you've got at quarterback," Young had raged at the coach, "ought to be in the jailhouse!"

The coach had taken a moment to spit tobacco juice casually. "*I'm* doing the quarterbacking," he finally said softly, then spit again. "If there are bonehead plays, I'm to blame."

Young had crawled away, the lesson stuck in his head forever. "From that day to this," he told the intern, "I sit and look. I jot down what is news, and let it go at that. I do no more quarterbacking."[2]

Fay Young's connection to the *Chicago Defender*, which had been arguing for the betterment of African Americans for almost fifty years, suggested he was rooting for the Globetrotters, despite his call for sportswriting objectivity. That partisanship was the legacy of Robert S. Abbott, the *Defender*'s founder, who had started the newspaper in his Chicago landlord's kitchen in 1905 on a budget of twenty-five cents, which was just enough for three hundred copies of a four-page weekly.

From the start, Abbott attacked segregation, using red ink to highlight stories of rape and lynching. It was five years before he could hire his first full-time paid employee. By 1915 the circulation was a quarter million and extended beyond Chicago. Pullman porters carried the *Defender* on trains into the South, where it was passed from person to person and read aloud in barbershops, in churches, and on street corners. Eventually, the *Defender* had a Chicago and a national edition, with a readership of over half a million.

It was Robert Abbott's *Defender*, depicting the North as a land of opportunity and promise, that helped bring one-and-a-half million southern blacks to Chicago. In Abbott's mind, and on the pages of his newspaper, they were "the Race . . . designated for great things." In sports, they were "Race men," and Abbott was dedicated to equality for all "Race men" in sports.[3]

Frank A. Young joined the *Defender* in 1912 as a volunteer. He wrote his sports stories nights and weekends while he worked as a dining-car waiter on the Northwestern Railroad. A year later he signed a regular contract with the *Defender* at $15 a week, and because of his habit of signing his stories with the initials of his name, he was quickly tagged with the nickname "Fay."

Underpaid and overworked, Fay Young waited tables, freelanced as a sports publicist, refereed college football, and sponsored boxers in order to supplement his meager income as a sportswriter. He talked very little about his own athletic past, and his sportswriting was never an instrument for reliving his own athletic glories. It was instead a force for integration, especially major league baseball. But from the *Defender*'s very beginning, when Robert Abbott had established a newsboy basketball team to boost circulation, basketball had been in the blood of the newspaper, and when young Abe Saperstein formed his New York Harlem Globetrotters, he immediately began hectoring Fay Young and the *Chicago Defender* for publicity. Young quickly decided that Saperstein was a pest and tried to ignore him. When that didn't work, he tried to discourage him. Basketball,

Young argued, was too new to have an audience among blacks, who preferred boxing and baseball.[4]

Young's arguments failed to discourage the aggressive Saperstein, and the *Defender* finally caved in and began to publicize the Globetrotters. At the same time, Young began to see the importance of basketball in the landscape of integration, and when the New York Rens came to Chicago for the first time in 1929, Young could hardly hide his own excitement when he wrote, "Interest [in basketball] on the South Side has reached fever heat."[5] It wasn't just what he described as the Rens "dash and pep" that was so exciting. This was the same African American team that had beaten the all-white New York Celtics at the height of their glory, and the whole world had been forced to take notice of what "Race men" could do on a basketball floor.

Eventually, it was Saperstein's powerful Globetrotters, whom Young had initially discouraged, who had the dash and pep that Young admired. Their cleverness on basketball courts worldwide and their numerous victories against all comers would do more for integration, Young felt, than hours of tedious speeches on race. "Damnfoolishness," he called such speeches, especially when they were delivered at the ballpark. "Folks came to see a ball game," he wrote, and speeches were like ice water dashed in their faces.[6]

The lesson was in the game itself. And Saperstein's celebrated Globetrotters were "Race men" whose basketball victories were the best polemic in the world for repudiating the racists who argued against integration in athletics. After years of covering sporting events, Fay Young knew as well as anybody the arguments that racists gave for keeping blacks and whites separated on the playing field.

The bigots began by quoting Thomas Jefferson, who had once said that "Negroes were inferior to whites in the endowment of both mind and body." If that wasn't enough to seal the argument, they could also quote Abraham Lincoln, who insisted, "There is a physical difference between the white and black races." By the end of the century, so-called scientific studies claimed to prove what those differences were: blacks had limited reasoning power, inferior muscle strength, a love of ostentation, as well as small lungs and an inferior nervous system. It meant that blacks had poor endurance and were too lazy and shiftless to be good competitors. There were other studies meant to prove that blacks were deficient in the qualities that made for great athletes. Even the "scientific studies" that eventually conceded there were star athletes among the "Negro race" discussed their heavy bones and small lungs. It was hardly the right anatomy for the demands of basketball.

Then in 1941 Dean Cromwell, who had coached the American Olympic team and Jesse Owens in Berlin in 1936, wrote that the black athlete excelled in certain athletic events because he was closer to primitive man than the white man. It meant that he could box, yes, but only because the sport required the brute strength of the jungle savage. Otherwise, African Americans had neither the courage nor the endurance for athletic competition. Furthermore, well-intentioned white philanthropy, which had helped blacks succeed elsewhere, had left them without the competitive will to succeed at sports. Meanwhile, in literature African Americans were depicted as fools and sycophants. In movies they were portrayed as buffoons and servants. They were musical and superstitious and superreligious, and their suppressed anger made them deceptive and potentially violent. Integration, particularly on a basketball court where intense battle lines were already drawn, only invited violence. As long as the races were kept athletically apart, the separatists could go right on arguing that blacks, with their lack of competitive will and their small lungs and inferior nervous systems, had neither the stamina nor the deft touch as shooters to prevail against superior whites on a basketball court. They surely wouldn't have the skills to defeat the powerful Minneapolis Lakers.[7]

The free-throw lane is only six feet wide, to which is appended a free-throw circle. The circle and the lane together form the shape of a lollypop keyhole, which is why it is called "the key." Though Goose Tatum could slip through the lane with one or two long steps, he sets up now on the free-throw line at the top of the key, his back to the basket, George Mikan directly behind him. Mikan makes no effort to prevent Goose from setting up there or receiving the ball, and he stands almost passively behind the Globetrotters' center, waiting and watching. It is only a matter of seconds, and a few whipped passes on the perimeter, before the ball flashes into Goose, who protects it now from Mikan's pawing reach by clamping it to his belly, the ball the size of a grapefruit in his huge hands. Two, three, four

9

Globetrotters whiz by Goose, circle around, whiz by again, all the jerseys on the floor, offense and defense alike, turning like a colorful pinwheel, around and around, until nobody is cutting anymore and Goose is alone, only Mikan a threat to him.

Goose puts down a dribble, intending to do exactly what, nobody knows for sure—his slow windmill hook shot? Some disappearing ball trick? Slip around Mikan for an easy layup?

He does none of these. One dribble sideways and he stops and tries to pass the ball to a teammate by bouncing it through the legs of a Lakers defender whose back is turned. But in the shuffle of legs the trick pass is deflected, and the ball rolls into a Lakers' hands. He picks it up and nods at Goose, as if to say, "Thank you. And so much for your tricks."

Lakers' ball. Still no score.

2

Ma Piersall

February. For Anglo-Saxons it was the "Mud Month," and by February 1948 in the United States, it was the perfect metaphor for the dirty injustices being perpetrated on the streets. Chicago police were still looking for the six white men who had jumped from their car on Halsted Street and beaten a black man to death with a baseball bat. On Calumet Avenue, a family of four was described as living in a state of hysteria after a mob of 150 howling white hoodlums gathered in front of their home with burning torches and bricks. In Lakeview, Georgia, the Klan performed a fire dance in a show of racist force. That same Klan threatened the life of the Lakeview High School basketball coach for his opposition to them. The coach, an ex-marine, countered with his own show of force by posing for an Associated Press photo that appeared throughout the country. It pictured him standing in front of his team bench with a six-gun tucked into his belt.[1]

It was unsettling to see the great American game of basketball corrupted by guns. Whether it was that February picture of a gun-toting basketball coach or, more likely, Harry S. Truman's deepening convictions about civil rights, the president decided he had had enough. And at almost exactly the moment the ball rose for the center jump that began the Lakers-Globetrotters contest in Chicago, Truman stepped to a microphone at the annual Jefferson-Jackson Day dinner at the Mayflower Hotel in Washington DC and reminded the huge audience of his commitment to the passage of his new civil rights program.

He had good reason to have other things on his mind. Gandhi had been assassinated. There was the troublesome issue of how to partition the new state of Palestine. In early February Czech Communists had seized the country in a coup. The Russians had stopped road traffic into Berlin, in the first act of what would be a long cold war. Elsewhere, the Soviets were committing diplomatic treachery as ominous as Hitler and his Nazis in 1938–39. So what did a little domestic turmoil amount to when the whole world was convulsing?

But what was most on President Truman's mind in February 1948 was the issue of American civil rights. For months African American parents in the nation's capital had been keeping their children at home, protesting Jim Crow practices in public schools. A black veteran, dragged off a bus by city officials in Batesburg, South Carolina, had been beaten and blinded. Four African Americans had been shot in the back by mob gunfire in Monroe, Georgia, and nothing had been done about it. Black soldiers returning to Mississippi after the war had been dumped out of army trucks and beaten. In Washington DC, a handful of angry southern politicians were threatening a congressional filibuster to defeat fair employment legislation. Even the Supreme Court seemed to be aligning itself with segregationists by refusing to order the University of Oklahoma to admit a black law student.

"I shall fight to end evils like this," Truman had vowed and then laid out his ten-point plan for civil rights, calling for federal legislation against segregated schools, poll taxes, discrimination in employment, and lynching. Truman tried to make it clear that he wasn't asking for social equality. It was equality of *opportunity* he was fighting for. Still, southern Democrats had met privately with the president to try to talk him out of his civil rights plan. But he insisted that his stomach had turned over when he discovered that black soldiers in Mississippi had been beaten.

Those same southern Democrats who had met with him now refused to show up for the Jefferson-Jackson Day dinner at the Mayflower Hotel. Senator Olin Johnson of South Carolina explained his absence by complaining that he and his wife feared they would be seated next to a "Nigra." Across the country, in Little Rock, Arkansas, half of the 850 Democrats who had gathered to listen to Truman's speech walked out when his voice first came over the loudspeaker system.

Truman said they were all "reactionaries" and likened them to "floogie birds" who flew backward and carried a sign that said, "I don't care where I'm going. I just want to see where I've been."[2]

The sarcasm only deepened the rift. "Damn democracy," southern governors warned, "if it means the uplift of the Negro." Mississippi Democrats threatened to withdraw from the Democratic Party and issued a call for "all true white Jefferson Democrats" to protest Truman's civil rights plan. Representative John Rankin complained that Truman was trying "to ram the platform of the Communist party down the people of the United States."[3] Governor Strom Thurmond of South Carolina pledged to defend white supremacy. Virginia's Senator Harry Byrd protested that federal civil rights laws would eventually lead to a dictatorship. "Hitler and Stalin," he insisted, "did this very same thing."[4] In arguing that lynchings were matters that should be handled by the states, editorialists of the *Birmingham News* felt that progress was being made in the South. "In the last ten years," they wrote, "only 37 persons have been lynched."[5]

Racial Pollyannas were pointing to Joe Louis in boxing, Buddy Young in football, and Jackie Robinson in baseball as proof that the athletic world was color blind. But the truth was that the racial divide in sports was still deep. As fans lined up to see the Lakers-Globetrotters game, Branch Rickey himself, who had signed Robinson with the Dodgers, charged that major league club owners had met at a hotel not far from Chicago Stadium in 1946 and voted to ban blacks. Led by Chicago Cubs owner Phil Wrigley, the owners denied any such vote had ever taken place, but segregation critics were incensed.[6]

Those critics didn't have to look far to find segregation elsewhere in sports. The United States Lawn Tennis Association had observed an unwritten rule against African Americans for sixty years. For the American Bowling Congress, the rules were *written* and barred blacks from tournaments. So, too, for golf, where the Professional Golf Association was making ugly news by refusing to accept the applications of two black golfers for a tournament in Richmond, California. In Greenville, North Carolina, scene in 1947 of a lynching that led to the trial of thirty-one defendants, the mere cancellation of a football game between white All-Stars and an air force team with five blacks hardly seemed newsworthy. Even boxing, where blacks and whites mixed both inside the ring and around it—even that apparently color-blind sport was under assault. Citing the controversial light-heavyweight fight between "Blackjack" Billy Fox and Jake LaMotta, which Fox won on a TKO after four rounds, Dan Burley, sports editor of the *New York Amsterdam News*, complained that whenever black boxers won, the white press tried to discredit them by circulating rumors of fixes.[7]

Back in January the *Chicago Defender* had written that the year 1948 "offered for the first time since Emancipation . . . a blueprint for racial democracy."[8] Now the editors of the paper joined Truman in attacking southern reactionaries who opposed that blueprint. "At no time in modern history," they wrote, "has our country been faced with so much political conspiracy and outright hypocrisy." Concessions that southern blacks were winning daily were being obscured, the *Defender* said, by "the sound and fury of the Dixie political leaders determined to make asses of themselves."[9]

With such racial sound and fury nationwide, especially in the world of sports, what was the point of trying to organize a basketball game between a team of black barnstormers from Chicago and an all-white team from Minnesota? It was a contest that seemed only to invite loyalties and comparisons, and eventually disagreements, based on race. It seemed especially unwise to risk staging a basketball drama that might be seen as an extension of the racial battles going on in the streets.

But only that week the *Chicago Daily Sun and Times* reported that basketball was enjoying its greatest year. It was the most widely played game on the planet, the *Daily Sun and Times* said. The only entertainment more popular were soap operas, Mickey Rooney movies, and comic strips. Ten million Americans played the game, one hundred million were fans.[10] With so many fans, why not a game at Chicago Stadium? It wasn't the grand stage for American basketball that Madison Square Garden insisted *it* was, but the enormous stadium was the perfect geographical center stage for a contest matching the two best teams in the country. But who were they?

Arch Ward, veteran sports columnist for the *Chicago Tribune*, had written that the Harlem Globetrotters were the best team in the world. *Esquire Magazine* thought that they were the "world's greatest basketball outfit . . . not just a passing phenomenon, like Philippine yo-yo spinners."[11] The Trotters had opened their 1947–48 season in Chicago Stadium with a lopsided victory against the "bewildered" Carlisle Indians. After the game, Arthur Wirtz, who owned Chicago Stadium and had booked the Globetrotters for two games that year, had asked Globetrotters' owner Abe Saperstein, "Who do you want next?"

"We'll play *anybody*," Saperstein said. Because his team could beat anybody, he boasted.[12] Six years earlier in Minnesota, Saperstein's Globetrotters had not even been able to beat a team of undistinguished Minnesota amateurs who called themselves the "Northern Pump Floormen," and his claim now that his team could beat anybody seemed like pure basketball chutzpah.[13] It caught the attention immediately of Max Winter, part owner and general manager of the brand-new Minneapolis Lakers and, not incidentally, Saperstein's good friend. After a slow start, Winter's Lakers were leading the NBL and were also being promoted as the best basketball team in the world. In January Winter met with Saperstein to agree on a Lakers-Globetrotters game as soon as possible in Chicago, and the two men began to work out the details. Neither one appeared to understand the racial implications of the game.[14] What mattered was proving which was the better basketball team.

The first announcement of the game in the papers came on February 12. For Lakers players, the news meant little. It was just a basketball side bet between Winter and Saperstein. Meanwhile, player contracts required them to "render skilled services whenever called upon to play." That included whatever exhibition games their owners arranged. But those exhibition games, no matter how big the crowds, didn't add a penny to their contracts. "We won't even get a cup of coffee for it," one of them complained. It only meant an additional night on the road and one more restless night's sleep in a strange hotel bed.[15]

As an indication of how seriously Abe Saperstein took the game with the Lakers, he merged the best players from his East and West Units to create what he felt was a powerhouse team. Newspapers pointed out that they had been on the road for five straight nights and speculated that they would be tired. However, the truth was that they played *every night*, night after night, and none of them could have counted how many straight nights they had been traveling. In just the month before this game, they had gone from Minnesota to South Dakota, down to Nebraska and Missouri, then out to California, on up to Washington, back down to New Mexico and Oklahoma, then they had worked their way north to Missouri, and finally the night before this game, they had played in Peoria, Illinois. So they were like traveling salesmen who wake up one morning beside their suitcases full of hair brushes or kitchen gadgets, their mouths still sour from the whiskey of the night before as they stare at the ceiling light fixture and try to figure out what city they are in.[16]

For Globetrotters players, whatever might have made this game extraordinary, it was difficult for them to see it or even care. Wherever they went they drew standing-room-only crowds, though not this large. They already believed they were the best team in the country, although they left it largely to Abe Saperstein and sportswriters to make that claim. What else beyond basketball was on the line, they weren't saying. But earlier in the week, the *Chicago Defender* hinted at what those stakes were when it proudly headlined a story announcing that the all-black basketball team from Wilberforce State College had beaten two "White Quints" from the boondocks of Ohio. Yet it was almost comic, the news that Wilberforce had beaten the mighty all-white teams of "Wilmington" and "Tiffin."[17] Who had ever heard of them?

The Lakers' Herm Schaefer walks the ball slowly up the floor again, and the banging of his dribble echoes in a stadium that is suddenly quiet.

This time Schaefer passes directly into George Mikan, who dribbles once as he jockeys for a better position from which to begin his shot, but collapsing Globetrotters sweep the ball away. There is a mad scramble on the floor for the ball. It squirts out and rolls to the feet of Goose Tatum, who picks it up with one hand and flips it casually to Marques Haynes.

Haynes heads down the floor slowly in a quiet that is ghostly. It is as if the fans, some of whom have stood in line half the night, have experienced that same pregame tension that winds athletes tighter and tighter with expectation, but now with the start of the game they are suddenly calm. Meanwhile, the lonely voices of the Globetrotters on the floor carry all the way to that third tier and bring isolated shouts of encouragement, as if they were meant to give support to a black preacher in a storefront church. Each lonely shout is half inarticulate yowl, half lyrical prayer. Similar lonely shouts echo from elsewhere in the cavernous stadium. The shouts all flame briefly like stick matches and then die out quickly in the suffocating silence.

How can such a mass of gathered humanity be so quiet? So many people under one roof, but the plumes of cigarette smoke rising here and there toward the ceiling are the only proof of their presence. Otherwise, they don't even move in their seats, and their faces are as fixed as paper masks, row after row of them banked up from courtside. Some of them have come expecting to howl and cheer for the entertaining drama of Brer Rabbit versus Brer Fox, featuring clever Globetrotters tricksters who outwit their powerful masters. But all promises of such an engaging drama have been scotched, first by the sight of Goose Tatum grinless in the jump circle and now by the endless methodical dribbles up and down the court, up and down the court.

For weeks newspapers in Chicago and Minneapolis had publicized the game. Without saying it directly, the issue was simple: Who was the better team? An all-white "quint," this one from the boondocks of Minnesota, or a black team of basketball traveling salesmen? But from Ohio to Massachusetts, black barnstorming teams had been playing and beating good white teams for decades. In the first World Professional Basketball Championship in 1939, the all-black New York Rens had defeated the all-white Oshkosh All-Stars. The next year the Harlem Globetrotters had won the same title.[18] Unfortunately, these victories weren't followed with the realization by the white major domos of basketball that skilled black players should be included in their plans for building basketball dynasties, and the sport remained largely segregated, especially at the professional level. Now here was this game, with these two unique, powerful teams, each getting national press and celebration. And here was the country, tossing and turning racially as it hadn't done since Emancipation. It was just this February connection of the world inside Chicago Stadium to the world outside it that made the game a likely barnburner, even if none of the parties to the agreement saw it or wanted to talk about it.

If race wasn't immediately in the minds of the players, it wasn't far from the game itself. The Globetrotters had arrived in Chicago late the night before and checked into Ma Piersall's, the small, two-story rooming house on Langley Street on the segregated South Side of Chicago. It was their home for Chicago-area games. The rooms were just ten by ten, with a steam heater that banged and clanked all night, a small dresser, and a single bed with no mattress and only sagging springs. The crude beds were hardly big enough for two players. But Ma Piersall, the motherly middle-aged black woman who owned the place, seemed especially fond of the Globetrotters and cleared out other guests to make room for them whenever they were in town.[19]

The Lakers had come into Chicago on Tuesday night, after beating Indianapolis handily, and they had checked into the popular Morrison Hotel. Contrasts between the Morrison and Ma Piersall's would have been stark, even without the incident of a month earlier that was still in the courts. Isabelle Cooley, the African American actress playing the lead in the award-winning drama *Anna Lucasta*, had made mail reservations at the Morrison before the play's Chicago run. But once she showed up, the hotel management had denied her a room and told her to find a room in a "South Side hotel for colored people." She had, but not without filing a damage suit against the hotel.[20]

It was a dark episode that threw an ironic spotlight in February 1948 on the Supreme Court, which was hearing what the press called "the dynamite issue" of the right of American citizens to buy a home and live where they wanted, regardless of race or color. The specific issue, which the Supreme Court deliberated behind closed doors, was restrictive housing covenants in Detroit and St. Louis, but if anyone had wanted to, it could have applied to the Globetrotters' confinement to the sagging beds of Ma Piersall's.[21]

It would have been unseemly to make an issue of anything so repugnant, in view of the pregame publicity and excitement for the Lakers-Globetrotters game. Chicago papers had been especially graphic in writing about the matchup. "George Mikan vs. Goose Tatum" the headlines trumpeted. It would be the basketball duel of the century. Noting that no Chicago pro game had ever drawn more than nine thousand fans, the *Daily Sun and Times* wrote that Saperstein's Globetrotters were the most "sought after team in the country." If the weather cooperated and the fire marshal looked the other way, more than sixteen thousand fans would show up in hopes of seeing George Mikan "cook the Trotters' Goose." The Globetrotters were "probably the ablest independent professional team in the country," other stories said. Best "independent" team? Arch Ward's judgment had been less qualified. They were the best team in the world. *Period!* Tributes elsewhere were just as unequivocal. Utah writers called them the "best in basketball." Fans in Honolulu and Arizona also thought they were the greatest basketball team in the world. Jimmy Powers of the *New York Daily News* insisted that he would back them against any pro team in the country.[22]

Saperstein's claim was that the Globetrotters had a 102-game winning streak going. And not all of the games had been won against "pushovers," sportswriters were careful to add. Meanwhile, the *Minneapolis Star* took issue with Saperstein and said the streak was only 93 games. The *Daily Sun and Times* set the streak at 98. The *Herald-American* put it at 99. *Time* magazine said 101. The *Minneapolis Morning Tribune* fixed the streak at 103.

However many consecutive victories it was, the mighty Lakers, the Chicago papers wrote, "may put the first blotch" on the Trotters' streak. As actors and performers, as tricksters, the Globetrotters were brilliant. But their play was all theater, not basketball. Goose Tatum was described as a "Negro pivot clown" who may have had arms so long Mikan would think he was confronting an octopus, but for the first time the Trotters would "have a basketball game on their hands." And basketball fans everywhere, the *Minneapolis Morning Tribune* said, would have "a means of comparing the Lakers with the classic Negro quint." The matchup was a "dream," they wrote, pro basketball's "Game of the Year."[23]

3

The Kangaroo Kid

The pinwheel turns rapidly again as the Globetrotters one after another circle by Goose Tatum. The Keystone Cops pace suggests that something hilarious is coming from the Globetrotters, perhaps the lost ball trick where Goose hides the ball under his jersey and the Globetrotters stumble around the court calling for it wistfully like it is a lost dog while the hapless officials fall in with the trick and stumble after them and the Lakers just stand there, leaving the innocent Goose undefended so that he can suddenly pull the ball from under his jersey, hammer two quick dribbles toward the basket, and score.

But despite isolated shouts that threaten to ignite the stadium, the pinwheel stops turning suddenly, and Goose flips the ball to a wide-open Marques Haynes just as one high voice in the stadium cries out, "Set down, set down!" as if he is supposed to fall into a courtside chair and rest while the rapid action continues around him.

A few in the crowd laugh at the idea because they don't understand that the call is not for him to *sit down* but to place himself for a "set shot," which he does with two hands from twenty feet.

The shot seems dead-on the basket, and Haynes is already backpedaling down the floor, confident that the shot is good, but the ball swirls around the rim and kicks out. The Lakers' Jim Pollard snatches the rebound and walks the ball up the floor. Crouched, protecting his dribble from his defender, he works his way to his left forward spot on the floor while George Mikan repeatedly bats Goose Tatum's octopus arms away.

Pollard suddenly picks up his dribble, faces Mikan, and lifts the ball over his head. He seems to be about to throw that same over-the-head bullet pass that slipped through Mikan's fingers, but this time he pulls the ball back at the last second and then cups it in his left wrist and swings his arm for the hook pass, as if he is a only a tetherball pole and his arm is the rope, whipping around in a wide arc. When he lets the pass go, the ball is spinning like a top and is far off the direct line between him and Mikan, perhaps headed out of bounds again, but Mikan doesn't move, and he tracks the pass carefully as he sets himself to receive the ball, which ricochets off the floor at such a sharp angle from its spinning English that Minneapolis sportswriters who have tried to describe this pass from Pollard to Mikan insist that the whole thing is an optical illusion.[1]

Illusion or not, the pass spins straight to Mikan, whose subsequent shot is already so famous that in an effort to illustrate it for every high-pockets string bean in the country who hopes to follow in his huge footsteps, pictures of it have appeared in stop-action frames in newspapers, which describe it as his "drop-step hook shoot" but which is less a hook shot than it is a layup. However it is described, it is unstoppable and the main reason why he has broken every scoring record, college and professional, in the country. And it means nothing to him now that Goose's long arms are tangled around him like tentacles, trying to dislodge the ball from his firm grip. He pauses only a second after receiving Pollard's dogleg pass and then fakes left with his head at the same time he "drop-steps" with his right foot. That drop-step hooks around the legs of Goose, who realizes suddenly that he has been drawn into the fake to the left, and he tries to move back where he should be, but Mikan has already lifted the ball and started his pivot right toward the baseline for the shot, his right elbow preceding him like a spearhead that knocks Goose on his heels and clears the way for an easy basket.

Lakers 2, Globetrotters 0.

His parents were Croatians who ran a tavern in the industrial section of Joliet, Illinois. After work at the nearby Texaco refinery or the Coca-Cola plant, dirt-streaked men with names like "Monkey Joe" or the "Crazy Serbian" came into Mikan's Tavern to have their *kannuppers*—a shot of whiskey with a beer chaser. There were bloody fights while the jukebox blared, and one night the mob sent two goons in to collect protection money. It was Monkey Joe and the Crazy Serbian who broke their beer bottles on the bar rail and drove the goons out.

As a young man George Mikan tended bar and waited tables at his parents' tavern. Patrons described him as "uncommonly tall," and his vision was so bad that, without his glasses, he said it was like looking at the rainy world through a windshield without wipers. His two brothers were also tall, and together they fixed a beer-barrel hoop to a wooden backboard and started shooting baskets with a plastic beach ball behind the tavern. Piano lessons, which his mother insisted on because he had huge hands, gave him strong fingers and a soft touch. But the coach at Joliet Catholic High cut him from the team because basketball wasn't a sport for players with glasses, he said, no matter how tall they were.

He transferred that fall to Quigley Prep Seminary in Chicago, with the intention of becoming a priest. The only basketball competition he enjoyed during that period was with the Catholic Youth Organization leagues in Joliet, but after he broke his leg and spent nearly two months on crutches, he grew half a foot to six feet six inches, and he was invited to join the Quigley team.

His glasses taped to his head now, with tangles of thick black hair, he could have been a double for the silent-screen comedian Harold Lloyd, and he was just as conspicuous on a basketball floor. Two scouts from the athletic department at DePaul University noticed his size and cornered him after a Quigley game. What were his intentions for college, they wanted to know.

He told them he intended to study to become a priest. But by the fall of 1941 he knew that his calling was basketball, not the priesthood, and he enrolled at DePaul University. He was only seventeen years old, but he had grown to be a six-foot-eight-inch 215-pound giant. It was impossible not to notice his size and his basketball potential, and scouts from Notre Dame who spotted him at DePaul in 1941 persuaded him to try out for a *real* team.

The Notre Dame tryout was a disaster. Hobbling on a broken arch, Mikan repeatedly bobbled low passes deliberately thrown at his feet to test his agility. Impressed by the bookish look Mikan's glasses gave him, Notre Dame coach Frank Keogan told him that his future was as a scholar, not a basketball star. But Keogan's assistant was one of his former stars, a gap-toothed pepper pot named Ray Meyer, with fat cheeks and an infectious smile. It was Meyer's first year as an assistant at Notre Dame. Because of his own modest physical skills, Meyer was determined at the start of his coaching career never to measure an athlete's promise by his appearance. It was his heart that mattered the most. And after watching Mikan try again and again to handle the passes thrown at his feet, Meyer was certain that the young athlete had a heart as big as a boiler room.[2]

A year later Meyer accepted the head coaching job at DePaul and again confronted the unlikely-looking Mikan, who lumbered up and down the floor, lurching as if he were running a creek bed filled with slippery boulders. It was Meyer who transformed Mikan from the lumbering giant who drew Frankenstein jokes into a pivot Hercules. It came slowly, the transformation, beginning with Meyer insisting that Mikan learn nimble footwork by always dancing with the smallest girls. The simple drill that completed the change became as famous as his unstoppable hook shot and eventually helped transform legions of gawky giants into nimble stars. It was called the "George Mikan Drill" and was just a series of baby hook shots with either hand—right hand, left hand, right hand, left hand—one after the other, catching the ball out of the net and forming a figure eight on the floor as surely as if he were a figure skater drawing compulsory designs in the ice.[3]

He became a nimble offensive giant who eventually led the nation in scoring and won All-American honors three straight years. On the way to DePaul's winning the 1945 National Invitational Tournament, Mikan scored a record 53 points in a single game and was celebrated from New York to California as "Big George," the greatest player the game had ever seen.

His story was as old as the tale of Frankenstein, even if he hated the jokes. A mountain of bones had been transformed and received the gift of an athletic life. The press gave Ray Meyer credit for working the miracle, not with galvanism and flashes of lightning in the dark dungeons of a murky castle but with ingenious drills under the bright lights of a basketball court. Meyer felt, however, that the only thing he deserved credit for was having the ability to recognize an athlete with a huge heart when he saw one.[4]

Marques Haynes misses another set shot. Jack Dwan rebounds the missed shot and again walks the ball up the floor for the Lakers. He passes to forward Jim Pollard, who crouches, then drops one foot back as if he is preparing to propel himself on a drive for the basket. But when his defender retreats, he straightens himself quickly, dips slightly from both knees, and releases a one-hand set shot that rips the net.

Lakers 4, Globetrotters 0.

The Globetrotters' Babe Pressley misses a field goal.

Don "Swede" Carlson grabs the rebound and trots up the floor behind his dribble. But as soon as he tries to pass into Mikan, the ball is deflected and skitters among a collapsing clutch of players as if it were a pinball before it finally winds up in Pollard's hands again, in his forward position on the left side of the basket. Babe Pressley crowds him now, determined not to let Pollard have room for another set shot. Because of Pressley's closeness, Pollard has to turn his right shoulder to protect the ball. Then he cups it in his wrist again and draws his left arm back in preparation for the tetherball whip pass that will spin like a top and eventually reach Mikan. But just at the release point of the pass, when Pollard's arm has shot forward and Pressley is stretching to block the pass, Pollard's arm stops while he is still cupping the ball. He quickly switches the ball to his right hand and he is off, driving straight for the top of the key.

The entire maneuver is a variation of what he calls his "California Fake," which is meant to make his defender reach or step one way to block the pass so that Pollard can drive the other.[5] It works beautifully, and Pressley shuffles his feet rapidly in a defensive slide to catch up to Pollard, who puts down one, two, three dribbles as he glides closer and closer to the free-throw line.

Pollard is still half a step ahead of Pressley when he reaches the free-throw line. But Pressley has recovered from his defensive mistake and is catching up quickly. He is already gathering himself for the defensive leap, anticipating the additional step Pollard will take before he can vault off his left foot for the shot.

That one additional step is all Pressley needs to close the gap so that he can jump with Pollard and, by virtue of his quickness and spring, slap Pollard's shot away just as it leaves his fingertips.

But a split second before Pressley can jump, Pollard leaps early and almost straight up. Off the wrong foot! Executed by anyone else the shot would be a disaster, a clumsy, lurching, rushed flail. But from Pollard, who some say is the smoothest, most graceful player ever in the game, the shot is a floating ballet move during which his arms and hands and legs all seem to be moving together effortlessly despite the wrong-foot vertical launch.

Pressley's late leap brings him flying at Pollard a split second after the ball is gone. He reaches with one arm in a desperate but futile attempt to swat the ball away. The reach twists him in the air so that he can follow the lazy, soft arc of Pollard's shot to the basket.

The ball slips over the front rim like a soft free throw that sticks for a moment in the net before it drops to the floor.

It is too soft and delicate a shot to deserve rude clapping, and the huge crowd expresses its wonder by *ooooooooooo*-ing, as if they have had the wind knocked out of them. Only a high yowl that comes from somewhere in the stadium seems to express the audience's full appreciation of the shot.

The scoreboard blinks: Lakers 6, Globetrotters 0.

"Field goal," the announcer says and then pauses to make sure everyone understands that the graceful shot was not a simple free throw, "by Jim Pollard."

His father was a carpenter who carved ornamental doors by hand, and James Clifford Pollard's hands on a basketball were as soft as his father's working a wood chisel. What else he might have inherited he never learned because his father and mother separated early on. He had much older brothers and sisters who had already left home, and he grew up in Oakland, California, living with his mother, Susie Pollard, in an apartment building that she managed in order to have a place to live. There was money for food but little else, and he never forgot the hardships of his boyhood. He had had just two pairs of pants, he would recall later—one for dress, the other for everyday.

The dress pants were for church services at the Salvation Army temple where Susie Pollard volunteered as a church officer. He went to church twice on Sunday and every Wednesday night. In school he was quiet and not particularly studious. By the fourth grade, he was the tallest student in his entire grammar school. When he started playing basketball in grammar school, the rules called for a center jump after every score, and his height and jumping ability made him an immediate standout.

His best friend was Eugene "Lefty" Rock, who was a year older but also an athlete and a promising basketball player. Jim towered over Lefty, who was speedy and tenacious, and the two friends earned the nickname "Mutt and Jeff" among their classmates. They played mumblety-peg regularly, and together with Lefty's brothers

they performed dramas in Lefty's basement, charging neighborhood kids a penny apiece to watch.

Performing the neighborhood dramas came easy for Jim, but
he remained otherwise quiet and seldom volunteered conversation.
Meanwhile, his touch and jumping ability on a basketball floor were
so extraordinary that he learned to tip the ball into the basket from
jump balls at the free-throw line. He was popular with his classmates, and the 1937 photograph of the student body officers at
Woodrow Wilson Junior High pictured him as Boy's League president, towering over student body president Eugene "Lefty" Rock.

In spite of his basketball promise at Oakland Tech High School,
he remained close to his mother, who expected him to keep his loyalties to the Salvation Army church, where he was the tallest member
of their basketball squad. It was a ragtag team of players who looked
as indigent as the poor people the church served. Their team uniforms didn't match, and they all wore floppy, dirty socks. But when
he posed for the team picture, his already large but soft hands delicately cradled the basketball, and his solemn face reflected how seriously he took his responsibilities as team captain, even if the church
itself meant little to him.

So it came as an utter surprise one day during the Christmas
holidays when Lefty Rock and his brothers went into downtown
Oakland to see a movie. They knew Jim Pollard was going to be
a basketball star. They also admired his quiet self-confidence. But
they knew little else about him. And as they approached the movie
theater, suddenly there he was playing his trumpet with a Salvation
Army brass band, wearing a flashy dress hat and a uniform with gold
buttons, mop epaulets, and braid piping.

The band drew a crowd of Christmas shoppers, many of whom
stepped forward to drop coins in the collection pot. But he never
looked up from his music to acknowledge the crowd or his friend
Lefty, who didn't quiz him about it until later.

"I didn't know you played trumpet," Lefty said, struggling to express his surprise, "with the Salvation Army?"

He shrugged. "I do it a lot," he said, without bothering to explain
that he did so out of devotion to his mother, not because he was
musical or religious.

As his high school athletic reputation grew, he had time for little
else in his life, and he drifted away from the Salvation Army church.

In basketball, his height, his speed and quickness, his soft hands, and his pin legs that could catapult him high into the air made him the talk of California prep basketball.

Newspapers eventually christened him "The Kangaroo Kid." He was chosen as a high school All-American, and college offers came from everywhere. His old grammar school friend Lefty Rock, who had moved to Southern California, tried to persuade Pollard to join him playing at the University of Southern California.

"There's nothing I'd rather do," Pollard said. "But my mom has a job near Stanford," he explained. And that was where he had decided to take his basketball talents, but not before he had spent six months at night school boosting his modest high school grades.

At Stanford, he renewed his friendship with Arilee Hanson, a vivacious and attractive brunette who was also from Oakland Tech and studying at San Jose State to be a teacher. She had been an athlete herself in high school and president of the Girls Athletic Association, and she hadn't failed to take notice of him. His first date with "Ari" was arranged after he spotted her coming out of a movie theater one night in Palo Alto. He invited her to a Stanford football game with him, but he couldn't sit with her because he had to work the game as a student usher. After the game, the two of them headed back to the East Bay, hitchhiking first to San Francisco because he didn't even have bus fare.

Meanwhile, his influence on Stanford basketball was immediate. Now six feet five inches tall, the bladelike thinness of his face hinted at penetrating speed, without beanpole awkwardness. It was that speed, along with his smoothness—they said he glided up and down the floor as if on skates—that led Stanford into the finals of the National Collegiate Athletic Association (NCAA) championship in 1942. Unfortunately, he came down with a raging flu bug the night before the final game against Dartmouth, and he could only sit on the bench, feverish and sweaty, too weak to even stand up to celebrate Stanford's eventual victory.

He was only twenty-two years old. He was the Kangaroo Kid, and stories about his jumping ability, fed by sportswriters who measured one of his driving basketball leaps at seventeen feet, bordered on the mythical. But with the world at war, he enlisted in the Coast Guard, and by June 1944 he and Ari were engaged. Two weeks before the wedding, his mother died suddenly. He had nowhere to call home now and no money. Only his skill at basketball seemed to separate him from those sad Salvation Army indigents for whom he had once raised money by playing his trumpet. And his one hope now was that he would somehow make his way in the world using that basketball talent.

Despite his quietness and his private nature, it was clear that the loss of his mother had shaken him deeply. For Arilee Hanson, the issue of marriage had already been decided. But she still asked his brothers and sisters if they felt it was appropriate now.

"Sure," they told her. "It'll be good for Jim. He'll have a home."[6]

4

Babe

After Pollard's field goal, the Globetrotters make their first substitution, Wilbur King. King is from Detroit. He is small but muscular and as good an all-around athlete—football, basketball, baseball, softball—as anybody in Detroit can remember.[1] White sportswriters in Detroit refer to him as "Willie," because Wilbur seems too backwoods for a player with such slick, blinding speed.

Willie King receives the inbound pass from Marques Haynes and takes off now with the ball at full dribbling speed. He slashes through two, three, four retreating Lakers whose backs are turned and are surprised to see him fly by them on his way to the basket. But his speed is so straight-ahead and unwavering that he is almost past the basket before he knows it, and he has to bend himself back to keep his layup from jamming against the bottom edge of the backboard. In the process, the ball rises straight up as he flies out of bounds after the shot.

The high rebound seems to be dropping lazily into several arms tangled in their reach for the ball when Jim Pollard's arm rises higher than the rest, hooks the ball, then curls it safely into his chest.

He breaks from the surrounding bodies as soon as he is back on the floor and races for the right sidelines, pushing his dribble ahead of him as he goes. At midcourt he faces a defensive interruption by retreating Globetrotters who block his path, and he is forced to stop and change direction by whirling himself around. The brief halt permits other players to stream past him—Lakers trying to catch up with his one-man fast break and Globetrotters racing to get back on defense.

Goose Tatum alone refuses to be swept up in the mad dash down the floor. He makes no effort to jog, or even walk, to catch up with his teammates. He merely stands hipshot at his own free-throw line, his long arms hanging at his side, watching as the action flows away from him.

His stance is so blasé it seems a prelude to a Globetrotters' "reem," the term Goose has coined to describe one of the team's comic routines.[2] While most of those comic moments are planned and tightly choreographed, Goose is left free to fall into one of his own reems whenever the mood strikes him, and now another high yowl rises from the crowd, in delicious anticipation of what will be an entertaining moment of comedy. Perhaps while the action rages downcourt, Goose will take the opportunity to stroll to the sidelines and relieve a courtside fan of her fancy hat and put it on his own head, then open her purse and use her tiny cosmetic mirror to preen and groom himself, his rubbery mouth twisting with sudden grins and smirks, then just as suddenly his eyes narrowing with seduction and intrigue. Or he will spot a beautiful woman at courtside wearing a thick fur coat, and he'll put it on and rise to his toes as if he's on high heels, then sashay and flounce in circles, his long arms straight down at his sides, his fingers delicately flared.

Whatever he intends to do, no one is watching the action, and every eye in the stadium is upon him. The longer he stands there, separated from the action, delaying the start of his comedy, almost sleepy in his indifference, the funnier the audience thinks the moment is. Other yowls from the fans, followed by high yips and hoots, focus the tension of the moment until a roar that starts as collective murmuring and then rises to laughter fills the stadium.

Goose refuses to move.

Downcourt, the Lakers force a pass into George Mikan. He is immediately surrounded by Globetrotters and has no room to maneuver for a shot. Marques Haynes slaps the ball away from him. It bounces toward the end line under the basket.

Muscular Babe Pressley grabs it just before it goes out of bounds.

Goose Tatum suddenly comes alive. One long arm shoots up immediately and flaps in the air like a flag.

He delivers a desperate call for the ball, before any of the Lakers can get back to cover him. The call is real, utterly unlike the burlesque cries of joy or shock he can deliver for laughs in the midst of furious action.

In a second, the comic tension disappears and is replaced by pure suspense.

Will Pressley hear the cry and recognize that Goose is wide open? Will the Lakers get back before he gets the ball and scores?

Pressley cocks one arm with the ball, then stretches the other as if he is hurling a javelin.

The pass is as flat and fast as a pitched baseball. There is a leathery smack as the ball reaches Goose's huge hands.

He is still wide open when he turns. It takes only one long dribble for him to get to the basket for the layup.

The Lakers racing to get back brake to a trot when it's clear they are too late.

"Field goal by Goooooooooo-sss Tate-ummmm."

Lakers 6, Globetrotters 2.

It was part of the character of the Globetrotters' offense, the occasional long passes to a sleeping Goose Tatum. In the first place, he had little interest in playing defense.[3] It was the dirty work of basketball. It meant all sweat and seriousness and putting himself at the offensive mercy of whatever player he was trying to guard. Where was the opportunity to lead and improvise? Where was the opportunity for performance and ingenious clowning? Even defensive rebounding held little interest for him, and he seldom even made an effort to jump. He was content just to hold his position on the floor among the struggling bodies by keeping a lock-kneed, flatfoot stance.[4]

It was offense that mattered, not just the opportunity to hang back and clown but the chance to shoot his incredible back-to-the-basket windmill hook shot, or deliver a blind pass to one of the cutting members of the pinwheel, or to fight and slash for an offensive rebound, leaping high to tip it in or catch it in the air and then hang there until the defenders fell away before he put it back softly off the backboard, proving that he could have jumped and rebounded defensively if he had wanted to.

Despite Goose Tatum's habits, it wasn't part of the Globetrotters' game plan against the Lakers to have him hang back on defense in order to perform courtside antics. It especially wasn't in their plan to have him loaf on defense, even if he did score on a full-court bullet pass from Babe Pressley.

Abe Saperstein may have been the Globetrotters' official leader, but it was the veteran Louis "Babe" Pressley who was the team's de facto coach. At a husky six-one, he had a physical presence that was commanding. He could shoot from the outside, and he was the team's premier defender. He preferred straight play but could fill in for Goose Tatum on those nights when Goose failed to show. He had been with the Globetrotters for over a decade and was the elder statesman of the team. Off the court he was easygoing and the team's practical joker. He dressed well and enjoyed smoking cigars in hotel lobbies. He knew the game of basketball inside and out, and he liked to talk strategy with the team's rookies and even the complete strangers who approached him in those lobbies. He was the team's natural leader, and his teammates easily deferred to his judgment.

It was Babe Pressley who had laid out the Globetrotters' plan for the game against the Lakers. That plan did not call for any long passes to a sleeping Goose Tatum. They were all expected to play both ends of the floor and to run the very same offense they ran night after night.

That offense was second nature to them. Goose Tatum stood at the high post with his back to the basket. Three players kept continuously cutting off him, and a fourth cornerman often came out of nowhere to finish each play. It was an offense that looked buffoonish in its merry-go-round simplicity, especially against a team of stooges playing only passive defense. But the truth was that on those occasions requiring serious basketball, what might have looked simple became an intricate ballet with split-second timing, variations off the high-post theme, and sudden individual improvisations that the others fell in with immediately because they had lived together on a basketball court night after night for years. A head tilt meant one thing. A squinch of the eyes something else. Bent legs, a dipped shoulder, changes in dribble speed—each signaled a sudden solo performance that might have looked wild and impulsive but was in fact part of an intuitive script.[5]

Against the Lakers, there was no point in trying to go inside with the ball, the Globetrotters knew. Mikan's height, as well as Pollard's ability to leap high and swat shots away, required an outside game. Besides, the Globetrotters felt that their speed and quickness could only be used to an advantage on the outside in the open court, where there was room to stop and start suddenly, then spin and change directions until they were open.

For the Lakers, it was just the opposite. Their game plan was to set up deliberately and go inside to Mikan as often as they could. With the pressing action of their busy NBL schedule, Lakers coach Johnny Kundla hadn't had time to scout the Globetrotters. He knew little about them, other than that they were gifted showboats and tricksters. But the word on the basketball grapevine was that they neglected defense. Even if they didn't, Kundla thought the Lakers' offense, and especially George Mikan, was too potent to stop, and they were expected to get the ball into him frequently. If he received the ball at the high post, the action called for high-post crisscrosses involving the two guards. There was the "JG" play—a simple pick-and-roll between Pollard and Mikan. There was "Pensacola," with one of the guards feeding Mikan at the high post, and then while Mikan faked maneuvering for his shot, the guard ran a loop route past two screens and took a backdoor return pass from Mikan for a layup.[6]

Before the game, the only question for the Globetrotters was who would guard Mikan. Globetrotters coach Abe Saperstein argued that with Goose's long arms, he would have the advantage of being able to deflect the passes into Mikan. But only if he intended to play aggressive defense. And that was always a question with him. So the other candidate for guarding Mikan was Babe Pressley, the Globetrotters' best defender. But then who would guard Pollard, who the Globetrotters believed was an even greater threat? If they had any chance at all of beating the powerful Lakers, it would be by stopping Pollard. Only Pressley had the defensive quickness to do that, and so he had to take Pollard.

The Globetrotters finally decided that the matchup would be exactly the one the newspapers had been touting, Goose Tatum versus George Mikan. The Globetrotters' guards would collapse around Mikan to frustrate him whenever he got the ball. But that was all they could do, they knew, delay him, make him hesitate. Or maybe they would get lucky and steal the ball because Mikan had the bad habit of not protecting it when he got it, or worse, putting down a dribble.

The Globetrotters thought that no matter what they did, Mikan would eventually get his points. Meanwhile, Pressley would do his best to contain Pollard. Two other matchups were important: Ermer Robinson would take the Lakers' playmaker Swede Carlson, who was the only other real scoring threat for the Lakers; and speedy, dribbling genius Marques Haynes would guard Herm Schaefer, the Lakers' veteran guard and floor leader. There was no talk of a zone defense by either team. There were just too many deadeye, two-hand set shooters who liked nothing better than being left free on a zone defense to set themselves for a long, high shot.[7]

Even George Mikan loves the opportunity to set himself and then release a long, graceful set shot off his fingertips, and occasionally, if their lead is big enough or it is late in the game and victory has already been secured, he will slip to the sidelines of the court where his defender will seldom follow him.[8] He will be left alone then, without a defender trying to push him away or slashing at him and no need to clear the way for his baby hook shot with a crude armbar that makes him seem like nothing but a strong-armed brute who is utterly without grace.

He is left alone on the sidelines now, and he calls for the ball. Once he has it in his hands, he brings it to his eyes, peers over it, and takes aim. Goose takes a slap step out toward Mikan, as if to scare him, as if to break Mikan's deep concentration on the shot, but then he retreats to the pivot, as if to say, "Go ahead and shoot, George. If it goes in, it will be nothing but blind-ass, preposterous luck."

Mikan pushes with both hands.

The arch of the ball is exaggerated, and there is no way to know whether it will go in or even be close. As soon as the ball is released, Mikan stands only for a second with his hands extended, fulfilling follow-through obligations that are proof of the shot's finesse. Then he breaks for the basket to join the knot of players pushing and struggling for a rebound that is sure to be the result of such an improbable shot.

But the shot is good.

Lakers 8, Globetrotters 2.

Mikan hitches up his pants, as if to say the improbable shot is all in a day's work. Trotting beside Goose back down the floor, Mikan has a broad smile, and Goose refuses to look at him.

Goose sets up at the low post with his back to the basket and raises one hand like a flag again. It is a signal that he wants the ball for his famous hook shot. It is his answer to Mikan's bold shot and, on the surface at least, much beyond Mikan's for sheer improbability. It is in fact an impossible shot. But Goose has practiced it over and over again for years so that he can make dozens in a row and sometimes even bank one in from as far away as the sidelines.[9] No matter how many times he might miss showboating the sidelines shot in a comic game, just one good miracle shot is enough to bring the house down.

He receives the ball now with his back still to the basket. For once there are no cutters, no turning pinwheel blades, and it gives him all the floor space he needs. He begins dribbling slowly away from the basket at an angle, taking long, deliberate, flatfoot steps with each dribble. He does not even look back for the basket or appear to care where it is behind him, and his dribble away from it seems an unlikely prelude to a shot. It leaves Mikan at first confused, and he follows tentatively, as if he fears he is being sucked into a trap. But when Goose is nearly ten feet from the basket, still moving away from it, he picks up his dribble in midstride, and it is suddenly clear that the deliberately slow retreat from the basket marks the beginning of a shot.

It starts with the ball at his knees in a two-hand grip. Then he swings the ball, both arms picking up speed as they move in a great looping hook-shot arc that makes the ball seem like a planet orbiting him.

Sportswriters around the country have given the windmill-like shot various names, but whatever they chose to call it, it is best described as "Goose's Prayer" because he doesn't even look at the basket until the last second, when he leaps into the air and suddenly twists himself to zero in on the target.

Mikan rushes out at him and jumps. He stretches to his full height, his fingers clawing the air like a bamboo rake. Just as the ball is rolling softly off Goose's fingertips, a burst of flashbulb light turns Mikan whiter than white. From the snowy satin of his uniform to the ivory of his skin, he is a towering obelisk that seems about to crush Goose, whose skin in the instant illumination turns slick, blacker than black. He is a broken, ravenlike figure, twisting and flapping, trying desperately to escape death.

But it is too fleeting and serious an image to register anywhere except inside the camera. And those who have seen it happen before—

the shot banking in by some miracle of Goose's talent that lies hidden beneath the laughable impossibility of the shot—begin raising a whoop in anticipation of another miracle. After all, Mikan has no hope of blocking the shot. Even if he had jumped in time, he can't reach it, not only because Goose is retreating as he shoots it but because his arms are so freakishly long that the arc of the shot keeps the ball outside any other human being's reach.

Goose is fifteen feet from the basket when he alights on the floor. Half of the stadium is on its feet, already celebrating the miracle.

But the shot caroms off the backboard, whirls the rim so violently that the net thrashes, then kicks out.

The score remains Lakers 8, Globetrotters 2.

5

Goose

He was as mysterious a figure as High John de Conquer, the mighty hero from African American folklore who walked on a singing drum.[1] It was the murkiness of Goose Tatum's past that bred the mystery. What few facts were known about him hardly explained who he was. Or why he was such a loner. Or where his talent for clowning had come from.

He was born Reece Tatum in New Jersey in the spring of 1921, one of seven children of a Methodist minister. While he was still a baby, his family moved to Calion, Arkansas, then to El Dorado. His boyhood was a closed book. Exactly who had given him his peculiar nickname remained a mystery. He was just "Goose." It seemed to fit, if for no other reason than when he unfolded his freakishly long arms and flapped them, he looked like an immense bird trying to take off.

Abe Saperstein spotted him early in 1940 clowning on a baseball diamond, effortlessly stroking a clean hit with a level swing, then streaking for third base with his head tilted back and flapping those long arms. Even his remarkable arm span wasn't certain. But the unofficial figure was eighty-four inches from fingertip to fingertip, so long that he could stand straight and still clutch his knees. If his long arms and clowning struck some observers as apish, he didn't object, telling people only, "My goal in life is to make people laugh."[2]

After Abe Saperstein failed to get a baseball franchise promised him in the Negro Leagues, he started his own professional baseball league and signed Goose Tatum to play left field with a team in the Twin Cities. He was as good an athlete as he was a clown, and Saperstein signed him to play center for his Globetrotters basketball team in June 1942. His toothy smile, elastic face, and Raggedy Ann body made him even more successful at basketball clowning, and he was soon the comic center of the Globetrotters.

Whether he was in the army or the army air corps during the war remained another mystery in his life. When he returned to the team in 1946, he was billed as the "Clown Prince" of Globetrotters' basketball. But he continued his baseball routines with the Indianapolis Clowns in the National Negro League, and he did comic skits on the field with "King Tut," who played with an oversized catcher's glove. In 1946, at Crosley Field in Cincinnati, newsreel cameras captured Goose Tatum in eight minutes of diamond clowning that broke up the world.[3]

But it was on a basketball court that his comedic genius was most apparent. He had all of the gifts of a virtuoso comedian: that elastic face and body, perfect timing, a relentless exhibitionism, and a keen eye for absurdity and farce. Snatching a courtside camera and then turning it on himself, his supple face would travel from theatrical sorrow to suspicion and intrigue in seconds. He would steal a businessman's bowler hat and briefcase, then take a crosscourt walk that ridiculed pretension everywhere. He would stand dumbfounded before a fat official who had just whistled him for mauling his defender. Then he would follow the oblivious official around the floor, mocking his self-importance. He would sit in an empty chair beside an attractive woman, then mimic every nervous move or expression she made, as if he were her mirror. In all of it, he would lose himself immediately and actually become the pompous businessman or the glamorous woman or the martinet official. He made silly faces and strange noises, and as he romped and parodied and clowned on a basketball floor, whatever identity he might have had as Reece Tatum from somewhere in Arkansas disappeared.

It was his grandest illusion, because off the court he was somebody else entirely, moody and sullen and distant. On the road he seldom spoke to anybody, even his teammates. He was always the center of the pregame publicity surrounding every Globetrotters' appearance. Before a game the local papers usually featured a posed picture of Goose in a crouch, his long arms dangling almost to the floor, a basketball in each huge hand. But he refused to give interviews to anybody, and he would growl at autograph seekers, "Get the fuck away!" On the bus, he slept or read local newspapers. In the locker room, while the others played poker or gin rummy, he sat alone reading his newspapers or just staring.

It wasn't that he had any special animosity for his teammates. He didn't appear to like *anybody*. And off court, he wanted to be left alone. The source of that withdrawal and anger was his deepest secret. Was the unfocused rage an understandable scar of self-hate left by years of discrimination and humiliation? If that were true, then where did that comic court persona come from? It seemed too deep and genuine to be the reflexive, tap-dancing, happy-go-lucky submission of the black minstrel.

Surrounded by so much mystery, anecdotes and rumors abounded: they said that once on a Globetrotters' swing through North Dakota, he jumped off the train and disappeared for weeks; it was rumored that he had a wife from Gary, Indiana, another from Kansas City, Missouri, and a woman friend from Detroit who was a dancer; he was often in the company of a woman as mysterious as he was, known only as "Lottie the Body" by the other Globetrotters; in Buenos Aires, he had been arrested outside the team hotel after causing a ruckus with a local woman; in the Negro Leagues, he had once stabbed an opponent with a screwdriver; finally, in an argument with a basketball promoter, he had pulled a gun.[4]

It all made him as mysterious and powerful as High John de Conquer, promising laughter and hope. Meanwhile, white audiences especially failed to realize that beneath his comedic talent and that happy-go-lucky court clown lay the gifts of a magnificent athlete. Beneath that ropy, Raggedy Ann body there were lightning reflexes and the instincts of an All-Star. He could shoot as well as anybody. When he wasn't playing the flatfoot pivot clown, wandering the floor as if his feet were stuck in glop, he had half a dozen moves around the basket—a jump hook shot that was years ahead of its time, his unstoppable windmill hook, spin moves, leaping fallaways that required a delicate touch, and just the opposite, power plays where he went right over the top of his opponents and strong-armed the shot. Defenders complained that with his long arms, "he could pick your pocket while scoring." If they tried to reach around him, he pinned their arms. "You thought you were in jail," they joked.[5] He could read rebounds and slide around defenders to quickly tip the ball in and then disappear down the floor. Newspapers described him as a "fabled scoring ace." His 57 points to open the season against the Carlisle Indians was a Chicago Stadium record. On the Globetrotters' West Coast trip in the weeks before Chicago, he broke the single-season scoring record for Saperstein's team with 1,341 points. After critics argued that these were all against stooge teams or local squads as hapless as the Carlisle Indians, he countered by holding seven-foot Don Otten of the Tri-Cities Blackhawks scoreless while he poured in 17 points.[6]

The truth was that he was as mighty on the basketball court as he was funny. But because he romped and clowned and made silly faces and strange noises, he fed the belief of white audiences that he was the stereotypical, happy-go-lucky Negro clown, oblivious to insult and humiliation. And as much as he was the comic center of the Globetrotters, he was also the center of the argument that the Globetrotters were tricksters, not basketball players.[7]

Swede Carlson rebounds Goose's Prayer and dribbles for a corner of the floor in an effort to free himself from Globetrotters trying to steal the ball. Marques Haynes follows him and fouls him before he gets to the corner.

Carlson converts the free throw.

Lakers 9, Globetrotters 2.

The Globetrotters take a time-out. They stand in a close circle on the court. They are wild and animated and full of energy. Abe Saperstein stands in the circle, trying to talk, bobbing his head and bending and twisting. But Babe Pressley eventually does all the talking, speaking quickly and jabbing a finger at players as he does. They are only minutes into the game, but Mikan has already scored twice. The long field goal from the corner was a fluke, yet the ease with which Mikan swept Tatum aside with his drop-step hook shot spells trouble for the rest of the game, and Pressley volunteers to take Mikan.

No one objects. It goes without saying that Goose won't have it any easier trying to stop Pollard, but Pressley says he'll be inside now to help if Pollard drives the key as he has done already. Meanwhile, he reminds Haynes and Robinson to help plug the key and foil passes to Mikan.[8]

Down the court the Lakers are stock-still in their huddle and don't even bother to towel off what little sweat they have generated.

From the high tier of the stadium, they look as frozen and immobile as garden figurines.

Time-in again. Globetrotters' ball.

The ball goes straight into Goose Tatum at the high post to start their pinwheel offense. But after the first cutters have gone by, he whirls suddenly, slips around Mikan, and heads for the basket.

Mikan is caught by surprise and chases after Goose. Pollard is also racing to the probable spot of Goose's layup, preparing to leap and bat it away. But Goose gathers himself and then brakes suddenly. Mikan crashes into him from behind and sends the ball one way and Goose another.

On the free-throw line, Goose bounces the ball one, two, three, four, five times. Then a sixth. He pauses. Takes aim. Finally, he changes his mind and takes a seventh bounce as an afterthought. Laughter and whoops rise from the fans, because he seems about to do the rubber-band trick, in which the free-thrower shoots and the ball sails for the basket and everybody leaps, then the ball "boings" right back to the shooter like a paddleball.

But his free throw is serious, and he misses.

Mikan rebounds the ball. The Lakers set up deliberately and try to run Pensacola, but Mikan's bounce pass to Carlson looping back-door along the baseline leads him too much and the pass goes out of bounds.

Globetrotters' ball.

They race down the floor, trying to force the action, but the Lakers are already spread out and waiting, so the Globetrotters again start their pinwheel offense. They cut and circle and cut again. Goose offers each cutter the ball as they fly by, then he withdraws it to wait for the next cutter. Mikan backs off to let his defending teammates slide through as they follow the cutters. He is also prepared to back up even farther if he has to in order to defend against whatever cutter Goose finally decides to hand the ball off to for a driving layup.

Suddenly there are no more cutters. Goose shovels a pass out to teammate Ermer Robinson, who is standing all alone almost thirty feet from the basket. Isolated from the others, way beyond the range of what would be a decent shot, he is an incongruous figure who seems all out of proportion, a misconstruction of nature. His face is too long, his ears are too low, and his mouth is too wide. His eyes are shadowy and deep, and his mustache is just two tiny separated patches above his lip. He has muscular thighs but skinny arms and no chest whatsoever. Nothing seems to fit on him. His trunks are too big and are bunched beneath the belt buckle. The top eyelets of his tennis shoes are left unlaced and open and make his shoes look too big. He wears stiff kneepads that refuse to follow the contour of his knees and seem meant for somebody twice his size.

He is the unlikeliest-looking shooter on the floor, out of whack and misaligned and ungainly. But as soon as he has the ball, the call comes from somewhere in the stadium for him to "Set down! Set down!"

It is an unnecessary call, because he is already dropping his left foot back in preparation for a one-hand set shot. He holds the ball almost at arm's length, as if he is offering it to Swede Carlson, his defender, deliberately taunting him, inviting him to reach to take the ball before Robinson can snatch it back with one hand and shake Carlson's hand with the other.

Carlson is determined not to be fooled, and he edges cautiously out to Robinson, who bends both knees slowly. By the time Carlson realizes the extended ball is not meant to make a fool out of him, it is too late. Robinson is already pushing the ball away in a graceful, one-hand set shot.

Carlson makes a desperate leap with one hand high, but the ball is long gone.

Robinson backpedals down the floor as he watches the ball sail toward the basket.

"Field goal, Errrrr-merrrrrr Rob-in-sonnnnnn."

Lakers 9, Globetrotters 4.

6

Ermer

Friends from the neighborhood in San Diego where Ermer Robinson grew up in the 1920s and 1930s sometimes called it "Garlic Center," because on hot days the smell of families cooking with garlic hung in the air as thick as soot. It was a settlement of immigrant families along J Street and K Street and L Street, an alphabet soup of Italians, Greeks, Irish, Jews, Armenians, Japanese, Chinese, Hispanics, and half a dozen African American families, all living in tiny box homes out around Stockton Elementary School and Guadalupé Church.

The Robinsons lived on Thirtieth Street between J and K, in a tiny, two-bedroom shotgun home in the middle of the block. Like all the other homes in the neighborhood, it was hardly big enough for a family, which included Ermer's three brothers and a sister. No one in the neighborhood ever saw Ermer's father, and they knew his mother only as "Mrs. Robinson," a tiny woman with sad eyes who worked as a housemaid in San Diego.

There were no luxuries in Garlic Center, but for the Robinsons it was better than a racial ghetto that bred defeatism and anger, and Ermer wore a frequent but thin smile, even if nobody had said anything funny. It was as if he knew something ironic or amusing that you didn't. It was as if he knew that, for him, there could be a whole lot worse places to live than Garlic Center.

The neighborhood game was softball, which the boys played on a field behind Stockton Elementary School. But by the time they were at Memorial Junior High on Logan Street, they had graduated to basketball on the asphalt courts connected to the school. To get there from Garlic Center, they had to walk across a forty-acre dirt field they called "No Man's Land," because neighborhood bullies often ambushed them in the field and then pummeled them.

Ermer Robinson was the smoothest and the quickest of the players. He was also the most inventive, and while the others tried to master two-hand set shots, he was the first to began experimenting with a one-hand shot. Eventually, he learned to drop his left foot back, then with the ball positioned off his right shoulder, he flexed his knees and sprang forward and up as he shot. Once in the air, his left hand dropped away while his right hand pushed the ball on its way.

By the time he was in the tenth grade at San Diego High, he was good enough to make the varsity basketball team. Meanwhile, his one-hand shot was still evolving. He would set up for it carefully, planting his left foot the way he had learned on the asphalt court beside "No Man's Land." Then he would carefully lift the ball to his eye-line. It was all so slow and deliberate that it invited defenders to come close and try to block the shot, but just when they did he shifted gears in a split second and was gone on a lightning drive to the basket.

Merrill Douglas, the basketball coach at San Diego High, was the athletic product of an era that featured *only* two-hand shooting, and Douglas had reason to be apprehensive about Ermer's one-hand shot when he first saw it. But he wisely refused to forbid it or even tinker with it. Whatever adjustments were necessary, Ermer was determined to work those out on his own, bragging to teammates and his coach that he took five hundred practice shots daily on the asphalt court next to "No Man's Land." It suggested that he was dangerously possessed by basketball, but he delivered that news with his characteristic thin smile, reflecting his confidence that he was getting good, particularly at shooting his one-hand shot. The source of his confidence was his discovery that he could still get the ball there from long range with one hand if he cocked his right leg at the peak of his jump, as if he were climbing a step ladder, then kicked to give the shot impetus at the same time he released the ball. And he could take himself right up to the edge of lifting off the floor for the shot before he suddenly yanked the ball back and took off for the basket.

Opponents couldn't stop Ermer Robinson his senior year at San Diego High, whether he released his one-hand shot from long range or pulled it back and drove for the basket. In mid-December 1941, just days after the Japanese attack on Pearl Harbor, Ermer and his San Diego High teammates went to the Chino Invitational Tournament. During the three-day tournament, Ermer slept head-to-feet in the same bed in a Chino boardinghouse with Rigo Rodriguez, a teammate also from Garlic Center.

A gifted athlete himself, Rigo's friendship and basketball competition with Ermer had begun on the courts next to "No Man's Land." Rigo had watched Ermer's one-hand shot develop from an awkward, tentative hurl to a deft, unstoppable shot. No one stood more in awe of Ermer and his shot than Rigo, but the first night at dinner in the Chino boardinghouse, Ermer was refused service.

"This is bullshit!" Rigo exploded.

"Let it go," Ermer told him quietly.

"Well, it's bullshit!" Rigo repeated, then noticed that the kitchen help were all Hispanic. He grabbed Ermer's arm. "C'mon, we'll eat in the kitchen."[1]

Ermer followed reluctantly, and the two of them were put at a table against the wall in the kitchen. Despite growing up in the ethnic mosaic of Garlic Center, this was the real, ugly world of prejudice, separation, and exclusion. And no matter how talented Ermer Robinson was as a basketball player, the episode stood as a reminder that his talents faced restrictions as irritating and unjust as confinement to that kitchen.

Still, Ermer Robinson and Rigo Rodriguez led the Hillers to victory in the first three games of the Chino tournament. That Saturday they met their archrivals, the Hoover Cardinals, in the tournament finals. Both teams were undefeated, and it was the matchup that fans of the two schools had been waiting for.

Meanwhile, San Diego sportswriters who saw Ermer Robinson's one-hand shot had begun describing him as a "flashy Negro forward."[2] It was as if his revolutionary shot was a reflection of something gaudy in his character. It was as if he were just another jaunty and theatrical African American who might have been an entertaining, tap-dancing minstrel on a basketball court but otherwise deserved the humiliation of eating his supper with the kitchen help.

Despite the "flashy" epithet, he remained quiet and unassuming, no matter how formidable and unusual his shot was. And how to stop that shot became the chief concern of the Hoover Cardinals, whose strategy began off court, in the same Chino boardinghouse where they were staying with the Hillers. In the middle of the night, before the final game of the tournament, several Hoover players jumped into Ermer and Rigo's room covered with bedsheets. It was a stunt that sprang from the bigoted belief that all blacks, no matter how "flashy" they might have been, stood in mortal fear of ghosts, and the next morning the Cardinals bragged that the night of sleepless horror had surely exhausted Ermer. Their hope was that he would be useless in a basketball game.[3]

"Who the hell are they kidding?" Rigo spoke for both of them. "They didn't scare anybody."

The Hillers lost that afternoon, not because Ermer had been terrified and tired—he led all tournament scorers—but because the Hillers couldn't stop a superior Cardinal team. The Hillers had time over Christmas vacation to lick their wounds and look forward to evening the score against the Cardinals in the new year. That chance came on January 13, at Big Gym on the Hillers' campus. The San Diego papers didn't give them much of a chance. Hoover's team was the most powerful in the school's history, they wrote, maybe the "greatest court unit in the state of California."[4] They had rambled through eight straight victories, including a "whipping" of San Diego High with their "flashy Negro forward." But this time they couldn't stop that flashy forward, whose one-hand shots from the deep sidelines were described as "dazzling . . . sensational," and the Hillers won easily.[5]

It meant that a third and deciding game at the end of January 1942 would settle the issue of who was the better team, Hoover or San Diego High, and fans of both teams streamed into Big Gym for the afternoon contest. A warren of three-feet-deep trenches had been dug on the athletic fields, for protection from artillery shrapnel.[6] It brought the war especially close to home. Ermer Robinson's one-hand shot was erratic, and his play was flat. Using a figure-eight weave, Hoover jumped out to a comfortable halftime advantage. But Coach Merrill Douglas knew just what to do, and he put Rigo Rodriguez in the game to stop the Cardinals' leading scorer. Rigo played with a defensive ferocity that indicated he was finally getting even with Hoover for their crude prank in Chino with the sheets.

Still, the outcome of the game was in doubt until Ermer, fired up by Rigo's play, dribbled the full length of the court, weaving his way through defenders. Thirty feet from the basket, he stopped as if he intended to pick up his dribble and shoot his deadly one-hand shot. But just as two Hoover defenders converged on him, he took off dribbling again. When he was clear of the defenders, he jumped into the air off one foot. He was still a long way from the basket, and to make sure the ball carried to the target, he cocked his right leg at the top of his leap, then straightened it quickly again, just as he had learned to do practicing five hundred shots a day on the asphalt court beside "No Man's Land."

Despite the leap and the violent midair kick, the shot floated into the net softly and sealed the victory. After the game, jubilant San Diego High students streamed onto the floor in a wild celebration. It wasn't just that Ermer Robinson had beaten their archrivals in the rubber game, it was the *way* he had done it, flying forward at full speed yet shooting without slamming the ball into the backboard. He had taken his already novel one-hand shot to an even higher level of originality, shooting it on the run, and San Diego sportswriters said he was the best prep forward in Southern California basketball.[7]

The boys from the Garlic Center neighborhood liked to spend their lunches together at the outdoor tables at San Diego High, on the Balboa Park mesa overlooking the city. They would split a sweet cinnamon pastry they called a "cowflop" as they talked about the latest heroic deeds of Joe DiMaggio or Archie Moore, who lived off Market Street not far from Garlic Center, or Ted Williams, who had come from Hoover High.

None of those icons had gone to college before entering professional competition. They hadn't needed to. For them, the next step up from high school had been the minor leagues or amateur boxing arenas. But for the best prep forward in Southern California basketball, the next step up would have to be college play. Yet, as that incident in Chino had indicated, the world outside Garlic Center was racially divided, especially in the world of college education. And with the world at war, the racist view that African Americans were uneducable found an ally in those who believed that America's defense industry didn't need more college-educated, white-collar bureaucrats and management professionals. It needed riveters and assembly-line automatons. African Americans made good factory workers, the argument went.[8] They could sweat and labor. What few there were in college were wasting their time.

It meant that the world of college basketball was almost purely white, and there were few places in that world for an African American player from "No Man's Land" in San Diego. Even if Ermer found a college that would admit him, how would he pay for it? There were no college recruiters prowling Garlic Center or San Diego High looking to recruit him, because there were no athletic scholarships for a thin, hardly six-foot African American with a flashy one-hand shot.

His goal in life, he had written three years earlier, was to be "an artist or a carpenter."[9] Despite his court glories, nothing had changed, and he was at the end of the basketball line. At eighteen years old, his life seemed to have peaked.

Ermer Robinson graduated from San Diego High in 1942. Along with Rigo Rodriguez and thousands of other San Diego young men, he became just another soldier caught up in the tumult of world war. He washed pots and pans, stood in line, and learned how to peel potatoes. He learned how to salute and make his bed and fire a gun. He spent the end of every month on his bed in the barracks or nursing a cheap beer in the PX, waiting for payday. The glory of that running one-hand shot in San Diego that had beaten Hoover seemed from another life, and in his new life he was just an inconspicuous mite marching across a parade field with a sea of troops. It seemed ludicrous to imagine that he would ever enjoy the same athletic glories of white icons like Joe DiMaggio and Ted Williams.

He was playing basketball with a team from Fort Lewis, Washington, when his one-hand shot caught the eye of Abe Saperstein, whose Globetrotters were barnstorming the West Coast. It was an odd shot that Saperstein had never seen before, and he told his players beside him on the bench, "We don't shoot that shot up here."[10]

It was a shot only for awkward amateurs, Saperstein wanted it understood, and he did not want to see it from any of *his* players.

But the Globetrotters couldn't stop Robinson. Again and again he scored with the odd shot, planting one foot on the floor, then hurling himself forward and up into the air, or running and then leaping and delivering that bizarre midair kick, the way he had done to beat Hoover, as he let the shot go.

Finally, Saperstein wondered aloud, "What's his name?"

Since graduating from high school, Robinson had grown two small patches of mustache no bigger than ditto marks. It seemed to emphasize his gravity and diminish the effect of his thin smile. On the court he was all basketball and dead serious. Despite his scoring ability, there was nothing about him that suggested a flashy court clown who would fit in one of the Globetrotters' reems, and Saperstein's sudden interest in him took the team by surprise.

"What's his name?" Saperstein repeated.

One of the Globetrotters checked the scorebook. "Ermer Robinson," he told Saperstein.

"*Ermer?*"

Yes, that was his name.

From where?

From someplace in California. Los Angeles? San Diego maybe? Nobody knew for sure.

Why hadn't anybody heard of him?

There was no explanation for that either, beyond the fact that he was an African American from "No Man's Land" in a far corner of the country. And until the war, he had never been farther from Garlic Center in his young life than Chino, California, where they had tried to put the fear of ghosts into him because he was an African American, flashy and superstitious and destined to take his suppers in the kitchens of the world.

Saperstein watched for another five minutes in complete silence as Robinson scored again and again with his one-hand shot and eventually beat the Globetrotters single-handedly.

"Jeez," Saperstein finally said, "I better get that kid."

7

The Fastest Runner on Sixty-first Street

After Robinson's long set shot, the Lakers again go straight to Mikan with the ball. He executes the same fake and drop-step hook shot, this time with his right hand. The fake so confuses Pressley that Mikan wheels for the shot unopposed, but the ball pops out of the basket.

Willie King grabs the rebound and takes off down the floor. At half-court he is fouled by Swede Carlson, but he misses the free throw. The Lakers score twice, the second basket a breakaway layup by Jim Pollard after a long pass.

Lakers 13, Globetrotters 4.

Pressley switches back to guarding Pollard. Just as soon as the switch is made, Goose Tatum picks up his second foul trying to stop Mikan.

Before he receives the ball to shoot the free throw, Mikan, with his eyes fixed on the basket, crosses himself, as if to direct the divine help he is asking for to the proper spot.

Mikan's free throw skips off the side of the rim. Despite the miss, the game has all the appearances of a rout. The only way for the Globetrotters to stop Mikan seems to be to foul him, and Pollard hasn't missed a field goal. The Lakers' only moment of weakness comes when Mikan is whistled for a three-second violation. Mikan reveals his disagreement with the call by glaring at the official for only a moment before he pushes his taped glasses back up the bridge of his nose and trots down the floor. Several players on the Lakers bench jump to their feet and flap towels in protest.

The Globetrotters' only baskets have been a cheap sleeper by Goose Tatum and Ermer Robinson's improbably long set shot. Surprise and improbability—neither one can be counted on to beat a team as good as the Lakers. And the Globetrotters' pinwheel offense is all sound and fury signifying nothing. At this point, the only thing that seems in doubt is how lopsided the final score will be.

But then Ermer Robinson and Willie King score. Marques Haynes scores twice, the second time after recovering a loose ball at half-court and driving to the basket for an easy layup. The Lakers score, but Willie King makes two free throws, and the game is suddenly tied:

Lakers 15, Globetrotters 15.

The quarter ends with Swede Carlson missing a field goal and the score still tied. Again, the two teams gather in front of their benches. For the fans, the change from lopsided rout to a dead-even game has come quickly. Their opening lethargy has been so deep that they have hardly noticed the Globetrotters' comeback. But now whooping and cheering rise steadily between quarters. It is cheering that is all out of proportion to the action on the floor, which is nothing but two teams huddled in front of their benches. Half of the shouting is meant to inspire the underdog Davids, the other half is a battlefield roar that expresses the pure power of a mighty army of Goliaths. The two produce one coherent explosion of noise that is for the game itself, for the balance and suspense of it. It is no longer a rout. It is a tense mystery that won't be resolved for three more quarters of agony. There surely will be no antics by the Globetrotters to provide comic relief. This will be serious basketball, because what separates these two teams, beyond the obvious fact that one is comprised of black players, the other white, is that they move differently. Not as individuals but as teams. As five men following a basketball script. The Lakers are fixed in a slow, sprawling dance. The Globetrotters bunch and then explode. Even as the two teams huddle on the floor at the end of the quarter, even as the roar of the crowd grows louder and louder, their differences are dramatic, the one calm, almost serene in its detachment, the other animated and stormy. That difference is so profound that it is surely an expression of something much deeper than basketball philosophies and game plans. It also seems deeper than race. It is a difference that reflects the geographic cradles out of which each team has come.

Minneapolis called itself the "City of Lakes and Parks." That identity was so powerful that the Mighty Mississippi curled back upon itself as it flowed through the city, as if it wanted to stop there and form a limpid pool. There were twenty-two lakes within the city limits and only one skyscraper, the Foshay Tower, a replica of the Washington Monument that seemed out of place in a bucolic city with no other towering buildings to turn the streets into cement canyons. Minneapolis was the city of sunshine and fresh air and green grass and lawnmowers and late sunsets when the evenings were so still that a single leaf falling off a tree alighted with a crash. Minneapolis was the city for people who loved the great outdoors. Its lakes and waterfalls inspired poets to write love songs. The most celebrated statue was neither a fiery politician nor a general on horseback but the figure of a violinist in Loring Park, drawing a bow across his bronze violin and filling the air with imaginary music. The city prided itself on being neat, clean, systematic. It was also a recreational paradise, and no rugged outdoor enthusiast complained about the harsh winters. Out of those harsh winters came abundant crops of golden wheat more valuable than anything in Fort Knox. Minneapolis was the milling capital of the world, its grain elevators breaking the flat plains like huge pipe organs that filled the air with more beautiful music. It was a city of half a million people and nearly five hundred churches where devout, God-fearing men and women of every faith lifted their voices in orderly anthems.[1]

Minneapolis was a city of Swedes and Norwegians, yes, but also of Germans and Czechs and Finns and Irish and Poles, not in ethnic enclaves but spread to the winds of the city. They worked and played and prayed together in their numerous churches. What was missing were African Americans. Not just in Minneapolis but in the entire state.

The first whites in Minnesota were settlers drawn to the state's "limitless and fertile prairies" by flyers meant to attract immigrants. But those same flyers also warned "that the wholly destitute will encounter at first greater hardships here than those they seek to escape."[2] To an emancipated slave looking to head north, it sounded like the miseries of sharecropping and tenant farming, only much colder, and in 1870 there were only 162 African Americans in the city of Minneapolis. By 1930 Minneapolis could count only some 4,000 African Americans in its midst.[3] Not even the massive migration of southern blacks to northern industrial centers in the 1920s and 1930s in search of jobs and a better life had much effect on Minneapolis. The few who did come faced restrictive housing covenants, unemployment, and social segregation, yet they did not raise their voices in violent social protest.[4] They remained, by and large, invisible. Going all the way back to 1913, not a single black face appeared among the proud faces of the state high school basketball champions.[5] And not a single black face appeared in the pages of *Minneapolis: A Story of Progress in Pictures*, which celebrated a century of progress in the city.[6]

Chicago could not have been less like Minneapolis. Chicago was the city of wind, fires, ethnic saloons, and jazz that rocketed along with a jagged, staccato beat and a buzzy edge. It was the city of gangsters and machine guns and mob massacres. Ads for the new movie *Northside 777* called it a city with a "bullet blasted past."[7] The poet Carl Sandburg wrote that it was stormy, husky, brawling. He said it was a city with big shoulders and as fierce as a dog. Its people were freight handlers and hog butchers and toolmakers who were "bareheaded . . . shoveling . . . wrecking . . . half naked and sweating."[8] Chicago was the city of con artists and ingenious stings and card mechanics playing the crimp. Chicago was the city of fan dancers and crooked baseball players. It was the city of Bugs Moran and Al Capone and Machine Gun Jack McGurn. It was the city of Big Bill Thompson and Bix Beiderbecke. It was the city where the only thing that looped back upon itself was the El, raising a racket as it circled its tracks. Noisy Maxwell Street featured open markets with live chickens and spirited haggling. "We cheat you fair," the signs said.[9] There were barkers and Gypsy fortune-tellers and scientists smashing atoms under football stadiums. Republicans and Democrats were always rallying there, not just because of its midpoint geography but because for years its streets had served as platforms for raucous debates between Yankee speculators, Marxists, socialists, advocates of free silver, and raging anarchists who argued with firebombs.[10]

Chicago was the city of Studs Lonigan. It was checkerboarded with ethnic neighborhoods—German, Scandinavian, Bohemian, Polish, Russian, Lithuanian.[11] There were Jewish enclaves and Catholic strongholds. In the 1920s it was the home of James T. Farrell's fictional hero Morty Aiken, who was the fastest runner on the whole South Side of Chicago.[12] Then he and his friends, eager to keep the South Side and Washington Park white, began chasing blacks. It was "The Fastest Runner on Sixty-first Street" who led the chase, running out ahead of his gang, "tearing along, pivoting out of the way of shocked, surprised pedestrians, running, really running . . . like a streak of lightning," until he was jumped and stabbed by blacks.[13]

With the industrial migrations of two world wars, and despite the bigotry of thousands of Morty Aikens, the South Side of Chicago eventually held one of the largest urban concentrations of African Americans in the United States.[14] It was the home of Richard Wright, a "black boy" trying to find his way in a white world. It was the home of a popular radio show called *Sam 'n' Henry*, featuring two white men playing their idea of happy-go-lucky blacks and who would eventually become "Amos 'n' Andy." But their Chicago programs would give no indication that there was anything like a Chicago South Side, a festering sore with people packed together like sardines in squalid projects.[15] Chicago became the home of African American protest marches and so-called Indignation Meetings behind closed doors. At these meetings, angry adults let off steam and fulminated about injustice, while outside, young African Americans, unable to find comfort in mere talk, fought white gangs with car chains and jack handles and sawed-off shotguns. Sometimes when they met for athletic contests, the only people who came to watch were cops and ambulance drivers.[16] Chicago was volatile. And it seemed a dangerous place to stage a basketball game between an all-white team from Minneapolis and a squad of African American clowns, no matter how funny they could be.

II

SECOND QUARTER

8

Blackie

George Mikan controls the tip to start the second quarter. He misses a fadeaway shot, and the Globetrotters rebound and fast break. Willie King drives full speed to an open spot in front of the basket and skids to a stop. Without leaving the floor, he releases a one-hand shot with a high arch. The ball misses the basket entirely and drops straight into Mikan's hands. He is surrounded by Globetrotters who try to steal the ball, but his elbows fly as he twists his body and clears space for himself.

The Lakers set up. Jack Dwan and Herm Schaefer trade several passes at their guard positions, searching for an opportunity to get the ball into Mikan, but Babe Pressley and Marques Haynes keep sagging off to frustrate the pass. Finally, Pollard gets the ball, drives the baseline, is blocked, then bounces a pass to Mikan, who scores an easy layup.

Lakers 17, Globetrotters 15.

Ermer Robinson misses a long set shot. Pollard rebounds. Dwan scores a field goal.

Lakers 19, Globetrotters 15.

Pollard steals the ball from Goose Tatum. Schaefer brings the ball up the court, and again he and Dwan trade passes, searching for an opening in the wall of collapsing Globetrotters to get the ball into Mikan.

For a moment it appears that the Globetrotters' strategy of blocking the passes to Mikan is working. In desperation, Dwan shoots a pass into forward Swede Carlson, who tries to drive the baseline. His defender slides with him, and when they reach the baseline, Carlson pivots and dribbles toward midcourt. He is immediately surrounded by three Globetrotters defenders and comes to a halt in midstride, apparently trapped. He pivots desperately and then leaps into the air, hurling the shot with a sidearm sweep as if the ball were a discus.

"Field goalllll, Sweeeeeeede Carrrrl-son."

Lakers 21, Globetrotters 15.

Another eerie quiet falls in Chicago Stadium as the crowd tries to understand how it is that even the Lakers' desperation shots are good. They are pulling away and threatening again to make a rout of it. The game won't even be close. The Lakers are too mighty and blessed with deep talent to stop. Yet they are not even six months old as a team. Athletic dynasties take years to form, even decades. They don't suddenly streak across the sky like meteors. They are more like comets, whose promise can be seen only as a faint glow that slowly draws stargazers and then one day fills the sky with fireworks. So how did a basketball comet as stellar and impressive as the Lakers appear in the athletic skies so quickly?

It was one of James Naismith's Massachusetts disciples who brought the gospel of basketball to Minnesota in 1892. Naismith himself appeared at the University of Minnesota in 1927 for the dedication of the "Old Barn," then the largest basketball arena in the country. Naismith congratulated the university for "being one of the pioneers in the development of basketball."[1] Shortly after the end of World War II, the floor of the Old Barn that Naismith had helped dedicate was elevated, putting the players on a stage that symbolized how important the game had now become in a state with a proud football history. It was time to start thinking about bringing a pro team to the Land of Lakes.

Two prosperous Minneapolis businessmen led the effort to create a team. Maurice Chalfen owned a Chinese restaurant in the city and promoted ice shows. A quiet, five-foot Polish immigrant named Ben Berger, who also owned a restaurant as well as a chain of movie houses, had promoted prizefights and wrestling matches in North Dakota. Neither man knew much about basketball.[2] But an enterprising twenty-four-year-old Minneapolis high school dropout–turned–sportswriter did.

His name was Sid Hartman. They called him "Blackie" because as a kid he had run a newsstand on Nicollet Avenue and always had black newsprint all over his fingers. Others said he had been given the nickname because he was always covered with soot from crawling through air vents to sneak into basketball games at the Minneapolis Auditorium. Whatever the source of the nickname, "Blackie" Hartman loved sports, even though he had never been much of an athlete himself, he confessed, except in softball games in North Minneapolis, Jews against blacks. He also admitted, "I'm not a writer. My spelling is bad, and my grammar is worse."[3] But that didn't stop him from writing about sports or promoting them, and on December 1, 1946, behind the promotion of Sid Hartman, Ben Berger, and others, 5,500 Minneapolis basketball fans turned out to watch the city's first professional basketball game, between the two Wisconsin towns of Oshkosh and Sheboygan from the NBL.[4]

The game proved that Minneapolis had an interest in professional basketball. But where to find a team? Not of transient barnstormers but a franchised team in an official league, with traditional rivalries and playoff races and the chance to create a local identity. Chalfen and Berger did not have to look far.

The Detroit Gems of the NBL were owned by a jeweler named Morris Winston, and they were losing every game. Winston felt so apologetic for his team's inept performances that one night, after only six fans showed up to watch his team lose again, he gave them refunds.[5] At one point Winston became so desperate to turn around his team's fortunes that as a bold experiment, he signed several African Americans. Attendance improved, but the team continued to lose, and the African American players were quickly released.[6] It meant that as Winston made plans to sell his team, there would be no awkward negotiations with prospective owners who might have balked at purchasing a basketball franchise with blacks on its roster. Who would pay to see blacks play basketball? White sports fans who experienced race separation almost everywhere else in their lives came to basketball games expecting to be entertained, not treated to bold experiments in integration.

The Gems finished the 1946–47 season with only four wins and forty losses. It was the worst record ever in professional basketball, and on July 6, 1947, Winston gladly unloaded his pathetic Detroit Gems to the Minneapolis partnership of Chalfen and Berger for $15,000. All of the Gems' players had already been assigned to other

NBL teams. The Gems had even dealt away their college draft rights. For Minneapolis, the new franchise in the NBL meant nothing but a trunk full of sweaty, tattered uniforms and scuffed basketballs.[7]

Chalfen and Berger considered it a blessing that the Gems came without either the players or the coach who had managed to fail so miserably. Still, with the 1947–48 season scheduled to open soon, the new owners had less than two months to hire a coach and build a team roster. It went without saying that the team would be all-white. It was in part simple obedience to the demographics of Minneapolis and Minnesota. But there was another, even more powerful force that would help determine the new team's roster. From the smallest high schools in the country through the universities and colleges to professional basketball, teams everywhere were largely all-white. Even if Minnesota was the country's northernmost state, stuck at the extremes of weather and geography, unique in so many ways, from the long vowels of its Scandinavians to its cornfields and silos, in basketball it was quintessentially American. And it was obvious that the brand-new Minneapolis Lakers would be as white as its ten thousand lakes were all deep blue.

To build a team, Chalfen and Berger turned to Max Winter, a Minneapolis native who had starred in athletics at Minneapolis North High, then Hamline University in St. Paul. Winter owned the 620 Club in Minneapolis, "Where Turkey Is King," his menus said. Winter's popular restaurant was a hangout for journalists, radio broadcasters, and an occasional gangster who enjoyed Winter's $1.50 dinner of Minnesota tom turkey with old-time sage dressing, snowy whipped potatoes, and sweet-sour cole slaw.[8]

Again, where was any promise of basketball expertise, professional or otherwise? Still, Max Winter, the turkey king of Minneapolis, became the team's general manager, and he set out to find a coach for a new franchise that didn't even have a name yet. His first choice was Joe Hutton, the successful coach from Hamline University. Hutton turned him down flat. The next name on Winter's list was a young former Minnesota basketball star from the 1930s named Johnny Kundla, about to begin his second year coaching at St. Thomas University, also in St. Paul.

Kundla was young and bright and virtually unheard of beyond the city limits of Minneapolis, but Max Winter sent Blackie Hartman to recruit him.

Hartman arrived one evening in Kundla's tiny, second-floor apartment in northeast Minneapolis. "I've got an offer to make," Hartman said, then laid out the coaching proposal.

Kundla had no interest. "What do I know about pro basketball?" he said. Besides, he argued, the university's basketball teams were very popular. Pro basketball wouldn't have a chance in Minneapolis. Hartman disagreed. "Pro basketball is going to be popular here." But Kundla explained that he was happy at St. Thomas. Professional basketball, he felt, was at best a precarious way to make a living, at worst, filled with promoters and con artists out to make a fast buck. He could be dumped at any moment. Married seven years, with two young sons, he had responsibilities in his life. He told Hartman that he wanted nothing to do with professional basketball, either playing or coaching.

Hartman would not take no for an answer, and several days later he caught up with Kundla again, this time at a twilight softball game where Kundla was playing.

"I'm gonna ask you again," Hartman said. "Have you changed your mind?"

Kundla shook his head, and now Hartman pleaded. "Johnny, will you just think about it?"

"I'm sorry, but I'm not interested."

They met one more time in mid-July after another softball game. Hartman went straight to the point. "We'll pay you six thousand dollars a year for a three-year contract. *Guaranteed*," he added, as if to allay any fears Kundla still had about being dumped.

That night in his tiny apartment, Kundla put the question to his wife, Marie. "How can we lose?" It was twice the money he was making at St. Thomas. "If the team folds," he said, without adding that he half expected it to, "I still get paid for three years."[9]

On July 15, 1947, Johnny Kundla met Berger and Chalfen in the team's office in the Loeb Arcade on Hennepin Avenue and signed a contract to lead a team with no name, no uniforms, no place to play, and no players. He was thirty-one years old, the youngest coach in the NBL, and not at all certain he had done the right thing. Meanwhile, sportswriters wrote that Kundla's selection was startling because they had expected a veteran coach. Since the team hadn't signed a single player yet, they wondered at Kundla's first press conference if *he* intended to play.

"Me play?" he grinned. "I doubt it. But you can never tell. I think I could get in shape."

Behind his wide, cheeky grin, it was hard to know if he was serious. But he went on to explain that while he preferred fast college games, "Minnesota style," he would adjust the game to his players. Meanwhile, he promised, the team would feature "local talent." Presumably, Minneapolis or Minnesota players the fans would already know.[10] It again went without saying that they would all be white.

Chalfen and Winters delivered on their promise of local talent immediately, signing Tony Jaros and Swede Carlson from the Chicago Stags for $15,000. Both players were from Minneapolis, and both had starred at the University of Minnesota. Jaros was scrappy and quick and already a Minneapolis athletic legend. He had a clever underhand shot that he used to slip the ball beneath the out-stretched arms of defenders. Carlson was a playmaker who had been the Stags' most valuable player the previous season. To get the two local stars, who were hardly over six feet, Chalfen and Berger had to pay as much as they had for the entire franchise, but it was proof of how deep they were willing to reach into their pockets to build a team the fans would appreciate.

And they weren't done signing local talent yet. Ken Exel, Warren Ajax, and Don Smith, three more ex–Golden Gophers stars, signed next. But Exel, Ajax, and Smith were also short, in addition to being talent gambles. It was time to look for a star.[11]

Their first choice was the Kangaroo Kid.

After his marriage to Arilee Hanson, Jim Pollard had signed to play amateur basketball with the Oakland Bittners, and in the spring of 1947 he led them to the finals of the Amateur Athletic Union (AAU) tournament in Denver.[12] San Francisco sportswriters said he was the "greatest active basketball player in the world."[13] A dozen professional teams battled to sign him. Then one day in late July, somebody named "Sid" called, representing the "Minneapolis Millionaires," a new pro team that would be playing in the NBL.[14]

For the Kangaroo Kid with the Salvation Army trumpet, it was overwhelming. But the more he thought about it, the more he liked the idea of playing with a brand-new team. He would not be following in the footsteps of some larger city's professional basketball history. In the icy extremes of Minneapolis, he and his teammates would be *making* history. And as he had been for every team on which he had played, he would be the new team's headliner.

There was one other consideration. "Is there anybody *else* out there who can help us?" Hartman had asked him.[15] The invitation to bring familiar basketball faces with him was exciting, and Pollard offered the names of three Bay Area pro prospects. Paul Napolitano was a rangy forward from the University of San Francisco and a high scorer with the Bittners. Bill Durkee had been a ferocious defensive player from the University of California (uc) at Berkeley who had given the Kangaroo Kid fits. Jack Rocker, also from uc Berkeley, was a talented, six-five forward who had already received pro offers from the Philadelphia Warriors. The three men, along with Pollard, were the heart of the Bittners' success. The idea that they would all go to Minneapolis together may have been Pollard's dream, but it threatened to gut the Bittners' team.[16]

Convinced he was about to lose the nucleus of his team, Lou Bittner, owner of the Oakland aau team, began making frantic phone calls. Napolitano and Rocker couldn't be found. But, yes, Durkee told him, he had received offers.

Pollard also admitted he had had offers. "But I want some other fellows I know to come with me," he said, without explaining who.[17]

It was enough to turn all of Oakland frantic, and Mayor Joe Smith called Pollard and pleaded with him not to abandon the Bittners. "You know, Jim," he said, "the Olympics are coming. We want the Bittners to represent America in Olympic basketball competition."[18]

It was the powerful carrot of patriotism, but Pollard still couldn't make up his mind.

"The team doesn't even have a name, or anything," he told Arilee. She let him think aloud.

"But Philadelphia's already got Joe Fulks, who's a great shooter." She shrugged.

The Chicago Stags had Max Zaslofsky, he reminded her. Rochester had the great Bob Davies. "I don't want to be battling for scoring honors."

She nodded. After leading Stanford and then the Bittners, it would be difficult for him to play second fiddle to anybody else.

"I think Minneapolis would be a good place to go," he said finally. "It'll be a fresh start."[19]

The Kangaroo Kid signed with the Minneapolis Millionaires for $10,000 on August 27, 1947. Napolitano, Durkee, and Rocker all followed suit. Proudly puffing a cigar, his head hardly above Pollard's waist, Ben Berger posed beside his new Minneapolis star, who told reporters the new team would win the NBL title their first year.[20]

9

The King of Basketball

Swede Carlson intercepts a pass from Haynes to Tatum.

Lakers' ball.

Carlson races up the floor and at half-court heads toward the key, but he is forced to stop when two Globetrotters defenders cut him off at the top of the free-throw circle.

Carlson's two-hand set shot only rattles the rim.

The long rebound comes to Willie King, who gathers the ball in stride and heads for the sidelines. He passes to Goose Tatum, who dribbles down the center of the court.

Pollard sweeps in from behind Goose and steals the ball.

Pollard and Schaefer counterbreak toward the Lakers' basket against a lone Globetrotters defender, who fouls Schaefer on the layup.

Schaefer makes the free throw.

Lakers 22, Globetrotters 15.

Globetrotters' ball.

Ermer Robinson heads for the basket on a driving layup that draws Mikan and Pollard to the spot where he is flying through the air. They come at Robinson from opposite directions, threatening to squash him in midair, but he manages to slip between them just before their bodies collide at the spot where he was, and their arms cross in the air like swords trying to cleave the ball.

"Fieeeeeld goal, Rob-in-sonnnnn."

Lakers 22, Globetrotters 17.

Lakers' ball.

The pass goes to Mikan, who begins backing into Goose, whose shoes slide from the force of Mikan. Goose turns his shoulder into Mikan and plants his feet for more purchase on the floor, but he slides farther, helpless against the weight of Mikan's pushing. Finally, Mikan turns to shoot without even jumping. Goose looks up to see Mikan's arms reaching to put the ball in the basket. Also without jumping, Goose reaches up with both arms in an effort to stop Mikan's shot.

Goose grabs one of Mikan's wrists and pulls down, as if he is working a pump handle. Mikan stumbles and struggles to regain his balance. The whistle shrieks. The ball never leaves Mikan's hands.

It is Goose Tatum's third foul, but he seems unconcerned as he positions himself in the first spot on the lane for Mikan's two free throws.

Pollard takes the middle spot beside Goose.

Both men take advantage of this break to bend over with their hands on their thighs. They grip the bottom edge of their trunks and breathe deeply.

Mikan delivers the first free throw with an underhand swing. Once the ball is in the air and headed for the basket, he continues to hold both hands out, as if to provide invisible guidance for the free throw.

The free throw is wide and dribbles off the side of the rim.

As Mikan prepares to swing his second free throw, Pollard straightens up. He turns himself slightly, crouches, and waits.

Mikan's second free throw bounces high off the back flange of the basket. The players on the lane are all leaning, preparing to jump for the rebound. But Pollard jumps a split second before the others. The long muscles in his thin legs have such hair triggers and his leap is so explosive that his jersey, which has been neatly tucked into his pants, flies out and exposes his belly just as a flashbulb flares from the camera of a photographer sitting cross-legged on the floor behind the basket. Pollard's hair, which usually remains neatly parted and combed even during strenuous action, seems electrified by the power of his leap.

At the peak of Pollard's jump, he is high above the others, especially Goose Tatum, who still hasn't left the floor. Both of Pollard's arms are outstretched, his fingers are flared, and he is spraddle-legged. It is as if his entire body has been jolted by his powerful spring.

The ball is dropping down just off the front lip of the basket when he cradles it momentarily on the tips of his turned-up fingers, as if he is a waiter balancing a serving tray instead of a basketball.

The flip of the ball back up toward the basket is too delicate to be noticeable. The ball just bounces softly off his fingertips, slips back over the front rim, and settles softly into the basket.

Lakers 24, Globetrotters 17.

They became the "Minneapolis Lakers" after fans picked the only name that made sense for a city with so many bucolic lakes. The team colors, royal blue and gold, were selected to reflect the city's Scandinavian heritage. In October 1947 twenty-six pro basketball hopefuls showed up for their first practices in a northeast Minneapolis community center. Eight of the prospects were familiar faces from the University of Minnesota, but all the others were strangers, from all points of the country's compass. They were tall and short, shooters and playmakers, rebounders and defenders, from New York to California. They were Italians and Poles and Swedes and Croats and Germans. What they had in common was that they were big-city boys mostly, all of whom had the opportunity to play college basketball, and all of them were white.

At the team's first press conference, sportswriters asked owner Ben Berger to identify the players. "I don't know *who* they are," he admitted, "but they're all good."[1]

New hopefuls came and went daily. Coach Johnny Kundla had to begin each practice with a round of introductions. The eventual scrimmages were disorganized, and Kundla's easygoing instructions went unheeded. Meanwhile, Minneapolis sportswriters predicted that the new team would give the city basketball at its best. Still, only eight season tickets were sold, and Ben Berger admitted he was still looking for a "big man," whatever that meant from his short perspective.

Johnny Kundla tried to be more specific. "One more good-sized man," he explained, "around six-nine, six-ten," was all the team needed.[2]

Only days before the Lakers' opening game on November 1 at Oshkosh, they signed Bob Gerber, the presumptive big man. But at just six-five and sporting a pencil mustache, he looked more like a silent-screen star than a basketball player. And he seemed an unlikely candidate to battle against Oshkosh's six-nine, 280-pound Leroy "Cowboy" Edwards, who played like a bronco buster.

So it came as a surprise when Sid Hartman in Oshkosh phoned Arilee Pollard to tell her excitedly, "We won! We won!" He explained that it had taken a dramatic last-second shot by Swede Carlson to capture the opening victory.[3]

"I'm happy," Johnny Kundla told the press. "We beat Cowboy Edwards. I'm surprised we can beat a team like that, after only two weeks of practice."[4]

He went on to predict that they would be in the thick of the race for the NBL championship. Pollard would lead them, he was confident. One incident halfway through the Oshkosh game had convinced him. Pollard had come to the bench with a bloody elbow. "What happened?" a worried Kundla had wondered. Had rugged Cowboy Edwards tried to break his arm? "I hit my elbow on the backboard," Pollard explained.[5]

Kundla had never seen anybody who could jump like the Kangaroo Kid or move with such grace on a basketball court. Everything seemed in place for a championship. If he was still hoping for the missing basketball giant, he didn't say it. Then the Lakers rolled over three of their first four opponents, with Pollard leading the way each game. Against Tri-Cities, he outscored and outjumped their seven-foot star, Don Otten.[6] It was clear that the Kangaroo Kid could play like a giant. Why did they need anybody else?

It wasn't until three weeks into the season that the giant finally appeared one night just before a game on November 20 in Sheboygan. He came into the locker room wearing a heavy black greatcoat and a banker's homburg that made him look even bigger than he was.[7]

It was George Mikan reporting for basketball duty with his new team.

Pollard's almighty leap and soft tip-in are followed by a moment of stunned silence, as it sinks in with the crowd that what they have just witnessed is deserving of praise much higher than mere shouting. Neither high yips of enthusiasm nor a general roar in which the excitement feeds on itself is appropriate now. Somewhere, someone starts clapping, and disciplined applause quickly fills the entire arena. It serves to express the awe that Pollard's tip-in deserves, but at the same time the mannerly applause strips the crowd of the howling enthusiasm it felt earlier for a spirited contest, and after the applause dies out, the arena is again filled with an eerie silence.

Globetrotters' ball.

Willie King misses a field goal.

Swede Carlson captures the long rebound and leads a fast break. He drives for the layup, and the ball hangs on the lip of the rim, balancing, not sure what it wants to do, roll in or out.

Just as the ball drops away from the basket, George Mikan pushes aside two Globetrotters and seizes the ball. He quickly shot-puts it back to the basket without leaving the floor.

Lakers 26, Globetrotters 17.

For George Mikan, the road from DePaul to the Lakers was tortuous. After his graduation from DePaul, he began postgraduate studies in law and signed with the Chicago Gears of the NBL in 1946. The gawky string bean from Mikan's Tavern now ran the floor like a handsome Clark Kent with taped-on glasses, and the Gears program for the 1946–47 season called him "The King of Basketball."[8]

Not long into that first season, however, he fell into a contract dispute with Maurice White, the owner of the Gears who had made a fortune manufacturing precision gears for the navy during World War II. While suits and countersuits flew back and forth in court, Mikan sat on the sidelines, and without him the Gears floundered.[9]

The contract dispute settled, Mikan returned to the team finally in January 1947, and the Gears eventually won the NBL championship. The success encouraged Maurice White to start a league of his own, and he began hatching a bizarre plan for a sports empire that he eagerly laid out one day to Mikan.

Mikan had led the league in scoring, White reminded his basketball king. He was clearly the magnet who drew fans wherever he played, and White explained his plan to start a new league that would capitalize on Mikan's extraordinary popularity. It would be called the American Professional Basketball League, comprised of seventeen teams, from Louisiana to Minnesota, from Georgia to Nebraska. The Atlanta Crackers, the Louisville Colonels, the St. Joseph Outlaws—it sounded like something out of a textbook on bigotry and violence, and the league folded in two weeks.[10]

The hapless Detroit Gems, which Ben Berger and Maurice Chalfen had bought for a mere $15,000 and turned into the Minneapolis

Lakers, had finished the previous season dead last in the NBL. That cellar finish entitled Berger and Chalfen to make the first pick now in the dispersal draft for all those basketball souls, including George Mikan, who had been set adrift by the collapse of Maurice White's improbable league.

Turkey king Max Winter met with the King of Basketball for three hours in the Lakers' offices in Minneapolis. Winter was joined by Sid Hartman, and Mikan was represented by his attorney. Winter and Hartman's initial offer didn't match what Mikan had been making with the Gears, and after three hours of fruitless negotiation, Mikan and his attorney asked Winter and Hartman to take them back to the Minneapolis airport for their return to Chicago.

On the way, Winter instructed Hartman in Hebrew to pretend he couldn't find the airport. While Hartman drove a circuitous course, Winter delivered a travelogue on the attractions of the bucolic city—the serene lakes, the parks with band shells and spacious lawns, the boulevards and rose gardens and winding creeks and streets with lush canopies of elm trees.

By the time they arrived at the airport, Mikan had missed his flight. But it was transparent stalling that amused Mikan more than it irritated him, and the next day he signed with the Lakers.[11]

Max Winter immediately called Johnny Kundla. "I've got good news," he told the Lakers' coach.

What could be better than the news he was already hearing daily that the Lakers with Jim Pollard were an unbeatable powerhouse?

"We've got the King of Basketball," Winter said.

Kundla was speechless. He had been too anxious about his team to even notice what else was going on in the world of professional basketball.

"We've signed . . . *George Mikan*," Winter explained, in case Kundla didn't understand.

"I don't believe it."

Winter assured him it was true.

"My, God!" Kundla said. "I've already got Pollard. Now I've got Mikan?"[12]

Yes, he had *both* men. In Pollard, he had a star whose superhuman, spraddle-legged flight had become almost mythical, decades before the appearance of Michael Jordan and the Nike swoosh that had been inspired by his miraculous basketball flight. And now

Kundla had the King of Basketball, too, a floor-bound tank of a player who, like Shaquille O'Neill also decades later, couldn't be stopped. Both Mikan and Pollard had had commonplace if not underprivileged pasts, the one in Oakland, the other in Joliet. In the context of such ordinary lives, it was hard to spot any privileges. But they were there nonetheless, especially if you measured their lives against those of their globetrotting opponents, none of whom had enjoyed the basketball opportunities they had. But in February 1948 few would have been willing to credit the black players with the mythical leaping powers of Jim Pollard or the relentless scoring might of George Mikan. Even fewer would have been willing to credit the Globetrotters with having overcome prejudice and basketball dispossession to reach the same level of basketball power as the Minneapolis Lakers.

10

The Crisco Kid

Globetrotters' ball.

At the center of their pinwheel, Goose Tatum walks.

Lakers' ball.

Herm Schaefer is fouled and makes the free throw.

Lakers 27, Globetrotters 17.

Globetrotters' ball.

Goose Tatum walks again.

Lakers' ball.

Babe Pressley fouls Mikan, who makes the free throw.

Lakers 28, Globetrotters 17.

Mikan's successful free throw is his first after three misses. It gives the Lakers an 11-point lead, their biggest of the game, and the Globetrotters take another time-out.

The time-out contrasts between the two teams are even more dramatic now. The Globetrotters' antic behavior in their floor huddle—all of them moving and talking, even Abe Saperstein gesturing wildly—suggests desperation. The Lakers' motionless, tight circle around Johnny Kundla reflects confidence in their commanding lead.

George Mikan appeared suddenly in Sheboygan in his greatcoat and homburg as a colossal caricature of himself, and there was no mistaking who he was. Still, he went around the locker room introducing himself to his new teammates. And when the King of Basketball shook hands with the Kangaroo Kid, their differences were deep.

It began with the fact that Pollard had never owned a topcoat in his life. Nor did he have the kind of glibness that seemed to have originated for Mikan in a Joliet tavern and then been polished by his law studies. Pollard's quiet boyhood had featured two pairs of pants and a Salvation Army trumpet. He told anybody who asked that he had had enough religion as a boy to last all his life.[1] Yet he could leap to the heavens and was the only Lakers player who dunked during warm-ups. "We know when he's been in the building," they said about him, "because the tops of the backboards are clean where he's raked them."[2] He had his smooth California fake, and he could make even awkward shots off the wrong foot look graceful. He was the natural. Everything he did flowed from instinct, swiftly and gracefully.

His glasses knocked cockeyed by defenders, lumbering up and down the floor in his knee pads, George Mikan was a basketball tractor, powerful and steady. He was also deeply religious. He crossed himself before all free throws, and during play he was as unflappable as a machine or that genteel British banker in his homburg. "You can't get him mad," they said.[3] Meanwhile, most of his basketball skills, from his soft touch to his ambidextrous hook shot, had been acquired by repetition and training and endless practice. He was truly a *study* in basketball.

But he couldn't fit in the trunks the Lakers provided for him that night in Sheboygan, so he wore his old Gears trunks. His trademark jersey was number 99, because ninety-nine cents wasn't quite a dollar, he said, and that helped to remind him that there was always a higher level to play to. But that night in Sheboygan, in front of five thousand fans, he played as number 21, and the Lakers lost by 14 points.[4]

The number change had little to do with why they lost. Mikan's reputation directed that the ball come to him. But posted too low in the key, he was boxed in all night by collapsing Sheboygan defenders who plugged the middle, fronted him, and stole passes repeatedly. When the Lakers could get the ball to him, they followed with two-man crisscrosses that further plugged the key.[5]

Pass and cut. For Johnny Kundla, it was sound basketball strategy from as far back as he could remember.

But Mikan complained, "It's jamming me up!" For his drop-step hook shot, he needed room to maneuver.[6]

Despite the addition of Mikan to the roster, the Lakers lost four of their next five games. Johnny Kundla felt lucky to have both Pollard and Mikan dropped in his coaching lap, but it was apparent that sheer talent wasn't the key to professional basketball success, and Kundla lost sleep wrestling with the problem.

Moving Pollard to a forward had been the easy part. It was where he belonged, facing the basket with plenty of room to drive and leap. But his quick fakes, his spinning hook passes that whistled at Mikan like ricocheting bullets, his sudden drives into the middle where Mikan had already positioned himself—they all took getting used to.[7]

Pollard told Mikan to keep his hands up. His passes could come any time. But they went right on through early December playing uneven basketball, losing as many as they won, without realizing the promise of having the two best players in the country. Pollard's play was especially disappointing. He scored just 2 points in one game and then sat out several games in mid-December because of a cold. "Pollard Back to Old Stride" the *Minneapolis Star* said after he finally returned to play.[8] But it wasn't a simple head cold that was behind the Lakers' troubles, and their disappointing play continued through December.

There were other difficulties. Pollard had come to Minneapolis as the Lakers' linchpin and earned well-deserved newspaper headlines and praise. From as far back as grade school, he had never been on a team where he wasn't the main story. It bred a quiet confidence that struck some as standoffish, others as arrogance. And now here was Big George Mikan in his fancy homburg, the King of Basketball, whose reputation was even more celebrated and built on championships and honors no less deserving than Pollard's. But on the floor during time-outs, Mikan often sat by himself toweling off or wiping his glasses while Pollard got a drink. It left Johnny Kundla talking quietly to just three players, calling for his "JG" play, featuring Pollard and Mikan on a pick-and-roll. But Pollard would zip a pass into Mikan, then stand waiting for Mikan, as if to say, "Go ahead, *you* do it." Mikan kept smiling and trying to score through the double- and triple-teams, bulldozing opponents with his armbar and trying to do it all himself. And Pollard went on leaping to the heavens. But they couldn't win consistently, and it took the veteran Herm Schaefer to straighten it out.[9]

They called him the "Crisco Kid" because he was "fat in the can."[10] He had come to the Lakers after he was released by the Indianapolis Kautskys. He had jug ears, a crooked, boyish smile, and he liked to play practical jokes on his teammates, but he had been in the NBL for almost a decade, and he took his basketball seriously. With his bowling-ball shape, he was not nearly the player he had been as captain and All-American at the University of Indiana or as the player-coach for several pro teams, but he was the oldest member of the Lakers, experienced and basketball smart, and he was immediately recognized as the team's natural leader.

On January 2, 1948, after a disappointing loss to Fort Wayne in front of almost eight thousand Minneapolis fans, Schaefer took Mikan aside in the locker room.

"Mikan," he said, "you're a fool."

The harsh words stunned Mikan. Stupidity was the last thing he expected to be accused of, *ever*. Nor did he expect to receive basketball belligerence from anybody. Ray Meyer had seldom gotten angry with him. Johnny Kundla, who felt a special connection to the churchly giant who crossed himself before free throws, never tore into players. They all liked Johnny's easy, patient coaching style, which was the polar opposite of coaches who thought verbal abuse was somehow inspirational. So why was Schaefer calling him a fool?

Schaefer explained that he felt Mikan and Pollard were at war with each other on the basketball court. Pollard was a brilliant player and passer. And Mikan was the King of Basketball. But as soon as the ball went into Mikan, that was the end of it. "George, you can't win games all by yourself," Schaefer finished. The ball had to come back out now and then. Learn to work together, Schaefer predicted, and the Lakers would win the NBL championship by ten games.

The next night, before meeting the team from Flint, Michigan, the King of Basketball and the Kangaroo Kid met to talk. The one was driven by a ferocious work ethic that compelled him to try to do it all himself, the other so blessed with natural grace that basketball sovereignty seemed his birthright. But the two men agreed on a head signal for return passes, then went out and beat Flint by 25 points. The next night they beat Flint again, this time by almost 40 points. Four straight victories followed, and they cruised to a 10–4 record in January.[11]

Herm Schaefer has the ball. He is standing at a shallow forward spot, his back to the basket, not quite close enough for his favorite shot, which is a right-handed hook shot from just outside the lane. If during the course of action he winds up with the ball anywhere near that spot, he will keep his dribble and back into his defender, sliding left and right as he backs up in order to get precisely where he has the most confidence in the shot. If he doesn't get in close enough, the eventual long hook shot will be as comic as Goose's Prayer. Yet if he backs too deep into the key, he risks having the shot knocked away with embarrassing authority by a towering center.

The Crisco Kid is only six feet tall. With his shape, it seems foolish for him to be trying hook shots as if he were a lanky center. Yet it is his favorite shot, the very same one he spent fifteen minutes demonstrating at a Lakers' clinic for Minneapolis kids one cold Saturday afternoon in late December. At the same clinic, Tony Jaros demonstrated his underhand scoop shot, Jim Pollard showed off his one-hand wrong-foot shot, and George Mikan executed his dropstep hook shot in a slow-motion ballet that made it look simple.[12]

It is only Schaefer's hook shot that doesn't seem to flow naturally from him. Nor does it bear much resemblance to the shot-put style of Mikan's hook shot. And as he maneuvers himself into position in the silence of Chicago Stadium, a rush of laughter rises from the fans, as if he is trying to mimic Goose's Prayer.

Yet Schaefer's is a true hook shot, in which he lays out his right arm and lets the ball roll off his fingertips. His arms hardly move, and it is entirely the flick of his wrist that gives the ball direction and impetus. It spins so rapidly that the expectation is that it will bite the backboard and squeal like a tire spinning on asphalt. But there is no sound at all as the shot, which is short, sticks for a second in the gap between the rim and the backboard before Babe Pressley leaps up to pull it free.

Globetrotters' ball.

Schaefer's impact on the team went beyond Mikan and Pollard. He preferred deliberate action with set plays, and it was usually Schaefer who started those plays with a high, slow dribble. He introduced a guard-forward pickoff play, which Kundla added to the plays they had neglected in their reliance on Mikan.[13] And Schaefer had a long, deadly two-hand set shot, which made it difficult for defenders to sag off on Mikan. Then the Lakers signed two more players to bolster their roster. Jack Dwan, whose set shot was even longer and deadlier than Schaefer's, came from the defunct St. Paul Saints after

Maurice White's basketball empire folded. Finally, they picked up Johnny Jorgenson, an agile forward who had been Mikan's teammate at DePaul.[14]

By the end of January, George Mikan had set a new NBL scoring record of 41 points in a single game, and the Lakers bore little resemblance to the team that had been so unsettled initially that practices had begun with introductions. Bob Gerber was gone, to return to swashbuckling motion pictures, one might have assumed. Only three of the numerous Minnesotans remained. Both Jack Rocker and Bill Durkee were gone from the California clique.[15] Like every other team in the NBL, there were still no blacks on the roster, and the only integration had been between Mikan and Pollard, who had reconciled their different styles of play. And with the arrival of February 1948, they began a win streak that would run to eight straight in the NBL. Nobody could beat them.

11

Olson's Terrible Swedes

There had always been something thrilling about barnstormers coming to town. Whether they performed frantic skits in barns, flew baling-wire biplanes, or shot baskets in country gyms, they seemed as free as the wind. Jews from Philadelphia and Swedes from the Midwest rode those winds from east to west and drew huge crowds playing exhibition basketball. "Rah rah rah!" the cheer went for a barnstorming team called Olson's Terrible Swedes. "They're terrible!" But it didn't matter that they weren't very good. Fans still came to see them play because they brought the razzle-dazzle world into a cracker-box gym. By turns through the 1920s and 1930s, globetrotting American Indians and Germans from Buffalo and modern-day Celts claimed they were the world champions of basketball.[1]

The most legitimate claim to the title came not from Germans or Swedes but a black team that had begun in 1923 on a dance floor in Harlem. They were known as the New York Rens, after the Renaissance Casino at 137th Street and Seventh Avenue. After the games, fans danced to Jimmie Lunceford's orchestra playing "Taint What You Do, It's the Way You Do It." The amazing way the Rens handled and passed a basketball brought claims that they were the best team in the country, and they were soon traveling up and down the East Coast. They weren't the first team of black barnstormers who matched their skills against white teams in a segregated society, but by the 1930s they were the best, playing to sellout crowds of blacks and whites seven days a week in New York and on the road.

Their ability to draw huge crowds should have been taken as a powerful economic argument for integration, but professional leagues refused to admit the Rens. Meanwhile, for some fans the basketball court was just another racial battlefield. When the all-white New York Celtics played the Rens, partisan fans rioted in the streets. One night in Akron, Ohio, a mob attacked one of the players. Elsewhere, crowds spit on them. The proprietors of an Indiana restaurant used a screen to segregate the Rens from regular customers. The Rens often ate cold cuts on buses and traveled hundreds of miles out of their way to find a hotel that would accept them. The team's traveling secretary took to carrying a pistol.[2]

Meanwhile, the connections between dancing and basketball seemed so natural that not long after the formation of the New York Rens, the Savoy Ballroom above a movie theater on Forty-seventh Street in Chicago gave birth to another team of black stars, this one called the Savoy Big Five. Late in 1928 they went looking for a manager-coach to get bookings for a barnstorming tour of the Illinois countryside. Despite the presence in the news of giant figures like Babe Ruth, Charles Lindbergh, and Gary Cooper, the Savoy Big Five picked a pint-sized Chicago Jew named Abraham Michael Saperstein to lead them. After Saperstein assumed team ownership, he had red, white, and blue uniforms stitched with the words "Saperstein's Original Harlem New York Globetrotters." Eventually they were simply the "Harlem Globetrotters," because he wanted to make sure that fans from as far away as Minnesota and New England realized they were a team of black men.[3]

At first they played serious and skillful basketball. Tiny Abe Saperstein was the Globetrotters' only substitute. He *looked* funny on the bench wearing a uniform under his winter coat, but the humor was unintentional. Then one night in a cold Iowa gym, the crowd roared when the uniform of one of Saperstein's players caught fire after he sat on a potbellied stove. Before long they were clowning regularly. White audiences in small prairie outposts, with nothing but the town's annual winter shoe-clearance to look forward to, were too busy laughing to turn nasty. The comedy also kept the games close and made sure that the Globetrotters got invited back.[4]

Whites may have been the target audience, but the *Chicago Defender* wrote about all African American barnstormers with pride. At first the clowns could not beat the powerful and serious Rens. When they finally did, on their way to winning the World Professional Basketball Tournament of 1940, the Globetrotters had learned to be comedic or straight, depending on how good the opponent was.[5]

Before games, they formed their Magic Circle and made the basketball hop like a movie-house bouncing ball by which Brother Bones whistled "Sweet Georgia Brown." Then they would turn the contest into a football game in which they drop-kicked the ball into the basket. They would wind up and hum basketball pitches at batters whose knees flapped with mock terror. They would make the ball disappear and then appear again suddenly, spinning on somebody's index finger. They would climb on each other's shoulders and tower over their helpless opponents, or they would become a circling, frenetic pinwheel of players, cutting for the basket one after the other and shouting as if they had been suddenly filled with the spirit of Jesus.[6]

The pass goes into Goose Tatum. He leaps high to receive the pass, bullfrogging his legs before he lands at the top of the key, his back to the basket. His knees are locked, and he is pigeon-toed as he pushes up against George Mikan, who uses the armbar of his hook shot to keep Goose at bay.

Suddenly Goose raises one arm high over his head. His wrist is bent sharply so that his hand is like a chicken claw cupping the ball firmly against his forearm. He juts his chin out, then opens his mouth, as if he is clearing his windpipes for a great belch.[7] But he delivers instead a chilling, strident howl that is half painful cry and half trumpet call.

It fills every corner of Chicago Stadium and signals the start of a reem. Goose's cry dies, and a muffled clamor rises from the crowd, as if they are all standing for the Pledge of Allegiance. But they are only straightening themselves suddenly in their seats, craning their necks. Because they recognize that this is it. This is the comic moment the Globetrotters have flirted with off and on. It is finally here.

Goose begins windmilling the ball, which is still cupped in his wrist. Mikan could reach up and take a swat at it if he wanted to. But he drops his armbar from Goose's back and steps away to enjoy the reem, just the trace of a smile on his face. The smile is too meager to reveal whether Mikan is truly amused or just trying to show that the only reason for him to be passive in anything, especially on a basketball floor, is in deference to Globetrotters' comedy. However he intends it, he knows enough not to interfere with a reem once it has started, because it is what so many fans have come to see, despite the promotion of the Mikan-Tatum matchup as the basketball duel of the century.

The Globetrotters began their pinwheel cutting. At first they circle off Goose in wide arcs one after the other. As they fly past him, he stops windmilling the ball just long enough to offer it to each cutter, then quickly withdraw it just as they grab for it. Once past him they shout their disappointment at not having received a handoff, and in a matter of seconds they are all nattering away as they keep circling, telling him they are open, they are *wide open*, why doesn't he give them the ball? But they still circle around and come cutting by him again, only to receive the same offer and rejection, after which they deliver the same plaintive cry of disappointment.

Goose moves the ball at the end of his stiff arm, up, down, out to the side, offering it and then taking it back again, talking to them as they flash by, congratulating them on their speed and form, encouraging them to come by one more time and he'll give them the ball, if they'll just come a little closer to him, tighten their cuts a little, don't be afraid, next time the ball is yours!

Occasionally, Goose slams down a dribble to reposition himself, sliding three steps left or right, moving himself with flatfoot slaps of his feet like a circus clown, utterly oblivious to the fact that he is on a basketball court, in possession of the ball, and flagrantly walking with it.

But no whistle blows, because it would be an intrusion upon a comic skit that has its own rules and script. Goose Tatum is the slaphappy jester, so simpleminded in his cheerfulness that he doesn't even know what the rules of basketball are. It is such an irrepressible part of his character, the cheerfulness, that it must be released in inarticulate yelps and howls, which are taken up by the other cutters. Even the Globetrotters' pinwheel offense, with its merry-go-round simplicity, seems silly and mindless. With each promise of the ball by Goose, with each refusal followed by an invitation to make their cuts tighter, the arc of their circling gets smaller and smaller and smaller, as if they are trapped in an invisible turnstile, until they are just a hilarious tangle of players staggering around each other.

The fans are laughing so hard, and so focused on the knot of bodies trying to disentangle themselves from Goose, that they don't notice Ermer Robinson standing isolated at the sidelines. Suddenly, he cuts along the baseline for the basket, and the pass from Goose

Tatum, which whistles by George Mikan's head, catches everyone by surprise. Mikan turns, but too late.[8]

"Field goal, Robinson."

Lakers 28, Globetrotters 19.

The comedy didn't insulate them from insults. Fans in Oshkosh shot staples at them or zinged them with paper clips shot from rubber bands. They were called "coons" and "shines," and one team walked off the court rather than lose to them.[9] They were accused of being disgraceful Uncle Toms dancing for the amusement of white audiences. Their critics insisted that the clowning was *all* they could do. And there were occasional episodes of violence. One winter night in Minnesota, a celebrated football coach playing with a team of All-Stars began swinging wildly when he saw that his rugged pigskin skills were no match for Globetrotters' slickness.[10] Another night at a high school gym in Portland, Oregon, police had to step in to stop the fighting.[11] They received growled racial slurs during the heat of play. Their antics drew jeers in Canada, and they suffered the same indignities as the New York Rens before them—long bus rides, restaurant refusals, seedy hotels. After they won the world championship in 1940, some of the players argued that they were too good to clown at all. By then, however, they were captives of their own reputation, and they stayed on the road night after night, clowning their way around the country.[12]

The longest they stayed in any one place was the ten days they bunked at Ma Piersall's in Chicago in October, to start their season. Abe Saperstein invited talented black basketball players from every quarter of the country to come to Chicago to try out for his celebrated team. He gave them each two dimes to ride the El to various practice sites, where they worked out behind locked doors. They polished their reems in the mornings, then drilled and scrimmaged in the afternoons.[13]

The standard contract for the players picked for the final traveling squad called for $400 a month, for as many games as were scheduled, sometimes two a day. Saperstein eventually had so many bookings throughout the country and so many good players who had nowhere else to go with their talent that he formed a West Unit to complement the East Unit of his club. He also had two farm teams—the Broadway Clowns and the Kansas City Stars—which he could turn to for additional talent if needed.[14]

They occasionally met good black teams seeking to dethrone them. And there were serious battles against all-white pro teams from the East. But most of the opponents were ragtag teams of old men, schoolteachers, and young basketball hopefuls trying to hone their skills. Then the AAU insisted that players would forfeit their amateur status if they competed against Globetrotters who were paid professionals. It forced Saperstein to create mainly all-white stooge teams that traveled along with his Globetrotters.[15] The stooge teams were under strict instructions to play passive defense and not interfere with the comic reems. It meant that when the *Chicago Defender* described the Globetrotters as the most sought after basketball aggregation in the country, with an amazing total of 2,886 victories during its twenty-year history, it was clear that many of those wins had come against stooge teams.[16]

Marques Haynes is the smallest player on the court, hardly six feet tall, only 150 pounds, more thin bone than flesh or muscle. He has a small face, narrow shoulders, and pin legs. Everything about him seems sticklike and rickety. Except his hands. His hands are huge and move as gracefully as paper fans. The palms are wide and deep, the fingers long and supple. The size and grace of his hands explain why he has become the most remarkable dribbler in the history of the game of basketball, and there is always one place in every game where the Globetrotters turn him loose, like a drummer finally getting his opportunity to solo. Haynes's showcase dribbling solos are often the high point of a Globetrotters' performance, engaging the fans even more than one of Goose Tatum's comic improvisations, which are often so sudden in their appearance and so unpredictable in their direction that the laughter is uncertain.

The wonder of Haynes's performance is that he dribbles through the legs of stooge defenders who chase him, or behind his back, or while stretched out on the floor with his legs crossed as if he is resting on a chaise lounge, the dribbles so low and rapid that the ball hardly seems to be moving but is just a blur, like hummingbird wings.[17] The wonder is also that the ball, an otherwise free object in space, has become a part of him. And the laughter and applause that eventually turn to cheering are for just that, for a moment that seems almost peaceful, not just because he is so relaxed lying on the floor dribbling but because two objects as different as a small round basketball and an angular, rickety human being have become one.

Now Haynes moves across midcourt and begins his dribbling solo. But the Globetrotters are behind by nine points, and this hardly seems the time for clowning. It is also too soon in the drama for him to begin his dribbling act. It should come, as it normally does, at some point in the second half when the crowd is primed and eager and swept up by two quarters of comic building that will lead them to explode with excitement at the first appearance of his dribbling magic.

Haynes seems tentative then as he begins darting in at the Lakers players, sliding to a stop on one of his kneepads, trying to entice one of them into guarding him. But having already been fooled by Goose Tatum's comic windmilling, the Lakers are determined not to be duped again by the comedy. They will not take the clowning bait. They will not be made into the very same stooges who have rolled over and played dead for countless Globetrotters' victories. Besides, the serious basketball tone of the game has already been established. Both teams are in it for the drama, not the comedy.

Even Haynes's teammates seem baffled as he probes deeper and deeper into Lakers defenders, thirty feet from the basket, twenty-five feet, now all the way to the top of the free-throw circle. Each time he darts in and flirts with defensive danger, laughter rises suddenly from the crowd. It is like laughter being pumped from a bellows, and it subsides as soon as Haynes retreats. Finally, he penetrates almost to the free-throw line and pretends to lose control of his dribble. He stumbles after the ball, recovers control, then loses control again as if he is a dribbling klutz.

Herm Schaefer raises one arm and lunges at him. Haynes gains control of the ball immediately and retreats again with a clumsy dribble that sends the ball bouncing high over his head so that he has to reach to control it. Schaefer follows him for only a few feet in a half-hearted effort to contest Haynes's ludicrous dribble, then straightens, puts his hands on his hips, and refuses to come any farther out. He stares at Haynes, as if to tell him that he can dribble all night at half-court if he wants to, he can pretend all night that he is a dribbling klutz, but if he tries to score, he'll face a smothering defense.

Haynes drops onto his knees, dribbling still, offering the ball to Schaefer as he dribbles, daring him to try to steal it. All of the Lakers are standing straight, watching, hands on hips, together in their refusal to play Haynes's little game.

It is the age-old tale of the rabbit and the fox, and it produces a gradual swell of cheering that rises to the loudest of the night. Haynes is the animal trickster of African fable, turned into Brer Rabbit, turned again into a slick, basketball-dribbling wonder.[18] It is a comic reversal of reality and history—a tiny trickster is using guile to outwit authority and power. Beleaguered Brer Rabbit is about to humiliate the mighty fox. But Haynes is also every underdog David who has ever battled a powerful Goliath, and there isn't anyone in Chicago Stadium who isn't swept up by the drama of it.

The crowd roaring its approval, he stretches out on the floor now and doesn't even look at any of the Lakers. It is the ultimate temptation, and several of them edge closer to him until they are only a few feet away. With Haynes flat on the floor, they are tempted to sweep in and steal the ball, if only they could be sure that Haynes wouldn't instantly pop to his feet and dart away like a jackrabbit and make a fool of them. If only they could be sure that they wouldn't be outwitted again by the rabbit's teasing cleverness.

12

Sambo

It was an old joke:

A slave rides his horse deep into the forest in the company of his master's wife. Once they are hidden in a sylvan glade, she dismounts her horse and tells him, "Do everything I do."

She quickly takes off all her clothes.

He dismounts and does likewise.

Next, she lies on her back on the ground. "All right, big boy," she calls to him, "get in the saddle and go to town."

He jumps back on his horse and rides naked into town.[1]

The joke's cruel rationale extended deep into the game of basketball. Racists argued that blacks were "Sambos," too simpleminded to ever master the complicated tactics or the competitive zeal the game called for. And the monotony of the Globetrotters' merry-go-round offense wasn't just a comic device. It was meant to be simple enough for African American players to master. Basketball was a game of brains, the argument went, which explained why some of the best early barnstormers were Jews, who were smart by nature. The sportswriter-turned-novelist Paul Gallico wrote that the reason basketball appealed to Jews was because the game placed a "premium on an alert, scheming mind, flashy trickiness, artful dodging." Others argued that Jews were good at the game because they were built low to the ground, which gave them excellent balance and footspeed.[2]

Two Lakers surround Marques Haynes when he is still on the floor and the ball goes out of bounds. A chorus of boos arises from the stadium, disapproval over the fact that his amazing performance has come to such an inglorious end.

Lakers' ball.

Herm Schaefer dribbles up the court with unusual guardedness now, bent low, protecting his dribble, although no defender is near him. It is as if he is still smarting from the mistaken relaxation that led to Goose Tatum's trick pass to Ermer Robinson, flashing along the end line toward the basket.

Schaefer passes to Jim Pollard, who dribbles immediately for the baseline, whirls, takes one long step toward center court, switches his dribble back toward the baseline, and glides under the basket for a reverse layup.

Field goal, Pollard.

Lakers 30, Globetrotters 19.

It could get emotional, the argument over who was naturally the fittest for what sport. Slavic hulks like Bronko Nagurski from Minnesota's Iron Range had the brute strength and size to make the best football players. Grantland Rice maintained that the American Indian had all the gifts of a natural athlete. "His reflexes are sharp," Rice wrote, "he rarely gets excited or off balance."[3] His cool composure was all part of his outdoor heritage, Rice felt. Barroom orators argued that Scandinavians made good long-distance runners, Greek strength was legendary, Germans had bulldog tenacity, Italians like the great DiMaggio were born graceful, the Irish had stamina, Orientals were quick and reflexive, nimble-footed Brazilians made the best soccer players.[4]

One solid truth lay beneath the spurious claims. Sports had long been an entry point for immigrants and outsiders seeking assimilation into American society. They were the butt of crude jokes—the Irish drunkards Pat and Mike, the naive Swede who called himself Yonny Yonson, Jake the scheming Jew, dimwitted Polacks, crude Italians—but they had all used sports as one way to escape the jokes that were meant to disable them.[5]

The exception was African Americans, for whom sports remained forbidden territory. Racists feared that white supremacy would be undone by African American athletic achievement, and the rationalizations for their continued exclusion from American games were as shallow as those promoting Greek strength or Oriental reflexes. In basketball, it wasn't just that they were simpleminded Sambos who could never learn the plays, they weren't *built* for the game. They were as angular and asymmetrical as Goose Tatum with his freakish arms. Sure, they might have had speed and a dancing quickness, but they were too stricken with ropy muscularity to have the soft touch of good shooters.[6]

After Pollard's reverse layup, Ermer Robinson receives the inbound pass from Marques Haynes and flies immediately up the court, pushing the dribble ahead of him, rushing to catch up with it, dribbling again, passing one, two, three tiring Lakers as he goes. Finally, only Swede Carlson is shoulder-to-shoulder with him, struggling to keep pace as he reaches to try to steal Robinson's dribble.

Robinson approaches the basket at such breakneck speed that it seems unlikely that he can stop or even slow down to gather himself to jump for the layup. Because of the momentum of his hurtling body, he seems to have no choice but to slam the ball at the basket in a desperate shot that in all probability will crack the backboard.

Ten feet from the basket, he slows suddenly. Carlson slides away from him, unable to slow down as quickly. Robinson jumps off his left foot and rises above Carlson's defensive reach. The shot travels a high arc with exactly the softness that seemed impossible. If anything, it is too soft, imparted with a floating, knuckleball lightness, and it lands on the flange of the basket and trickles off to the side.

Jim Pollard sweeps in trailing Robinson and curls the rebound to his chest.

Lakers' ball.

Pollard misses a field goal. Goose rebounds. The Globetrotters fast break. Marques Haynes drives toward the free-throw line. He easily eludes his defender and is heading at full speed straight for George Mikan, standing in his way at the top of the key like a human portcullis. For a split second it seems as if Haynes is headed for such a bone-shattering collision with Mikan that it has to be the start of another brief comic moment, because nobody as small and fragile looking as Haynes would deliberately hurl himself into a barrier as solid as Mikan. It is foolish pratfall comedy that only circus clowns and blacks perform because foolishness is fixed in their character.

Mikan drops his arms and braces for the collision.

But Haynes stops on a dime and then slides on his back knee, which acts as a floor brake to keep him from crashing into Mikan. He quickly retreats a step, and before Mikan can raise his arms to their full defensive height again, Haynes pops a one-hand shot that loops over Mikan's arms.

Field goal, Haynes.

Lakers 30, Globetrotters 21.

Teamwork, cooperation, sacrificing the self for the good of the whole—none of those qualities were included in the stereotype of blacks. They were performers—the Globetrotters' reems proved that. They loved to dramatize and imitate and sing and dance. They were by nature tap dancers and singers who "wheeled about and turned about and did jis so, and ebery time they wheeled about they jumped Jim Crow." Never mind that it was a white minstrel in blackface who jigged to that old English ditty. The minstrelsy captured the truth of a race. Everything blacks touched wound up transformed.[7] It made them brilliant jazz musicians, but they were too wedded to the self-glorification of improvisation and performance to accept the responsibilities of teamwork. The singing, the dancing, the self-glorification may have been a perfectly understandable reaction to the abuses of slavery, but it was nonetheless a part of African American character, and until it could be undone— after perhaps another thousand years of evolution—African Americans would never be successful at a game that required sacrifice and teamwork.

They weren't coachable, the argument continued. They were as devilish and cunning as Brer Rabbit, always looking for ways to outwit authority and power. It was in their folklore, all the way back to Africa. If they obeyed authority at all, it was only as a disguise for the outrage and bitterness they felt. Look how they danced in the streets after every Joe Louis victory over a white fighter.[8] It was revenge at last. Meanwhile, their deep anger was too generalized ever to be properly focused by a coach on a basketball rival. It left them sullen and uncooperative, a lazy and shiftless race whose playfulness and tricks disguised a sharp defiance.[9]

They also lacked the competitive fire that made for premier athletes. Whether as Sambo or Stepin' Fetchit or the black clown Willie "Sleep & Eat" Best, whose nickname was meant to define a race, song and dance were in African Americans' genes. It was the irrepressible joy of a child who was impulsive, easily frightened by ghosts, irrational, too quickly distracted to keep his mind on one game, and like the Globetrotters, inclined to foolishness and clowning.[10]

Finally, they couldn't play defense. Or they were too lazy and shiftless to want to. What glory was there in defense? Who noticed those subtleties during a game? Baskets drew the loudest cheers, dramatic baskets, done with panache and flair—just look at how Goose's Prayer could bring down the house. Abe Saperstein recognized that truth when he told his players, "Anybody can make a basket. It's *how* you make the basket that matters."[11] Meanwhile, there was no room for flair in defense. It was done one way, the correct way, on most good teams the coach's way. Where was there a place for defense in the Magic Circle?

George Mikan battles over the top of two Globetrotters to put a missed Lakers shot back in the basket.

Lakers 32, Globetrotters 21.

The Globetrotters miss, and the Lakers set up slowly. The ball circles the perimeter, then goes into Mikan. He tries to execute his drop-step hook shot, but Goose refuses to bite on the fake and is already waiting for Mikan when he wheels to begin his hook shot.

"Hey, George," he growls loudly enough for those who are at courtside to hear, "where you goin'?"

Goose's long arm reaches out and slaps the ball from Mikan's grip.

The ball bounces free of Mikan, and Goose palms it off the bounce.

Mikan is rarely cut short in the execution of his hook shot, and Goose's superb defensive maneuver catches the Lakers entirely by surprise.[12] Even the Globetrotters are stunned, and for a brief moment everybody on the floor freezes, waiting to see what Mikan will do.

In the standstill, Goose suddenly sets off at a fast-break dribble down the middle of the floor. He passes the Lakers Herm Schaefer, who swipes at the ball futilely. Three more long dribbles and Goose is crossing half-court before anyone thinks to chase him.

His dribbling seems precarious, just on the verge of being out of control, but he picks up speed. The flatfoot gait is gone, there are no unintelligible howls, and his whole body seems to have lost its gangling angularity.

When he reaches the basket, he is fifteen feet ahead of anyone else. He glances over his shoulder, realizes how completely he has caught the Lakers by surprise, and stops.

Schaefer and Jaros are approaching at full speed.

Goose grins and sticks out one arm at them, the ball stuck in his palm, tantalizing them. Come and get it, come and get it. Steal it back if you can.

They cross the free-throw line and are closing fast when he turns and lifts his arm with the palmed ball and flicks his wrist to let it go.

Field goal, Tatum.

Lakers 32, Globetrotters 23.

In January 1948 the *Baltimore African American* newspaper had begun running basketball plays in their sports section.[13] Designed by successful coaches at all-black universities, the complicated plays, featuring teamwork and screens and passing, flew in the face of those who argued that blacks were too undisciplined and in need of self-glorification to learn difficult plays. But neither complicated plays nor demonstrations of pure talent would have ever convinced the racist detractors who argued that the Globetrotters were only fun-loving Sambos, Stepin' Fetchits, Rochesters, Amos 'n' Andys, or paint-faced Jim Crows wheeling and turning and doing "jis so."

African American newspapers acknowledged that, yes, the original Globetrotters had been laughable as basketball players, but no more. Not with all their victories.

The victories proved nothing! the detractors shot back.

"The Trotters keep rolling along," the *Pittsburgh Courier* wrote. They were "sensational . . . a mighty club."

But mighty only against hapless stooges.

No, they were "fabled masters of the hardwood court," the *New York Amsterdam News* boasted.

Sure, the critics agreed, if you mean the Sambo of African American fables.

The *Pittsburgh Courier* disagreed. The Globetrotters were "undoubtedly the most colorful cage aggregation in the world."

Colorful! That was the point. As entertainers. Performers. Meanwhile, their basketball talent was dubious.

Yes, the *New York Amsterdam News* conceded, the Globetrotters were a "clever cage circus . . . with hilarious antics." They were a mixture of Barnum and Bailey and baseball. But they were a solid ball club, capable of holding their own against any company.

Cleverness. Antics. Barnum and Bailey. Precisely! Where was the good, hard, serious basketball?

Finally, it didn't help at all that, almost in desperation, the New York paper wrote that Goose Tatum "grimaced, clowned, passed, finagled, and had the time of his life" on a basketball floor.

It only deepened the argument over whether the Globetrotters were really good basketball players or just tricksters.[14]

Dribbling into the Lakers frontcourt, Herm Schaefer cranes his head to check the Chicago Stadium scoreboard, its clock face almost obscured in the haze of cigarette smoke.

Ten seconds left in the half.

Schaefer picks up his dribble and rifles a pass to Swede Carlson. He redirects the pass to Mikan so quickly that it seems like a deflection.

Whether it is the dwindling time or the fact that his last fake ended in disaster, Mikan receives the pass and begins wheeling for his hook shot all in one motion. His shoulder bangs Goose in the chest.

Goose stumbles backward and lifts his hands, pleading his defensive innocence to the official. But Mikan continues the rugged sweep of his shot, determined this time not to be stopped, his fingers curved like steel tongs as he squeezes the very life out of the ball.

The shot is too strong and slams off the backboard on the far side of the rim.

A horn sounds. Halftime.

Lakers 32, Globetrotters 23.

III

HALFTIME

13

Johnny and Abe

The organ for Chicago Stadium was so big it took an entire freight train of boxcars to get it to Chicago in 1927. At full strength, each of its 3,675 pipes billowing musical smoke like a locomotive, it could match the volume of twenty-five big brass bands and shatter light-bulbs and windows. It was so powerful that once, after a controversial boxing match, the stadium organist had stopped a fan riot by playing at nearly full volume.[1]

Given the power of that organ, the halftime music seemed restrained now, neither the barrelhouse tunes that would arouse the fans nor a musical thunderbolt that would settle them. It was as if the organist was following the lead of a game that couldn't decide whether it wanted to be a breathtaking, seesaw battle or a lopsided contest. And it was out of character for a stadium that had been nicknamed the "Madhouse on Madison" because of its history of frenzied athletic contests and stormy political conventions during which the whole stadium shook with rambunctious music.[2]

In the Lakers' dressing room, the organ music was only a distant drone that drifted in and out like band-shell music from across a lake. The tame music may have been out of character for the stadium, but it was the perfect accompaniment for Johnny Kundla's patient halftime talk.

They were ahead by 9 points and had never trailed, he reminded the Lakers. Mikan and Pollard were already in double figures. In their confusion over how to stop Mikan, the Trotters had switched defenders, then switched back again. Goose Tatum had three fouls. The so-called duel of the century wasn't proving to be much of a matchup. Goose's "sleeper" basket had been cheap, Kundla finished. It was up to the Lakers guards to make sure it didn't happen again.

Other than that, there was nothing to worry about. The Globetrotters were proving to be exactly what some had predicted, no match for the mighty Lakers.[3]

Even if they hadn't been comfortably ahead, it might have been appropriate for Kundla to turn dramatic at that point, before they returned to the floor. It was one of the sacred conventions of coaching, a stem-winding pep talk. But Kundla had never been much for intensity. Pregame Gipper speeches, emotional halftime perorations, angry bench tirades—he doubted they did anything except inspire movie fans.[4] And none of them would have fit with the cheeky smile that had been his trademark from boyhood.

Johnny Kundla's life was right out of American legend, as central to the athletic folklore of whites as Goose Tatum's was to blacks. He was the cheerful and ambitious Nobody from Nowheresville— in Kundla's case, Star Junction, Pennsylvania—who rises to athletic stardom and fame. His parents, eastern European immigrants, had separated when he was young, and he had come to Minneapolis with his mother. She worked as a cook in the tea shop at Dayton's during the day and studied for her citizenship at night. He spoke Czech at home and wore cheap cardboard shoes to school. But by 1933, after he graduated from Central High at only sixteen, he had already made a name for himself in Minneapolis as a prep athlete, and his smile and cheerfulness smothered anything that might have been deep and dark in his character.[5]

That smile got him his first real job after graduation as a desk clerk at the Field Hotel on Eighth Street in Minneapolis. He mopped floors, answered the phone, and greeted guests with a genuine and infectious grin. It seemed exciting enough work, especially for a kid from Star Junction. But then his mother announced that she and Johnny's stepdad were moving to Tacoma, Washington.

"I'm gonna stay here," he told her.

His mother's disapproval was immediate. He had made it a habit after school of stopping by the Dayton's tea shop, the two of them visiting and talking while she cooked. They had become very close, and the idea of leaving him behind in Minneapolis was unthinkable. He was still just a boy!

"I'll be ok," he reassured her. "Don't worry about me."

"You don't have any money."

It was true. He didn't have any *saved*. But he had steady work and an income. "I'll be all right," he insisted.

She recognized his determination to remain in Minneapolis and eventually bid him a tearful farewell, leaving him to fend for himself in the Big City. He got a room in a boardinghouse and traveled with a gang of friends who used penknives to pick the locks of the Minneapolis Auditorium in order to sneak into college basketball games. After he enrolled at the University of Minnesota, he became a walk-on basketball star who got goose bumps every time eighteen thousand wild fans cheered one of his two-hand set shots in the Old Barn, and he had to remind himself that he was still just the kid from Star Junction.[6]

It seemed as much a part of him as his smile, the conviction that, despite his growing reputation, he was nothing special. But after a game in Madison Square Garden, even New York papers recognized that he *was* something special, comparing him to Stanford's All-American Hank Luisetti.[7] Back in Minneapolis, the newspapers were soon crediting the "gangling forward" with reviving University of Minnesota basketball.[8]

He met Marie Fritz, whose smile was as broad as his, in the university library. He took her to Dinkeytown for cupcakes, then walked her to the city limits so she wouldn't have to pay added streetcar fare to St. Paul. He gave her a ring in the Irwin Cobb Hotel in Paducah, Kentucky, where he was playing Class D baseball. He was scheduled to move up to Class A in Elmira, New York, eventually the Brooklyn Dodgers, but he and Marie were married, and he returned to Minnesota for graduate study in education.[9]

His first coaching job was as an assistant to Dave MacMillan at the University of Minnesota. MacMillan was volatile and often abusive to his players, and it was the cheerful, even-tempered Kundla who was expected to keep MacMillan under control. "Take it easy, Mac," he had to warn his mentor time and again, "take it easy."[10]

It was the catchphrase for Johnny Kundla's life. "Take it easy. Keep smiling." And he became convinced that anger and abuse were recipes for getting the worst, not the best, out of basketball players. He vowed that as a head coach someday, he would never battle with his players.

Patience, cheerfulness, a disarming modesty—these qualities separated him from self-important coaches who used anger and militancy to force players to adjust to their so-called brilliant tactics. Instead, Kundla focused on what his players could do, and he was immediately successful as a coach. He won a city championship with a parochial grade school team. Then, after he coached a high school team to the state Catholic championship, basketball observers flattered him with the prediction that a great coach was in the making and that more would be heard about him in the future.

First, however, he had to go to World War II, as a green ensign on an LST ferrying infantry troops to combat beaches. The ulcers began in Borneo and the Philippines. After numerous beach assaults and months of no milk and bad coffee, he came home from the war chewing antacid pills like candy.[11]

The ulcers and painful stomach cramps could not break the spell of his relentless, easy grin. That grin was especially prominent at halftime in the locker room of Chicago Stadium. He was grinning not only because the Lakers had a comfortable lead. He was grinning just as much over a picture that had been in his head now for almost ten years.

He had been traveling in 1939 with a basketball team called the Galloping Gophers, playing exhibition games throughout Minnesota against the Harlem Globetrotters. One ice-cold night at a game in Bemidji, he and his teammates had been walking into the gym when the Globetrotters drove up. Abe Saperstein was at the wheel of a touring van, his entire team packed inside, the long legs of his players sticking out every window like the clowns' car in a circus.[12]

In a state so overwhelmingly white, it was a stark and telling image that perfectly defined the Globetrotters. They may have been capable of brilliant, slapstick basketball, but they were proving to be no real challenge for the mighty Minneapolis Lakers.

Abe Saperstein never went anywhere without his accordion leather briefcase stuffed with papers, and he almost staggered with the weight of it now as he led his Globetrotters into the locker room at halftime. He wore high-top shoes with thick soles that were meant to add stature to his squat, five-foot-three-inch frame, but his dark double-breasted suit and wide tie made him look even stouter than he was.[13]

He hurried into the locker room, dimly lit by two bare lightbulbs in a forked socket of the low ceiling. He swung his briefcase onto a taping table, as if he might have intended to open it and pull out papers with ingenious basketball plays that would rescue his team from its predicament. Or rescue him. He had been the one who had trumpeted to the press about how invincible his Globetrotters were. He had been the one who had kept reminding the press of their string of victories. He had been the one who had boasted publicly that his team would play *anybody*, then challenged his friend Max Winter to bring on the Minneapolis Lakers. And if that stuffed briefcase didn't contain the answer to stopping George Mikan and Jim Pollard, then what would they do?

The answer surely wasn't immediately in Abe Saperstein's head, as the nominal coach of the Globetrotters. The athletic recognition he had won on Chicago playgrounds and at Lake View High School surely hadn't turned him into a master basketball strategist. What few suggestions he made to his players—"move the ball more . . . set up Goose"—stood mainly as evidence that the Globetrotters were his team. For the rest, he was happy to defer to Babe Pressley.[14]

What was never far from Saperstein's mind was the success of the Globetrotters as a business venture. It was a legacy of his father, Louis Saperstein, a Polish Jew who had fled to England, where Abe was born in 1902. In 1911 the family had come to Chicago, home of one of the largest Jewish populations in the world. They might have been expected to settle in the heart of the Jewish immigrant area around Halsted and Maxwell, with its old-world open markets. Instead, Louie Saperstein bought a nine-room, two-story house in a neighborhood of Irish Catholics and Germans on Hermitage Street in North Chicago. It meant driving elsewhere for kosher meats and being cursed as dirty Jews during Christmas, but it was a neighborhood that Louie felt offered him the best business prospects as an expert Jewish tailor for the neighborhood Gentiles.

Meanwhile, there were pogroms and anti-Semitic regimes in Europe, and America would be described as an "Eden for Jews."[15] But Louie Saperstein did not want his children to forget that it was a hard world, and he told his nine children at the supper table—over chicken soup with *gnadles*, or chopped liver, or kreplachs—that the point of seasoning their food with biting horseradish was "to remind us of the hardships faced by others under the tyrants."[16]

If he saw any value in sports and recreation, it was only as a business proposition. Sure, Jews and blacks were fellows in tragedy, but he worried over Abe's venture with a black basketball team. "Are you going to make enough money to live?" he wondered.

Abe worked seven days a week proving that he could. His first office was in the basement of the home on Hermitage Street, on a cold cement floor, among laundry tubs, a washing machine, a grimy coal shed, and a furnace that popped and roared in the winter. In time he moved up to a bedroom office in the house on Hermitage, where he put his sister, Fay, to work typing letters for him to get bookings for his traveling basketball and baseball teams.[17]

"Papa," she pleaded to Louis Saperstein, "it's Saturday. I want to go out with my friends."

"Abie needs you," her father told her.

Work and the entrepreneurial spirit became godheads for young Abe Saperstein. His hard work and enterprising genius began to pay off, and he set up an office on State and Lake Streets in Chicago and covered the walls with pictures of Abe Lincoln. In his work he was often a solitary white face in a landscape of black athletes. Friends and business associates described him as "color blind," a "purely democratic soul."[18] The *New York Amsterdam News* wrote that his activities were proving "his interest in the development of Negro sports."[19] There were contrary views, especially from some team members who objected to the characterization of him as a democratic soul, but public grousing would never have fit the team's slaphappy image, and the critics kept quiet.[20] Meanwhile, he was fastidious about his clothes, wearing only tailored suits with four-button vests. And at civic receptions for his team, dressed in a bow tie and a tuxedo and flashing a broad smile, he could have passed for the ambassador of racial goodwill that many claimed he was.

He married, had children, and moved into a comfortable house on the North Side in the Ravenswood District, a block from his father's tailor shop.

Louie Saperstein watched Abe indulge his own son with expensive toys. "You're *spoiling* him," Louie warned.

"I want to give my children everything I didn't have," Abe answered.

It was the only time his father became angry with him. "Abie, I gave you a roof over your head," he said. "I gave you clothes on your back and food for your stomach. What more does a man need to live?"[21]

Indeed, what more did he need? He had the roof and the clothes and the food. He had no outspoken critics. His keen business instincts had helped him recognize that the razzle-dazzle tactics of his black basketball team would entertain white working-class immigrant audiences.[22] Through hard work and dedication, he had built a basketball empire with worldwide fans, and he had a fat briefcase stuffed with promises of prosperity.

The only thing left was unequivocal proof that he had the best basketball team in the world, black or white.

"We should run 'em!" Babe Pressley told the Globetrotters as they discussed what to do in their locker room. "Push it up the court. Tire 'em."[23]

Everybody agreed. If they were desperate or worried, nobody expressed it. The only hint of worry lay in the fact that a halftime discussion of strategies was a departure from tradition. On the road night after night, their plays and reems were so scripted there was nothing to discuss. Goose Tatum usually repaired to a corner of the locker room to read or stare into space. For the rest of them, the only thing that ever seemed pressing at halftime was who had the deal in the running card games they took from town to town.

But they sat in a group now and planned what to do, organ music floating in from the distance. They all knew that no team played as many games as they did or could match their conditioning. Meanwhile, Pressley reminded them that they were down by 9 points. Coming out for the second half, the Lakers would be cold. Tatum and Pressley would double-team Mikan. Robinson, Haynes, and King would pick up their men at three-quarters court. And they would fast break on every possession—turnovers, free throws, made baskets . . . *everything*. "Mikan's slow getting up and down the court," he went on. "He won't be able to keep up."[24]

Nobody disagreed with that either, even if it wasn't true. Mikan was in superb condition and could run the floor with any team.[25] But the Globetrotters believed that the King of Basketball especially would suffer from the faster pace. He was big and slow, they felt.

Because of his size, transition from offense to defense was difficult. If you ran in front of him down the floor and blocked his path, he wasn't agile enough to negotiate around you. He would be the first of the Lakers to tire.[26]

"Push it up the court," Pressley repeated before they headed back out on the court. "We know we're in better shape."

He turned to the three men whom he expected to do most of the running. "It's up to you," he told them and nodded first to Willie King, then to Marques Haynes, finally to Ermer Robinson.[27]

IV

THIRD QUARTER

O

14

Bucky

Fay Young did not leave the scorer's table during halftime. It was always a struggle to get through the smoke and crowds to the vendors' booths for a cup of coffee or a hot dog, no matter how appetizing the smell of mustard that drifted onto the stadium floor and drew hungry fans like flies. And once he had mingled with the crowd, there was also the possibility that perfect strangers with smirks on their white faces would recognize his familiar face and ask him to explain why *his* team was losing.

He watched the Globetrotters return to the floor for the second half. They were trailing badly, and they seemed utterly without the dash and pep that had made them so celebrated. There seemed little hope that the game in Chicago Stadium would do anything but give the racists something to crow about. Young's best hope now seemed to be that, in defeat, the Globetrotters would carry themselves with the dignity and poise befitting "Race men."

It is the summer of 1932, and Democrats singing "Happy Days Are Here Again" gather in force in Chicago Stadium and pick Franklin Delano Roosevelt as their candidate for president. That same summer gloomy Republicans, resigned to certain defeat in November, fill only a third of the stadium's seats with delegates and nominate a somber and colorless Herbert Hoover as their candidate.[1]

To start the second half of the Lakers-Globetrotters game in February 1948, it is as if the audience has just relived those two wildly different political conventions from the stadium's past. The game has gone from a colorless rout to a dead-even contest, then back to a rout again. And a crowd that gathered with high expectations has instead been whipsawed from apathy to enthusiasm, back to apathy again. They are volatile and edgy now, and the simple act of George Mikan controlling the tip to start the second half brings a great roar from fans who want emotional consistency. No more wild swings, from happy days to tedium. No more emotional disorder. If the game itself won't produce one continuous mood, then the audience is determined to impress its mood upon the game, and they keep right on cheering as the Lakers set up their offense.

The effect of their enthusiasm is immediate. Babe Pressley bats away Schaefer's attempted pass into Mikan, then dives on his stomach for the loose ball, skids across the floor, and sweeps the ball to Willie King.

"Go, go, go!" Pressley hollers from the floor.

At half-court, Willie King and Marques Haynes crisscross, and Haynes winds up with the ball in the middle. He heads straight for the free-throw line, where he faces two Lakers defenders who are backpedaling frantically.

It is a classic three-on-two fast break, with Willie King cutting for the basket from the left side and Ermer Robinson from the right, both of them also moving at full speed. Haynes veers slightly to his right, and his large eyes seem to double in size as he fixes on Robinson for the pass.

Both defenders slide toward Robinson, but without changing the rhythm of his dribble and his eyes still fixed right, Haynes whips the ball to his left.

Willie King is wide open for an easy layup, but the deception is so complete that the pass catches him by surprise and sails out of bounds.

The crowd explodes with still louder cheering. Even if it has backfired, Haynes's pass is trickery with a new intent. And it signals what is in store from the Globetrotters. However amazing, there will be no more dribbling wizardry that exalts only Haynes. There will be no more personal miracles like Goose's Prayer. There will be no more simpleminded pinwheels that collapse into a gaggle of players. In an instant, the character of the game has changed from one that has had the heavy beat and mood of organ music to one that knows only the double-time tempo of Chicago-style jazz. The new mood promises frenetic, fast-break basketball with catapulting players, sudden stops, and wild pivots.[2] It creates a supercharged atmosphere of tension and urgency and the possibility of rough-house, perhaps even violent play.

Violence in sports. In basketball, it was as old as the game itself, when officials dared not enter the cage inside which the battle was fought, and it provided a convenient argument for those who wanted to keep blacks out of the game. On the same floor with whites, the poor souls would be killed.

It was raw racism masquerading as compassion, and the black basketball pioneers who were determined to play despite the warnings nearly were killed. The first in professional basketball was a small, studious-looking violinist named Harry Haskell Lew, whose ancestors were musicians going all the way back to fifers and drummers at the Battle of Bunker Hill. Nicknamed "Bucky," he was clearly more than just a sweet violinist, and he had a reputation for tenacious defense and a good set shot.

In 1902 he signed to play professional basketball for $5 a game in the New England League with a team from Lowell, Massachusetts. As a player, Lew endured catcalls, boos, insults, knees in the gut, and elbows to the rib cage.

"Once they knew I could take it," he said later, "I had it made."

Not quite. Playing the next season with a team from Haverhill, Massachusetts, opponents refused to take the floor against him. Disguising the racism as awe, they said his defense was too formidable. But in another game with Haverhill, racial insults from the stands grew so threatening that one of Lew's teammates had to stop the action. "If there's one more sound the rest of this game," he shouted at the fans, "we're leaving."[3]

Somehow, Bucky Lew survived twenty years of jarring New England basketball. It should have put to rest the argument that sports weren't safe for blacks, but fans of early professional sports signed petitions threatening mob action and "much bloodshed" against blacks.[4] Other fans threatened to riot if blacks were permitted to compete.[5] In a much-publicized incident at New York University in 1940, students staged a sit-in to protest Jim Crow practices in football and basketball. But the advocates of the "gentleman's agreements" that kept blacks out of athletic competition argued that it could be *dangerous* if blacks competed, an invitation to lynching.[6]

The Jim Crow laws and "gentleman's agreements" were to protect African Americans.

Those "gentleman's agreements" were what had kept the NBL all-white. The league had begun in 1937 with teams whose clumsy names—the Indianapolis Kautskys, the Firestone Non-Skids, the Fort Wayne General Electrics—seemed to promise roughhouse, industrial-style basketball that was dangerous enough, those "gentleman's agreements" said, without bringing blacks into the battle. But with the start of World War II, three NBL teams were forced to drop out of the league after losing players to the military draft during the 1941–42 season. It left the league with just four teams, and one of those—the Toledo Jim White Chevrolets—was also in danger of folding for lack of players. The future of the league itself was at stake.[7]

Sid Goldberg, who owned the troubled Toledo, Ohio, franchise, told the other owners that his roster had been almost wiped out by the war. His leading scorer was gone. The only way he could build a competitive team, he insisted, was by signing blacks. And he intended to do just that.

If the other owners objected, they said nothing.

Goldberg eventually signed four players to start the 1942–43 season, including a former Toledo prep star and ex-Globetrotter named Bill Jones, who was fed up with the inconveniences of constant travel.

Before their first game, Jones warned his teammates that white opponents might try to bait him. "But don't let that upset you," he said. "I can handle it."[8]

The stage seemed set for sinister events, but without a full roster of players and no real star, the team lost its first four games and then folded before anything serious could happen.[9]

Meanwhile, the Studebaker aircraft plant in Chicago had agreed to field a team in the NBL. With high hopes they christened themselves the Studebaker Champions, then began looking for players good enough to *be* champions. One day a former Globetrotter named Roosevelt "Roosie" Hudson waited outside the Studebaker plant while his friend Duke Cumberland, another ex-Trotter, went inside the plant to apply for a job. At only five-eight but cat quick with alert eyes and an easy smile, Roosie Hudson was a fixture in South Side Chicago basketball. As a kid he had played three-on-

three playground pickup games from dawn until dusk. By the time
he went home his shoes were so sweat-fouled his mother refused to
let him in the house. From there he had graduated to playing prelim-
inary games for the main attractions at Chicago's Savoy Ballroom.
Finally, in the late 1930s and 1940s he was traveling the country as
a peripatetic Harlem Globetrotter, who looked back on his days of
pickup basketball games on the South Side as the purest fun he had
ever had. [10]

Outside the Studebaker plant, a company official recognized
Hudson immediately. "We're looking for players," he said. "Can
you get other Trotters?"

Of course he could. As in Toledo, it didn't take much searching to
find Globetrotters who were unhappy over the constant travel and
eager to enter the world of organized professional basketball. Pro
leagues, which had been the exclusive domain of white players—
either by those "gentleman's agreements" or quiet fiat—were now
open to blacks. Instead of barnstorming antics and silly pinwheel
offenses, there would be new opportunities for serious, hard-nosed
competition. Better still, it would defy the bigots who had been
forced to concede that black teams versus white professional teams
may have been good for attendance but who still continued to argue
that whites and blacks on the same team was integration lunacy.

Eventually, six African Americans, including Roosie Hudson and
Duke Cumberland, took jobs as drill press operators and machinists
and stewards in the Studebaker plant, turning out engine housings
and wheel assemblies for army air corps bombers headed for historic raids on ball bearing factories in Germany. But another kind
of history was being made on the basketball court, where the Studebaker Champions played as the first truly integrated professional
basketball team in U.S. history. This wasn't just the case of a lone
wolf bucking the system the way Bucky Lew had done. This was a
team of four whites and six blacks who played hard together without
incident. [11]

Playing their games in Cicero, Illinois, where it was dangerous for blacks to walk the streets, they lost more than they won
in the NBL. And fueled perhaps by those who still insisted that integrated teams were a bad idea, rumors circulated that the Studebaker
Champions were split by racial tension. What little dissension there
was involved basketball, not race. Mike Novak, who had starred at

Loyola of Chicago, thought that Wyatt "Sonny" Boswell, a streak-shooting guard from Ohio, was as much of a "gunner" in basketball as his namesake Wyatt Earp had been on the streets of Tombstone. Over Novak's objections, Boswell continued to shoot even when his hand went cold. "Wait until I get into the groove," he told his teammates, expecting them to indulge his cold shooting.[12]

For the bigots, the dissension stood as proof that interracial competition was a bad idea, doomed to failure because it defied the history of racial separation. Meanwhile, its roster gutted more by the wartime draft, the Studebaker Champions folded at the end of the season.[13] It appeared that the brief integration of professional basketball was over. The only place for blacks in the professional game, no matter how good they were, no matter how much they shot and finally got in the groove, was globetrotting and running those silly pinwheels.

Lakers' ball.

The cheering does not subside but grows in intensity as Ermer Robinson begins leaping in front of Jack Dwan, semaphoring his hands wildly in an effort to block the inbound pass to Herm Schaefer.

Marques Haynes keeps one hand lightly on Schaefer, who darts and dodges in an effort to free himself to receive Dwan's pass. But Haynes moves as if he is the mirror image of Schaefer, and several seconds pass while the official marks time with an arm chop and Dwan finally abandons the idea of inbounding to Schaefer. Instead, he shoots a desperate pass to Jim Pollard, who has come back to rescue the two guards.

Pollard turns up the floor immediately, comfortable with this new pace of racehorse, galloping basketball. At the half-court line, he whirls suddenly to elude Babe Pressley, but Pressley reaches in from behind and uses his arm like a hockey stick to poke-check the ball away from Pollard.

Tony Jaros, who has substituted for Swede Carlson, picks up the loose ball just before it goes out of bounds at the sidelines. At six-two, Jaros is muscular and hairy and dark. He has grown up in north Minneapolis, among laborers and machinists. He has a hard, angular face, and there is nothing about him that suggests deftness or cleverness. The suggestion is only of drillpunch basketball, of straight-ahead, coarse play that will flatten defenders in his path.

Nothing could be further from the truth. He is in fact an agile all-around athlete—football, basketball, baseball—and a Minneapolis prep legend who plays Triple-A baseball with the Minneapolis Millers in the off-season. In basketball, he is slick and cunning, and his hard physical image is all part of the deceit. His dodges and feints, and especially his quickness, catch defenders by surprise. His young Minneapolis fans worship him and swear that he has so many moves on a basketball court that he never shoots the same shot twice. Except one.[14]

It is a shot Jaros adopted years earlier after watching Johnny Kundla play basketball at the University of Minnesota. Kundla calls it an "underhand scoop shot" and credits his idea for the shot to John Wooden, who used it to draw fouls at Purdue.[15] From Wooden to Kundla, the shot is so simple that it seems old-fashioned, if not crude. But in the two clever hands of Tony Jaros, and disguised brilliantly beneath his hard exterior, it is a work of basketball art.[16]

Using his quickness, he moves easily up the open floor now toward the basket. He appears to have a straight line for a head-on uncontested layup, when Babe Pressley suddenly cuts him off. He wheels, but Pressley is there again. Jaros skips on one foot, then takes a long stride during which he picks up his dribble and lifts his head and eyes to the basket. Pressley raises his arms to swat the shot, but Jaros holds the ball with two hands and scoops it under Pressley arms, which drop too late.

The underhand scoop shot is good.

But behind Jaros and Pressley a whistle shrieks. Traveling! No score.

Lakers subs jump from their bench and flap towels again in disgust. How about blowing a whistle on Goose Tatum? one of them shouts. With his flatfoot shuffle, he walks every time he gets the ball!

Johnny Kundla stands with his hands in his pockets, his head cocked slightly, smiling indulgently at the official for being so childish he can't tell the difference between walking and a clever shot. Boos and catcalls from fans contribute to an atmosphere of incipient violence. Could it happen here? On this colossal stage? With all the thunder and sweep of the powerful stadium organ?

Globetrotters' ball.

They fast break, and Babe Pressley shoots a running hook shot from the right side that banks in.

Lakers 32, Globetrotters 25.

Lakers' ball.

It is obvious that the Globetrotters are going to run and press, and before the Lakers inbound the ball, Johnny Kundla hurriedly replaces Jack Dwan with Johnny Jorgenson for more Lakers speed.

The substitution completed, Herm Schaefer steps out of bounds with the ball and looks down the floor. Two Globetrotters are scrambling to cover Jorgenson, while Pollard is left alone. Pollard breaks for the Lakers' basket and is all by himself at half-court when he gathers in the ball over his shoulder like a long pass in football. He puts down one dribble and lengthens his stride and then takes off in a broad jump, sweeping the ball up and off the backboard softly before he lands out of bounds.

Field goal, Pollard.

Lakers 34, Globetrotters 25.

It is a "Take that!" basket and stands as the Lakers' defiant answer to the new pace, which is obviously not too fast for them.

The crowd roars its approval again, not only for Pollard's brilliant, flying broad-jump basket but for the fact that the Lakers will not retreat from the Globetrotters' challenge to a faster game.

15

Pop

Globetrotters' ball.

This time on their fast break they try to run up the heels of the Lakers, who are all scrambling to get back on defense. Ermer Robinson stumbles through a clutch of players, and his shot slams off the backboard.

The ball caroms into the hands of George Mikan, who struggles to regain his balance before he throws an overhead pass to Johnny Jorgenson.

Marques Haynes fouls Jorgenson, who steps to the free-throw line. The memory of Jim Pollard's spectacular leaping tip-in off a previous missed free throw is still in the minds of the Globetrotters as Johnny Jorgenson draws a bead on the basket for his free throw. Goose Tatum is inside Pollard on the lane, Willie King outside him. The two of them intend to sandwich the Kangaroo Kid to prevent a repeat tip-in.

Across the lane, George Mikan is inside Babe Pressley, but Pressley is crowding him, threatening to push him out of bounds before Jorgenson even releases the free throw.

Mikan digs in to hold his position. The missed free throw bounces toward him, and as he jumps to grab it, Pressley pushes into him and jackknifes him in the air. Mikan has the ball for a second, bobbles it, has it again, then has it knocked away by Pressley.

In the melee of players diving for the loose ball, a hog pile of writhing bodies forms. Babe Pressley is the last to jump on the hog pile.

The whistle shrieks. Everyone in the pile stares at the official, pleading innocence.

Foul on Babe Pressley.

Herm Schaefer converts the free throw.

Lakers 35, Globetrotters 25.

The new pace has not narrowed the gap. Instead, the racing players, the reckless broad jumps, the belly skids, the diving bodies, the dangerous hog piles, the whistle shrieking like a terrified voice in a horror movie—they have only heightened the atmosphere of urgency and tension that the fans feel. Whatever the Globetrotters do, the Lakers can match and exceed it. The mood is of attack and counterattack, of intensification and escalation leading inevitably to some explosive climax, of something even more dangerous and breakneck yet to come.

Meanwhile, it is the Globetrotters' ball. Two long, quick passes take the ball the full length of the court. If they are frustrated at all by their inability to close the gap on the Lakers, they show no sign of it. Their faces are expressionless, and they have stopped the chatter that accompanies their pinwheel offense. The occasional moments of razzle-dazzle are also gone. There are no windmills of the ball, no tricky knee-jacks or pirouettes at the end of a pass, no flashy fakes that send defenders flying. What is left is speed, not just the speed of their bodies hurtling up the court but the speed of the ball itself, which quickens in the Globetrotters' hands, bouncing and spinning and rocketing from player to player. Still, there is a calm at the center of it, like some soul-settling hurricane eye that keeps the team from flying apart.

The pass goes to Ermer Robinson, who is cutting along the baseline. He tries to come out with a shot from behind the backboard, but a defender slashes his arm and the ball flies free. There is no whistle, but the audience is so swept up now by the pell-mell pace that they can only murmur their disapproval before the play continues. It is nonstop action of missed shots, intercepted passes, loose balls, and one collision after another with no whistles, each bump and slap more violent than the previous one. It is too fast to permit the fans to react to any single episode, and their emotions began to pile up, waiting for a pause in the action in order to explode.

The chance comes after Tony Jaros sprints to recover a loose ball at midcourt. Willie King, also chasing after the ball, smashes headlong into Jaros. The force of the collision sounds a dull "whumpfff" in the stadium, like a horseshoe dropping into a sandy pit.

Jaros spins crazily on one foot but hangs on to the ball.

One official races to the site of the collision, drops to his knees, and slides into the action, his whistle shrieking as he slides. He makes a safe sign, as if he's calling a runner safe at home plate. But it is a signal for no foul! His call is that Jaros has walked again. The crowd erupts immediately with a volcanic chorus of boos, jeers, and shrill whistles. Jaros holds the ball and glares at the official, punishing him for having made such an unpopular call. Willie King tries to take the ball from Jaros, who is reluctant to give it up, and the two play a brief game of tug-of-war for possession of the ball.

It lasts no more than a second, their arms pumping back and forth as each tries to rip the ball from the other's grip. It is a brief outburst with no implications beyond what it means in the course of the game—Jaros doesn't think he walked, and King wants the ball so that he can quickly inbound it to start the Trotters' fast break. But the crowd falls instantly silent, as if their enthusiasm has suddenly run into a wall. The struggle on the court freezes them with the fear that on the heels of such a flurry of violent action, punches are going to be thrown. Granite-faced Jaros and speedy King will both drop the ball and square off. Their fight will be the realization of years of warnings and predictions—from Bucky Lew to Roosie Hudson to Sonny Boswell's shooting quarrels—that violence between the races on a basketball floor is inevitable.

The worst realization of that violence had come just a year earlier, after four teams in the NBL, in what looked like a great stride forward in basketball integration, had each signed a black player. One of them was William Penn Gates, who grew up in Harlem playing stickball and basketball on West 132nd. A muscular body and a mature face earned him the nickname "Pop" as a young man. After high school Pop Gates signed to play with the New York Rens for $100 a month, barnstorming the country. At six-three and two hundred pounds, he gained a reputation for implacable defense, rugged rebounding, and smooth scoring. There may have been better shooters, his admirers conceded. There surely were men much taller who could dominate play around the basket. But Pop Gates was the best *all-around* player in the country, they said.[1]

Pop Gates gave the Tri-Cities Blackhawks of the NBL steady scoring, powerful rebounding, and a clinging push-and-grab defense.

On February 24, 1947, 2,500 fans of the Syracuse Nationals showed up in the city's Jefferson Street armory to see the Blackhawks, with their talented black player, Pop Gates. Syracuse fans had a reputation for fierce loyalty to their beloved "Nats."[2] Courtside seats cozied up to the floor and gave the jeers and taunts from spectators an immediacy that was hard to ignore. Those same courtside seats made it convenient for fans to intercede on the floor when things were going badly for the Nats.

The Blackhawks came into the Syracuse Armory riding a seven-game win streak and driving to make the NBL playoffs. For the Nats, who were also struggling to make the playoffs, the key to winning lay in stopping Pop Gates. They gave that assignment to John "Chick" Meehan, who had been an all-around athlete and high school star in Syracuse. He graduated from high school in 1936 and took his basketball talents to the New York Professional Basketball League. After playing with teams in Rochester, Syracuse, and Newark, New York, he ended up as a seasoned pro with the brand-new Syracuse Nationals.[3]

For Syracuse fans, Chick Meehan was a homegrown star, the local boy who had made good, and he was instantly popular. He was as brash as he was handsome, with a bright smile and a pompadour of thick black hair that stayed perfectly groomed during basketball combat. Beyond his hot shooting, he had a reputation for pugnacious defense.[4] Nobody was too good for him to stop. And that Monday night in February 1947, against the Tri-Cities Blackhawks, he was determined to stop Pop Gates.

In spite of his defensive determination, Chick Meehan could not stop Pop Gates, and their matchup featured elbowing, kneeing, pushing, and shoving. With five minutes left in the game, Meehan went after a loose ball at the top of the key in the Nats' court. Pop Gates moved with him. Meehan was in midstride, hurrying for the ball, when Gates pushed him. The force of the shove, along with Meehan's speed, sent him straight to the floor. The left side of his face hit the floor hard and made a noise like a bowling ball striking a pin.[5]

The ball dribbled away, and all eyes were on Meehan now, as he pulled himself to his knees, then to his feet. He staggered, but finally managed to square himself to Gates.

"What the hell?" he said slowly.

Gates answered by delivering a solid right cross to the side of Meehan's head. The blow spun Meehan, and again he fell flat on his face, this time out cold.

A sudden hush fell in the armory. In an instant, every player on the floor froze as if they were part of a tableau. It was a fixity that seemed to last forever and made the scene all the more sinister.

Gates was the first to move. With both fists raised, he turned to face the players closest to him. In a matter of seconds, he and Syracuse's six-nine John Gee were swinging at each other wildly. Then John Chaney of Syracuse jumped on Gates's back, but Gates threw him off immediately.[6]

On the floor, Meehan still hadn't moved, and half-a-dozen Syracuse and Tri-Cities players stepped around him as they began slugging at each other. Players who entered the fracas to restrain others were quickly trading punches. Both officials began blowing their whistles in an effort to stop it. Meanwhile, Gates was easily identifiable as the figure in the center of the mayhem, swinging wildly at anybody who came near him, even his own teammates who attempted to restrain him.[7]

Still, the fight would have run its explosive course quickly and the fighters would have separated if it had not been for the presence of the fat gangster who sat in one of those courtside seats and was a fixture at Nats games. He was one of the team's most ardent supporters, and he jumped from his chair and headed for Gates, a knife in one hand.

He disappeared into what was now a melee of players, fans, police, and National Guard troops who had poured onto the floor.[8] The entire floor was now filled with fans punching out other fans, and as soon as the fighting settled in one spot, it broke out again in another, and the mob surged and heaved like a bed of kelp.

Gates was eventually surrounded by police and soldiers who dragged him from the armory, a gauntlet of fans punching and spitting at him as he was taken out. Chick Meehan's teammates managed to carry him to his own bench, lifeless and bloody. The floor remained filled with pockets of fighters, dancing and jabbing at each other.

It took fifteen minutes to restore order. When the floor was finally cleared and the courtside chairs filled again, the fat gangster was gone. His left eye swollen shut and a gash over his right eye,

Meehan was taken to Memorial Hospital in Syracuse.[9] The news the next morning was that there had been a "slugfest" involving players and fans in Syracuse. It all seemed to fit with the characterization of Syracuse fans as rabid and difficult. But exactly what had happened remained murky.

"Meehan got chesty with me," Gates later told friends, "and I decked him."[10] Gates insisted that Meehan had twice thrown him to the floor before he retaliated during the episode of the loose ball. Rumors elsewhere in the league were that Pop Gates had almost blinded somebody. Others claimed, "Pop broke Meehan's face."[11]

In March Pop Gates sent a letter to Chick Meehan, still in a Syracuse hospital following the incident between them. The matter had been on his mind ever since it happened, Gates wrote. Acknowledging that the two had been friends, he insisted that the trouble should never have occurred. He was sincerely sorry, he said.[12]

But by the end of the season Pop Gates was gone from the Tri-Cities roster.[13] The three other black players who had entered the league with Gates also disappeared, making the league all-white . . . again. Gates explained later that he had left the financially troubled Tri-Cities franchise over money.[14] But one rumor persisted, in the form of shadowy insinuation: there had been a deliberate purging of blacks from the NBL by frightened owners after the ugly Gates-Meehan incident in Syracuse.[15]

Chick Meehan did his best to minimize the issue of race in the episode. He and Pop Gates knew each other well, he explained. They had met often on a basketball court. "He's thrown everything in the book at me," Meehan said, "and the same goes for the way I've treated him." But he told reporters to "get one thing straight. This wasn't one of those racial affairs."[16]

Between Gates and Meehan, it may not have been, but race was the only explanation for why so many fans had jumped into the melee. A tiny basketball court had become a desperate battlefield for bigots. And no matter how much games were meant to be a relief from the pressures of the workaday world, no bucolic field, or worse, no confining gymnasium or stadium with fans packed to the rafters in a pressure-cooker atmosphere to watch on those rare occasions when blacks and whites competed against each other, could be free of the fear of violence.

It was not a remote possibility, the likelihood of racial mayhem in Chicago Stadium in February 1948. Even fans listening on the radio in faraway Minnesota sensed that the matchup had an intensity that went beyond basketball dominance. In an intense setting that featured a volatile mixture of a few racists along with fanatical team loyalists, some small but warlike incident on the floor—a shot blocked with the impact of a blackjack, a drive to the basket suddenly derailed, the push-pull episode between Tony Jaros and Willie King in the Madhouse on Madison—could detonate the mixture. The fear wasn't just that the players might start swinging at each other, as they had in Syracuse. After years of being taunted and clotheslined and blindsided, the Globetrotters had learned to ignore the court provocations of an occasional white hatchet man. And the Lakers were professionals, the kings of basketball, too celebrated, one hoped, to indulge in fisticuffs. But those fanatical fans, rabid in their partisanship or staking much more than mere basketball supremacy on the game, could find any rough incident on the court as an excuse to stream onto the floor, as they had done in Syracuse, and take matters into their own hands. It meant that mere courage wasn't enough for black athletes to survive the violence in sports. They also needed something tougher, something pugnacious, something the *New York Amsterdam News* had once chosen to call "guts," because a good part of the world was after their hides.[17]

After several quick push-pulls between them, Jaros and King realize that their behavior is unseemly, and they let go of the ball at once so that it bounces and rolls away harmlessly. High up in the stadium, a lone laugh pierces the silence, relief that an ominous episode has resolved itself.

The official recovers the ball and flips it to Marques Haynes, who steps out of bounds quickly. He spots Ermer Robinson breaking for the basket and pitches a long pass to him. Robinson is beyond the basket when he receives the ball, and he has to twist himself to keep from jamming the ball into the bottom of the backboard.

Field goal, Robinson.

Lakers 35, Globetrotters 27.

Lakers' ball.

The pass is to George Mikan. Goose Tatum and Pressley collapse on him from opposite sides like the faces of a vice. Mikan clamps the ball to his belly and twists himself to get free of the pressure. His elbows slice the air like rotary blades. Goose and Pressley raise their arms high, as if they are being shaken down. But they hold their ground as Mikan's sharp elbows slash across their chests. Finally, Goose drops one arm and slaps at the ball. The force of Goose's arm dropping onto Mikan's elbow pops the ball loose. Two Globetrotters seize it immediately, but the whistle has already blown.

Foul, Goose Tatum.

It is Goose's fourth foul. But as the Globetrotters take up their spots on the lane, Babe Pressley makes no move to replace him on the floor, and no one attempts to caution Goose. He seldom, if ever, fouls out of a game. And no one is worried that he will do so now. His defense is rarely aggressive enough to risk it, and when it is, his hands and fingers work as deftly as a pickpocket's to strip the ball cleanly.[18]

Mikan misses the free throw. Goose jumps high for the rebound and lands surrounded by Lakers but with his feet spread wide. It is his firm declaration that the ball is his, but several Lakers paw at him, trying to strip the ball from him.

His back is turned to the rest of the floor when he steps and jumps, as if he is about to deliver an improbable full-court hook shot. It is Goose's Prayer taken to its ultimate absurdity, and a brief spike of laughter rises over the continuous roar that now fills the stadium.

But it is a hook pass, not an impossible shot, and Marques Haynes gathers the pinpoint pass in at half-court and turns to begin his quick drive for the basket.

Herm Schaefer is waiting for him in the free-throw lane. It is an odd matchup, a pasty bowling pin in the path of a fleet rabbit.

Haynes makes no effort to go around him. Instead, he brakes in full stride, almost executing the splits as his front foot slides between Schaefer's feet.

Crouched, ready to jump to block the layup, Schaefer realizes too late that Haynes is reversing his direction and going to shoot falling away.

It seems foolish, a showboat trick shot in place of the surefire layup he could have had by just altering his course slightly and flying around Schaefer. But it is Haynes's favorite shot. He has rehearsed it as much as any of his incredible dribbling maneuvers, and he has more confidence in it than a layup.[19]

He skips a low dribble between his legs as he retreats from Schaefer with a rabbity skitter. He releases the ball with his right hand so quickly he doesn't even have to jump to avoid having it blocked.

The shot is so quick and magnificent the announcer's mispronunciation seems a deliberate effort to credit Haynes with basketball nobility.

"Field goal," he intones, "by Mar-keeeeeeeeezzz Hayyyyyyyynes!"

Lakers 35, Globetrotters 29.

16

Marques

"Flair," Marques Haynes liked to call it. "You take a tap dancer," he would explain and tap-dance lifelessly to demonstrate the *absence* of flair. Suddenly, he would begin dancing with animation. "But you get another dancer out there. He's tap-dancing . . . putting a lot of *flair* into it. He's selling it!"

In basketball, he felt, it was especially important. "You have to put some *flair* into it," he said. "Some showmanship."[1]

Flair. Showmanship. They were exactly the qualities that critics pointed to when they insisted that the Globetrotters were merely clowns and basketball tap dancers. But flair, as Haynes possessed it, was a plus that reflected his ability to make his body respond to the balletic demands of the game of basketball. He had had "flair" since boyhood in Sand Springs, Oklahoma. With huge eyes and thick eyebrows that he liked to lift suddenly to express melodramatic wonder or surprise, even his face reflected his theatrical gifts. In Sand Springs, his older brother had taught him the fine art of dribbling. Eventually, every snappy move he made on a basketball court, leading his high school to the National Negro Championships, was accompanied by flourishes so subtle they were almost imperceptible and gave his sticklike frame a baffling elegance as he moved.

He majored in education at Langston University, the Oklahoma institution created to provide opportunities to African Americans in higher education that were denied at other colleges. Haynes led Langston's basketball team in scoring all four years, and Abe Saperstein spotted him in the spring of 1946 when his Globetrotters team lost to Langston. Saperstein wanted him to join the team immediately, but Haynes was determined to graduate from Langston first.[2]

Meanwhile, he was good enough to have played with any professional basketball team in the country, but that only seemed to promise strife and tension. It was hardly the proper stage for a dribbling genius to perform his magic. And if he looked at it purely as a financial proposition, professional basketball players didn't make any more money than he could barnstorming. So what if it meant seedy hotels, bad food, and night after night on the road. That wouldn't be any different in the pros either.

So he showed up at 2:30 a.m. one night that summer at Abe Saperstein's door in Chicago, a basketball under his arm. A fancy dribbling demonstration in the middle of the night won him a spot on the Kansas City farm team, and he quickly moved up to the Globetrotters.[3] His dribbling exhibitions were what fans came to see, but he could shoot, too. There were many nights when he didn't miss, and his gift for "flair" made all his shots look less difficult than they were.

As much hummingbird as he was rabbit, he would seem to hang in the air over the floor, beating his dribbling wings, then flit sideways or backward. One night when the Globetrotters were left shorthanded because of fouls, he dribbled out the entire fourth quarter of a game. Another night on a makeshift floor of canvas laid over grass, he still managed to perform his dribbling act while others couldn't even get the ball to bounce.[4] With or without the ball, he moved everywhere on the court at full speed, stopping and sliding to his padded knees, then popping to his feet again and darting off in another direction. No rival was ever safe with the ball. If a dribbling opponent turned his head for a second, Haynes would appear from nowhere, steal the ball, and be gone. And he would come at a run from far out to hurl his thin body fearlessly into the giants who battled beneath the basket for rebounds.

He was, they said, the greatest Globetrotter to come along in years, and it was exactly his "flair," built on quickness and athleticism, that made him such a star.[5]

Lakers' ball.

Mikan receives the pass directly in front of the basket as he is sliding through the key. He would normally put down one dribble, continue through the lane, and complete his hook shot in a seamless sweep. But as soon as he has the ball, he is sandwiched again by

Goose Tatum and Pressley. He manages to turn himself just enough to target the basket over his left shoulder, then leap from both feet at once for a jump-hook shot that neither Goose nor Pressley can reach to block.

The shot is too strong and slams off the backboard, straight to the spot where the three of them are jockeying for position for the rebound.

They are still crouched, having had time only to throw up their hands reflexively, their fingers in the air like spikes upon which the ball is in danger of being impaled, when Marques Haynes sails over them from somewhere and bats the ball in the air before it reaches their fingertips.

The batted ball flies straight to Willie King.

This time the Globetrotters fast break is four men—only Goose Tatum stays back. Once they reach their basket, it is a four-on-one break, and they pass the ball needlessly, toying with Johnny Jorgenson, the lone Lakers defender, who scoots desperately from one to the other in a futile defensive effort.

Field goal, King.

Lakers 35, Globetrotters 31.

Lakers' ball.

Substitution: Swede Carlson back in for Tony Jaros.

Babe Pressley fouls George Mikan. Mikan misses the free throw.

Babe Pressley races to catch up to Willie King and Marques Haynes on the fast break.

Field goal, Pressley.

Lakers 35, Globetrotters 33.

Fans who have been coming to Chicago Stadium for years insist that a full house cheering wildly from all three tiers is the loudest noise they have ever heard *anywhere*. It is louder than the din of war, louder than the howling of a violent storm, louder than freight trains and earthquakes and breaking surf and mountain avalanches. Others claim that the pandemonium of Chicago Stadium is the loudest noise a human being can endure before blacking out from sheer pain.

One explanation for the almost unbearable noise is that it is a bizarre acoustical phenomenon produced by those successive tiers, which trap the sound, then compress it and shake it before it bursts from beneath each overhanging tier into the full stadium, where it mixes with the same roar coming from beneath the other tiers. But stadiums elsewhere have tiers that trap the noise, so why is it so much louder here? Why, at its loudest in Chicago Stadium, does it make your skin crawl and your bones shake? It is the *history* of the place, some answer. Years and years of rip-roaring title fights and frenzied hockey battles, with the huge organ pounding and soaring through it all, have left such a lasting mark on Chicago Stadium that just driving to it or standing in line to buy a ticket raises goose bumps of expectancy and excitement that turn to hysteria once you are inside the Madhouse on Madison.[6]

The courtside spectators, filled with that expectancy and excitement, are the first to stand and cheer now because the Globetrotters have come within 2 points. Like ripples expanding from a stone dropped in a still pool, fans in row after row jump to their feet. The ripples move back from the courtside seats to the second tier, finally to the third tier high in the stadium. Everyone in the stadium is soon standing, raising a deafening, earsplitting, uncomfortable cheer for the Globetrotters' remarkable comeback.

The cheering is so constant and obliterating that it subsumes all of the sounds coming from the court. From the third tier especially, the movement of the players seems distant and mechanical, like the action on a silent-movie screen.

Lakers' ball.

They set up slowly. The pass goes into Pollard, who looks at Mikan, then passes back out to Jorgenson, to Pollard again, looping crosscourt to Carlson, who also checks Mikan—still covered—to Schaefer, to Pollard, who holds the ball over his head and repeatedly jerks it toward Mikan but doesn't let it go because there are three Globetrotters collapsed around Mikan now.

Pollard misses his one-hand set shot.

The cheering rises still higher as Pressley rebounds Pollard's shot and the Globetrotters fast break again. But the Lakers retreat and stop the break, and the Globetrotters shift into their pinwheel offense. Swede Carlson picks off a pass and bolts up the floor, but Johnny Kundla is standing in front of the Lakers' bench, trying to say something, which nobody can hear, at the same time he signals "easy! easy!" with his hands out and his palms turned down, and Carlson brakes to a walk.

Mikan takes the pass in the key and twists himself to shoot without jumping. The quick shot catches Pressley and Goose by surprise but rims out. Mikan bulls his way through Goose and Pressley to grab the rebound, again without jumping. He forces the ball back up to the basket, and it swirls out of the rim again.

On his third effort, he takes time to clear away defenders by swiveling his shoulders and hips. From the violence of his whirling, his glasses slip off the bridge of his nose and hang by a stem off one ear. Suddenly he looks laughably gawky, a throwback to his days as a gangling Joliet schoolboy, but he manages to strong-arm the second rebound back into the basket.

Field goal, Mikan.

Lakers 37, Globetrotters 33.

Exhausted from its wild cheering and looking for an opportunity to gather itself for the next rampage of action, the crowd relaxes and the noise level drops. Mikan refixes his glasses to his head as he trots back down the floor. It is his first field goal of the second half. The double-team is working exactly as the Globetrotters intended, but if Mikan's repeated hammering away at the basket is any indication, he seems to have tripled his scoring determination. It will take more than the momentary undoing of his glasses to stop him now. His ferocious single-mindedness will have to be sacked. But by what? Surely not by mere mortals like the Harlem Globetrotters, who have only their long arms and their reckless courage. They might as well try to bring down Goliath with stones hurled from leather slings.

Globetrotters' ball.

They rush up the court, even though the Lakers have all gotten back and are waiting for them.

Marques Haynes easily dribbles around Herm Schaefer but then is blocked by Swede Carlson from getting any closer to the basket. Haynes retreats with his quick back-step, but from the bench Carlson has watched Haynes execute the same shot against Schaefer. Anticipating Haynes's retreat, Carlson jumps forward too eagerly and slams into Haynes as he releases the shot, which fails to reach the rim.

Foul, Carlson.

Haynes carefully places the toes of his sneakers behind the free-throw line, as if he is settling his shoes into sand, then swings the first free throw underhand.

Lakers 37, Globetrotters 34.

He swings the second shot.

Lakers 37, Globetrotters 35.

Lakers' ball.

The crowd winds itself up again like a high siren. Mikan pushes Goose and Pressley away, and in the brief instant he is open, he raises one hand to call for the ball. Pollard whips him a hook pass, but as soon as he has the ball Mikan is surrounded and can only flail a shot at the basket. Goose rebounds the ball and the Globetrotters are off, driven by the propulsive force of the stadium uproar.

Ermer Robinson misses, Pollard rebounds, and back come the Lakers. Johnny Kundla uncrosses his legs and stands up quickly. He holds out his hands again, as if he is playing soft piano music meant to suppress his team's wild impulses, but the pace is beyond his or anybody's control now. It is a spinning maelstrom of full-court action, sucking everything into it, and the only thing Kundla can do is sit back down and watch.

The two teams trade free throws.

Lakers 38, Globetrotters 36.

Then Mikan is fouled by Pressley. As he steps to the free-throw line, there are no waving arms or balloons or catcalls or sudden bugle blasts, and the fans fall silent. The silence is no deeper than any of the previous hushes for free throws, but it seems deeper now, coming as it does on the heels of the furious action and uproar that have been shaking the stadium steadily. In the silence, the only voices are of two stadium vendors. One of them is walking along the floor in front of the courtside seats. He wears a white paper cap with a dark cuff, and a metal chest is slung off the front of him by a wide strap. "Ice cream!" he calls. "Ice cream!" From one of the higher tiers of the stadium, another vendor's voice calls, "Hey, cold beer, cold beer!"

Neither one finds any buyers.

Meanwhile, the players take their places on the lane and wait for Mikan as he begins his slow free-throw ritual. The Globetrotters breathe deeply and are jumpy, in defiance of the cool, detached image that is becoming popular among young black men. "Playing it cool"—it is an idiom born of musicians moving away from the "hot" jazz sounds of the past to something cool and liquid.[7] The coolness is an argument, a defense, a projection of distance and self-composure.[8] It is a pose that says, "You can't hurt me no matter what you do to me, no matter how much you exclude me from your white society."

But the Globetrotters look anything but cool now. They appear to be irritated by this need to pause. They are eager to resume the headlong pace, and they are impatient with Mikan, who is in no special hurry. He bounces the ball once, twice, a third time before he lifts the ball to his chest slowly and aligns his thumbs and fingers with the seams. Then he puts his arms at full extension, as if he is offering the ball to the basket. The Globetrotters continue to fidget as he takes his own sweet time sighting over the ball to the rim. Finally, he bends his knees, swings the ball down between his legs and up again, and releases the free throw in a flat arc that bangs the front of the rim and drops into Babe Pressley's hands.

Pressley shoots a short pass to Haynes, and the Globetrotters are off again, all five of them running at full speed, impelled by cheering that explodes like a blast from the stadium pipe organ, passes snapping between them without a single dribble, not even from Haynes, who takes the ball in one step and releases it the next in a long bounce pass to Willie King that threads its way through a muddle of players.

Field goal, King

Lakers 38, Globetrotters 38. Perfect basketball equilibrium.

Time-out, Lakers.

Johnny Kundla tried to be heard over the noise of the crowd during the Lakers time-out. "Somebody has to be open," he shouted.

They didn't need to hear him to know it was true. With Goose and Pressley sandwiching Mikan and a Globetrotters guard also collapsing on Mikan every time he got the ball, he was like Gulliver with Lilliputs at his feet trying to rope him to the floor, and it was obvious that somebody had to be open. Pollard certainly. Probably Swede Carlson, too.

But there were other tactical considerations for the Lakers. Both Goose and Pressley had four fouls. And the Globetrotters had a short bench. None of the four sober-faced subs sitting with warm-up jackets slung over their knees looked prepared to fill anybody's shoes, either comedically or athletically. Foul out one or both of the two Globetrotters sandwiching Mikan, and it would be all over. Mikan would score effortlessly.

The rest of Kundla's directions were reassurances and gentle admonitions, delivered with his trademark smile: we know we can score; get back on defense; we can run as well as they can, but be patient, don't force it; yes, our lead evaporated, but we can get it back as quickly as we built it the first time.[9]

Lakers' ball.

Herm Schaefer goes straight to George Mikan with the pass. He is surrounded by Lilliputs and passes back out to Pollard, who drives the middle, straight at the bodies bunched around Mikan.

Pollard lifts himself off the wrong foot again and raises the ball over his head for the shot.

At the top of his leap, he spots Mikan sliding toward the basket with his hand up, and he shoots a pass to him.

Lakers 40, Globetrotters 38.

The Globetrotters fly down the floor, Haynes misses, the Lakers counterbreak, Pollard misses, the Globetrotters bolt back down the floor and miss again, but Pressley is fouled by Pollard on the rebound. Nobody is calm on the free-throw line now. Chests heave, cheeks balloon from the heavy breathing, and Pressley makes the free throw.

Lakers 40, Globetrotters 39.

The Lakers set up slowly, Pollard misses a jump shot, Pressley rebounds. Haynes is fouled by Swede Carlson on the fast break and converts the free throw.

Lakers 40, Globetrotters 40.

Tied again. Perfect equilibrium still. And no resolution in sight. The entire game is hanging in midair like a circus high-wire walker, his balancing pole dipping a little to this side, a little to that, the audience sucking in great drafts of air with each dip, as if they are watching a breathtaking performance.

Lakers' ball.

Less than a minute on the clock to the end of the third quarter.

Again, the ball zips around the perimeter of Lakers players trying to find an opening to complete a pass into Mikan, who grinds and pushes against Goose and Pressley like a horse scratching himself against a tree. They dig in and push back, and the three of them slide around in the key like loose cargo on the deck of a pitching ship. Mikan manages to keep one arm up, signifying that he is ready to receive the pass.

But there is no way to get the ball into him. Finally, when Herm Schaefer holds the ball up over his head, as if to flip the pass into Mikan, Haynes drops so far off him that Schaefer sets himself and delivers a long set shot.

The ball caroms off the backboard and the rim and arcs in a high rebound that Haynes leaps for. He has it in his hands and is still in the air when Mikan's hands also grip the ball. Their bodies hang against each other in the air like two loose suits dangling from a single peg, but the struggle for possession of the ball is momentary and fierce. With a heave, Mikan rips the ball from Haynes's hands. At the same time Haynes rips back with such a violent effort that when his hands slip away from the ball, the recoil sends him falling backward to the floor.[10]

While he is still falling, a gasp rises from the fans, like a siren inhaling suddenly. The clever and playful rabbit, impervious to pain or sorrow and the source of so much pleasure, is about to suffer injury.

When he hits the floor flat on his back, the thud is sickening. He rolls slowly on his side, and the only noises in the Madhouse are sounds of the smoke drifting lazily to the ceiling and the scoreboard clock moving silently.

Then he pops to his feet. Unhurt. Escaped. The playful figure free to perform his rabbity miracles again. The applause is long and hard, and when it is clear that Haynes hasn't been hurt, it slowly slides into cheering as Pollard scores.

Lakers 42, Globetrotters 40.

The action flies back the other way. Willie King misses, the directions are reversed again, Pollard misses, "go, go, go," the cheers rising higher and higher, as much from relief as excitement over the continuous, whirlwind action. Now Haynes misses, they turn around and head back, Schaefer misses, finally a bullet pass the length of the court to Goose Tatum, left behind in the seesaw mayhem, all alone under his own basket to score only his third field goal of the night, another sleeper, a peaceful little reach-and-flick shot that is out of place in the middle of such flat-out basketball.

Lakers 42, Globetrotters 42.

The quarter ends, the two teams retreat to their benches and stand with their hands on their hips, breathing deeply.

Marques Haynes has miraculously escaped serious injury after his frightening fall onto his back, but the fall seems to stand as a prelude to something even more frightening, and the crowd is silent now, breathing deeply also, gathering itself for whatever breathtaking drama lies still ahead.

V

FOURTH QUARTER

17

Ted

The Lakers toweled off between quarters while Johnny Kundla reminded his players again that both Goose Tatum and Ermer Pressley had four fouls. Even if they continued to double-team Mikan, the defense would be passive, which would be the same as none at all. Mikan would be able to score at will, Kundla said. "Keep going to George," he instructed his players. And no more sleepers from Goose, he lifted a finger and warned. He did not point the finger at anybody, but it was clear that he expected Swede Carlson and Herm Schaefer to make sure it did not happen again.[1]

In their huddle, the Globetrotters remained committed to the strategy that got them back in the game. "Keep running," Pressley said, "push it! Who's tired?"

He broke from the huddle without waiting for the obvious answer: with so many games, the Globetrotters were all in magnificent condition, and none of them were tired, no matter how hard and deeply they were breathing.[2]

Goose Tatum controls the center tip.

Globetrotters' ball.

Willie King dribbles straight up the middle and then seems deflected more by the black line of the free-throw circle than by any defenders as he takes a circuitous path to the basket. His layup is tipped at the last moment, and the ball pops high into the air. Jim Pollard rips the ball down with one hand, finds no one open to pass to, and heads up the court, stutter-stepping and spinning as he moves.

He is backing his way into the key, closer and closer to the basket, pushing against Pressley's defense, the force of his pushing reflected in the jackhammer pounding of his dribble, when he flips a backhand bounce pass off his dribble to George Mikan.

Field goal, Mikan.

Lakers 44, Globetrotters 42.

Globetrotters' ball.

Babe Pressley scores.

Lakers 44, Globetrotters 44. The fifth tie.

The two teams trade free throws again.

Lakers 45, Globetrotters 45.

Goose Tatum steals a forced pass into Mikan. The Globetrotters try to fast break but at midcourt lose control of the ball. They scramble to recover possession and in the process lose the fast-break opportunity. Instead, they drift quickly into a five-man weave, not the pinwheel cutting of earlier, with Goose Tatum at the free-throw line acting as the hub, but a flat weave just inside the midcourt line, all five players trotting around and around, tracing an elliptical course on the floor, going nowhere. The Lakers back up a few feet to keep a safe distance from the whirligig action. The ball never touches the floor as it passes between the Globetrotters, bobbing like a cork at the center of their lazy turning. It is as hypnotic as watching a fan belt or a bicycle chain, turning turning turning, and it is so interruptive of what has been the breakneck flow of the game that the Lakers stop any pretense of defense and just stand and watch this foolish reem in the center of a serious basketball game. It is so ill timed and inappropriate that it brings neither laughter nor applause from the crowd but a stunned silence, as if to say, "What the hell are they doing?" trotting in a dizzy circle like basketball nitwits.

Ermer Robinson makes a slow turn at the shoulder of the ellipse. He takes one step back along the fan-belt course, then with an explosion of speed forks off toward the basket. Marques Haynes cradles the cork in one hand before he flips it through the dazed Lakers, who move too late to intercept the pass.

Robinson takes the ball in full stride as he approaches the right side of the basket. Jim Pollard and George Mikan race to block his layup. Robinson springs into the air as Pollard and Mikan leap together, their arms forming a picket fence through which Robinson has to shoot. He lifts the ball, as if to push it through the pickets, then pulls it back and continues floating, twisting himself through the pickets, under the basket, floating farther still, waiting, holding the ball to his chest until he is free and clear for the shot, which he finally delivers by twisting himself again as he floats away from the basket.

Field goal, Robinson.

Lakers 45, Globetrotters 47.

It was the first Globetrotters' lead. The Lakers took a time-out but appeared calm. Meanwhile, the entire stadium came to its feet, the wave of rising bodies moving up from courtside again. They were celebrating in part the brief and fragile supremacy of the underdogs, but they were also cheering wildly for the unlimited possibilities of basketball, which had been a game with the architecture of football, featuring set formations and plays as rigid as road maps. Its guards and forwards and centers had been arranged in place with the fixity of baseball players. And the gurus of the game had described the sanctioned shots with a lexicon as strict as a dictionary.[3]

But exhilarating moments of basketball ballet and improvisation were appearing regularly—like Jim Pollard's earlier wrong-foot shot and now Ermer Robinson's floating reverse layup—and the fans were rising in celebration of it. That it came immediately on the heels of the hypnotic, wheel-chain motion was doubly electrifying, like an alarm clock clanging urgently in the dark.

During the time-out, the Lakers substitute Paul Napolitano for Swede Carlson. Of the four stars recruited from California, he and Pollard are the only two remaining.[4] Napolitano's defense and scoring potential have earned him a permanent spot with the team, and nothing is sacrificed by injecting him into the lineup.

Lakers' ball.

Mikan misses his drop-step hook shot and battles Goose and Pressley for the rebound. The three of them grab the ball together and then stagger around in a long and violent convulsion of heaving to gain firm possession. The Lakers substitutes rise again from their bench to protest the mauling they think Mikan is suffering at the hands of Goose and Pressley, but no whistle blows, and the ball finally pops loose. Mikan grabs it again but is too exhausted to put a shot back up immediately.

He dribbles once to steady himself, then bounces a pass out to Paul Napolitano.

In the struggle for possession of the ball in the key, other Globetrotters have collapsed around Mikan, and now Napolitano is wide open. His eventual shot reflects how strict and long lasting the influence of those shooting dictionaries have been. Yet it is Napolitano's pet shot, and in the Lakers' shooting clinic earlier in the year, where Pollard demonstrated his wrong-foot shot and Mikan his drop-step hook shot, Napolitano's pet shot is described as a "one hander, *using both hands.*"[5] The only explanation for this oxymoron is that the two-hand influence of his coaches has so stricken him with a basketball conscience that he doesn't feel free to shoot a purely one-hand shot.

Napolitano's eventual shot then is a hybrid that begins as a two-hand push off his chest, his big hands like hubcaps on the opposing sides of the ball. The shot doesn't become one-handed until the ball is almost at arm's length and his right hand takes over and completes the job of pushing the ball on its way.

Field goal, Napolitano.

Lakers 47, Globetrotters 47.

Napolitano's quick score after his entry into the game makes his substitution seem ingenious, but Johnny Kundla remains impassive on the bench, legs crossed, arms crossed, cradling his chin in one hand, as if contemplating a piece of sculpture instead of the Globetrotters racing back down the floor.

Mikan intercepts the pass into Goose but can find no one to throw the outlet pass to, so he takes off dribbling down the floor. His dribbling is a blend of chaotic reeling and momentum so powerful it would be foolish to get in his way, and he eventually drives all the way to the basket but misses the layup.

Trailing Mikan, Goose Tatum grabs the rebound, and the Globetrotters counterbreak again. Haynes misses, Pollard rebounds, and his immediate flight back down the floor finally brings Johnny Kundla to his feet, signaling "slow, slow, slow!" with his hands again.

Schaefer and Goose trade free throws.

Lakers 48, Globetrotters 48.

Pollard misses a field goal, Mikan rebounds and kicks the ball out, Schaefer misses, and Goose is in perfect position for the rebound when Mikan crashes into him from behind and captures the ball.

It is Mikan's third foul, but the frustration on his face as he takes a position on the free-throw lane reflects something much deeper than irritation over the call or even that Goose out-positioned him for the rebound. It is as if he is battling something in himself, and losing the battle, and for just the brief moment that the action has stopped again for a free throw, his chest heaves as he tries to catch his breath, and he is as much exhausted by the combat inside him as he is by the furious pace of the game.

Free throw, Tatum.

Lakers 48, Globetrotters 49.

Six minutes left on the scoreboard clock.

Lakers' ball.

Haynes steals the pass into Mikan and streaks down the floor. Donald "Ducky" Moore, substituting for the Globetrotters, misses the field goal. Mikan rebounds, and the Lakers need no directions from Johnny Kundla on the bench to set up slowly. The ball circles the perimeter of Lakers players like a small planet orbiting the sun of Mikan. He turns and keeps repositioning himself, to stay aligned with the ball planet. Finally, there is an opening for the quick pass, which leaves a flaming trail like an asteroid.

As soon as he gets the ball, he clamps it to his stomach, elbows out like sharp wing nuts, then pivots with the force of an auger to face the basket. There are no drop-step fakes now, no effort even to avoid the arms that are slashing at him. In his determined frame of mind, any deception at all would be a sign of weakness, an admission that he doesn't have the superiority to confront and overpower his defenders head-on and take back the lead. He has resolved the issue that was troubling him on the free-throw line, which is: who is going to deliver us from defeat evil? The answer is that *he* is! Sure, there are four other teammates on the floor, but he is the only one who grew up in Mikan's Tavern watching bloody fights between railroad workers and brickmakers. He is the only one who watched Monkey Joe and the Crazy Serbian break beer bottles on the tavern bar and then drive out mobsters trying to collect tribute money. He is the only one who has the bull-moose size and the silken touch.

He punches his shoulder through the slim opening between Pressley and Goose. They peel away from him. He bulls his way through the larger opening and lifts the ball. Pressley's and Goose's hands slide off it as if it is greased. Jumping only enough to clear the ball, Mikan releases a shot that is so soft it hangs over the basket like the moon.

Field goal, Mikan.

Lakers 50, Globetrotters 49.

Five minutes.

Globetrotters' ball.

Pressley ties the score again with a free throw.

Lakers 50, Globetrotters 50.

Lakers' ball.

Jim Pollard drives the middle from his forward position, Babe Pressley hounding him the whole way, slapping and poking at the ball as Pollard moves. As if anticipating Pollard's wrong-foot shot, Pressley jumps too soon and then hangs in the air over Pollard, his arms out like a spread-winged hawk casting a shadow over its prey. Pollard dribbles out from beneath the shadow and leaps as Pressley floats back to the floor. Pollard's shot, a sweeping right-hand hook shot, bangs off the backboard and rips the net.

Lakers 52, Globetrotters 50.

Globetrotters' ball.

Robinson misses a field goal, Mikan rebounds, and Pressley tries to wrestle the ball from Mikan's hands. The whistle shrieks. It is Pressley's fifth foul, and he leaves the game.

Ted Strong replaces Pressley. At six-five, 220 pounds, he is the one Globetrotter whose height and muscular frame seem to equip him to do battle against the taller Lakers. He has broad shoulders, a thick neck, huge hands, burly thighs that threaten to rip the piping of his stretched pants, and biceps that seem to have been inflated by tire pumps.

Strong is a twelve-year veteran of the Globetrotters, and by virtue of his experience and the authority of his size, he would seem to be the team's natural leader. But basketball is his second love, behind the pleasures of a stiff drink now and then and performing as a slugging outfielder for the Kansas City Monarchs in the Negro Leagues. Globetrotters' publicity pictures of him winding up with the basketball squeezed in his huge hand, one leg raised in the high kick of a flamethrowing pitcher, suggest where his real talent lies.[6] But as he rumbles onto the floor and heads for his spot on the free throw-lane, he cuts through the free-throw circle, where Mikan is waiting to be awarded the ball. As he passes slowly in the shadow of Mikan, who has popped his glasses and is cleaning them on his shirttail, Strong's powerful frame seems daunting, and the question is obvious: Where has he been?

18

The Wee Ice Mon

At the free-throw line, George Mikan aims, dips, and makes the free throw.

Lakers 53, Globetrotters 50.

Globetrotters' ball.

Marques Haynes walks the ball up the court. His slow pace appears to be an admission by the Globetrotters of defeat. Their whirlwind play has been a basketball tornado that sucked up everything in its path, including the Lakers. But the Lakers are pulling away again, and it is clear that the fast pace has been counterproductive. There is little for the Globetrotters to do now but accede to that "slow, slow, slow" pace that Johnny Kundla has finally forced upon the game with the soothing hands of a concert pianist.

Willie King makes several tentative probings of the Lakers' defense, jabbing and poking toward the free-throw line with a creep dribble. With each foray, the cheering rises suddenly as if in anticipation of something dramatic, but a noose of Lakers players immediately tightens around King. He tries to maneuver out of the trap by pivoting, but he drags his pivot foot and the whistle shrieks. No one on or off the floor can hear the whistle because of the crowd noise, and play continues, with King pivoting and wheeling desperately until he squirts a pass out to Ermer Robinson just as the frustrated official who has made the traveling call, his chest pumping like a bellows, skips into the center of the action in an effort to stop play.

Robinson shoots anyway, the basket is good, but both officials are prancing among the players, waving off the basket.

Traveling! Lakers' ball.

As they walk the ball up the floor, the continuous roar of confusion on the heels of the disallowed basket seems to have the opposite effect of earlier cheering. Instead of racing the action, the cheering is slowing it now, creating a clear atmospheric paste through which the Lakers have to swim as they try to score. Everything slows to a crawl. The vendors are hunched and sluggish as they try to howl out "ice cream" and "cold beer" over the cheering. The hands of the scoreboard clock that sweep down the minutes and seconds seem on the verge of grinding to a halt.

Mikan moves into his hook shot with an uncharacteristic indolence.

Goose Tatum rebounds the missed shot, and the Globetrotters are suddenly off. All five of them race down the floor as if they have come flying out of the bell of a Victrola, cranked up suddenly after a dead stop.

Marques Haynes drives for a layup from the right side. But before takeoff, he sticks one foot in the floor like an ice pick, then throws both his arms in the air, burlesquing a layup shot. A retreating Lakers defender bites on the fake and flies by him.

Field goal, Haynes.

Lakers 53, Globetrotters 52.

Lakers' ball.

They set up slowly. Double-teaming pressure by the Globetrotters is so frenetic there are two of them wherever the ball goes, and the impression is that they must have an extra player on the floor. Pivoting to pass out of that pressure, Herm Schaefer is fouled and makes his fifth straight free throw.

Lakers 54, Globetrotters 52.

The Globetrotters set up slowly again. The Lakers' defense is cautious and edgy. Their focus is not on the man with the ball, but like distracted daydreamers staring into space, each one is half focused on an invisible spot somewhere in the center of them all. They flick their heads this way and that, making sure they see everything else on the court, convinced that whoever has the ball is merely a suckering distraction for a scoring plot—a penetrating drive, a reverse cut, a screen—that is developing somewhere else on the floor.

Ermer Robinson crouches with the ball near the sidelines. Swede Carlson backs away from him, looking for that scoring plot elsewhere. Robinson straightens, sets his feet in tandem, and shoots a long, one-hand shot.

Field goal, Robinson.
Lakers 54, Globetrotters 54.

At the press table, Fay Young of the *Chicago Defender* made note of the fact that it was the tenth time the game had been tied. He also noted that Ermer Robinson had already scored 15 points. For a moment, he wondered if Abe Saperstein and the other Globetrotters were as aware as he was that it was the unlikely-looking Robinson, nothing but a bag of bones in a jersey, upon whom the Globetrotters fortunes seemed to depend.

Young had watched enough athletic contests to know that players slipped into hot streaks and slumps according to forces as mysterious as a sorcerer's spell. Nobody, least of all coaches, understood those forces, or worse, recognized them until it was too late. For a brief moment Young toyed with the idea of alerting Abe Saperstein and Babe Pressley to the fact that the hottest shooter on the floor appeared to be Ermer Robinson. Before it was too late, every effort should be made to get the ball to him.

But any signal from Young would have been exactly the kind of journalistic meddling and lack of objectivity that he had already warned the intern beside him to avoid, and the idea passed quickly. Besides, Young felt, this was a game determined to resolve itself according to a storybook script written by athletic gods in utter defiance of the will of any of the combatants and, most of all, in defiance of the will of any sportswriter. Just sit back and watch, he reminded himself.

Elsewhere at the press table, sportswriters scratching out game notes began searching for heroic metaphors that would appear in their stories on the game. Football clashes as desert warfare, boxing matches as biblical sagas, bantam golfers like the unflappable and tiny Ben Hogan portrayed as the "wee ice mon"—the point wasn't just to write something readable and dramatic, the point was to connect the deeds of athletes in brief games on tiny battlefields to something epic.[1]

But exactly what was the epic metaphor in Chicago Stadium? Twice the Lakers had taken comfortable leads. For the tenth time the Globetrotters had pulled dead-even. As soon as they did, the Lakers drew away again. If there was a metaphor in it all, it was as if the game were a horse race featuring a powerful but lazy thorough-bred who ran only as hard as it took to win. Challengers moved up to try to overtake the great horse. They raced dead-even for a few strides, or perhaps the champion allowed the challenger to stick its nose out ahead for a few strides before the champion shifted into high gear and drew away—but only as much as it needed to stay ahead.

And the mighty Lakers were that thoroughbred, loafing along just enough to stay ahead, toying with the Globetrotters, tantalizing them, inviting them to throw their whole heart into the battle, only to be crushed by superior strength and speed.

Lakers' ball.

Jim Pollard drives the full length of the floor, then stops at the free-throw line, plants both feet, and jumps.

Three Globetrotters have him boxed in as he jumps. He rises so quickly from their midst that they arch their backs to watch him as he goes up, their raised arms encircling him like palings. At the peak of his jump, his body poking up from the center of them, a flashbulb explosion freezes Pollard into a sculpture held high on a pedestal of Globetrotters. Despite the violent catapult of energy it took to lift him so high, he is perfectly still at the peak of his jump, hanging in the air with the serenity of a basketball angel.

His shot hits the back rim, and the ball gargles in the throat of the basket before it is spit out.

Goose Tatum gathers the rebound. When he turns to look down the floor for the outlet pass, Mikan chops the ball free from Goose's hands. Mikan recovers the loose ball and dribbles once to quickly steady himself. He is turning to shoot when the whistle blows.

Foul on Mikan.

While the others move down the floor for the free throw, Mikan remains under the basket, hands on his hips, staring into space, his face so deliberately expressionless it screams with anger. But over what? Not grabbing the rebound himself? The foolishness of his foul? The late whistle?[2]

Whatever it is, he permits himself only a second to dwell on it. Then he trudges off, following the others. But it has been enough of a pause for the announcer to find an opening in the booing and cheering to announce that it is Mikan's fourth foul.

The pendulum of victory swings back in favor of the Globetrotters. By virtue of their double-teaming of Mikan and a fast break predicated in part on the idea that they can run him into the ground, the Globetrotters have made Mikan the focus of their tactics. Now he is in danger of fouling out. Once he is gone, victory will belong to the Globetrotters. Never mind that Jim Pollard will still be out there. Never mind that the Lakers have a deep bench and other great shooters. The Globetrotters will have shot the Lakers' mightiest warrior. Goliath is dead! The battle is over!

Mikan is the last to take his position on the free-throw lane, and Goose shoots quickly without deliberation.

Free throw, Tatum.

Lakers 54, Globetrotters 55.

Lakers' ball.

Herm Schaefer shoots a bounce pass into Mikan, who has to struggle out from between Babe Pressley and Goose Tatum to receive the pass. The minute he has it securely in his hands, Pressley and Goose move directly behind him, shoulder to shoulder, anticipating that Mikan's relentless determination, which is apparent to everybody in Chicago Stadium, will again direct him to turn and try to slash his way between them on his way to the basket. This time, however, there is no daylight between Goose and Pressley, and they hammer back against the effort of his sharp shoulder to separate them like a splitting wedge. He retreats a half step, then batters at them again with his shoulder. They still refuse to separate and instead pound back.

It is a standoff. The crowd is roaring, and the players on the Lakers' bench have come to their feet. Mikan tries one more time and is bucked back. He pauses a second to gather himself from the third rejection. He makes no effort to find the Lakers player who has to be open somewhere. Nor does his face reflect the frustration of the Lakers' bench, howling in protest now over the way Mikan is being pummeled.

He twitches his head left in a silly fake that fools no one. Then he turns to his right, to begin the step and sweep of his hook shot. But Pressley has slid out and is waiting for him. The two collide chest to chest. Mikan has no choice now but to gather himself on both feet, then jump, with one of Pressley's arms laid across his wrists like a heavy beam.

It is as if Mikan is trying to jump against the weight of sandbags, and the effort makes him shudder, then suddenly go as limp as a rag doll. Only his arms have the will and the strength to keep rising against the drag. And once he finally releases the ball in a soft shot that sails over Goose's outstretched arms, he staggers and falls to his knees.

Score by Mikan.

Lakers 56, Globetrotters 55.

Johnny Kundla has to trot up and down his bench like a sheepdog to keep his players from swarming onto the floor in protest over the fact that there was no foul called on Mikan's desperation shot.

As soon as Kundla has them pushed back off the floor, Marques Haynes comes hurtling along the bench, dribbling toward the deep corner of the floor, where he slides to one knee and is immediately trapped.

Mikan has been slow coming to his feet after his miraculous shot, and he has been left behind by Goose Tatum, who wheels straight up the middle of the floor and into the key, one hand raised, calling for the ball because he is wide open. Still on his knees in the corner, Haynes can only rifle a pass out to Ermer Robinson, who sets himself for the shot immediately.

The shot skips off the front rim and the backboard, then rises almost straight up in a high rebound that seems to be dropping out of the cigarette clouds.

It comes as no surprise, the moment of crashing violence that has been hanging over the game as thick as that smoke. It comes as the unavoidable climax to the frantic pace, to all the collisions and re-bounding convulsions and sandbags and angry tug-of-wars. It comes as the inevitable result of tensions that that can't keep rising forever. It is as predictable as the "boing" of a pocket-watch mainspring after endless stem-winding.

The two who meet head-on in the pitch of battle also is no sur-prise. It is the same boyish David and mighty Goliath who have already banged bodies once. This time, Mikan comes at full speed up the middle of the floor for the rebound. Haynes comes flying in from the deep corner. As the ball drops just outside the free-throw lane, they meet high in the air. The noise of their bodies collid-ing raises a thunderclap like two saddles slamming into each other. They each get their hands on the ball at once and try to rip it from the other's grasp. The effort sends Haynes falling backward out of the sky again, windmilling his arms as he falls.[3]

He lands with the same sickening thud as the first time.[4] The midair collision also crumples Mikan, who drops to his knees as soon as he hits the floor. On his hands and knees, Mikan watches the ball skitter away from him toward midcourt. Behind him, Ermer Robinson's sad, impassive face is suddenly twisted with anger as he points a finger of accusation at Mikan.

It has been almost one year to the day since Pop Gates's punch took Chick Meehan by surprise and brought a sudden silence in the Syracuse Armory. In that martial atmosphere, the silence had also brought an eerie chill that lasted only an instant before the violence exploded. Now, the hush that falls in Chicago Stadium as Robinson points and points and points at Mikan is stuffy and oppressive, filled with hot anxiety.

Is Robinson going to leap onto Mikan and pummel him? Is Robinson's effort to shame mighty Goliath for crushing poor David going to make the giant explode with rage? Will both teams then jump into the hot fray and be swallowed by an army of angry fans?

But no one moves, except a lone photographer who scuttles onto the floor and explodes a flashbulb of light into the scene.[5] In the continuing silence, only the cigarette smoke above the lights and the hands on the scoreboard clock move, and Marques Haynes lies dead still on the catafalque of the floor.

19

David and Goliath

Still on his hands and knees, George Mikan lifts his head to point the loose ball like a bird dog. Herm Schaefer recovers the ball and breaks for what will be an easy basket, but one of the officials notices that Marques Haynes is still motionless on the floor, and his whistle sounds in the silence to stop the action. The official skips to the spot where Haynes is crumpled on his side. He straddles the motionless body and bends over it. Then he straightens up and begins waving frantically to the Globetrotters' bench.

Babe Pressley is the first to reach Haynes and kneel beside him. "Are you all right?" he asks.

His voice carries beyond the courtside seats and up into the first tier, but Haynes doesn't answer.

Pressley bends closer. "How do you feel?"

The only answer is the sound of courtside seats creaking as worried fans rise for a better look.

"Marques," Pressley shouts now, "how do you feel?"

Haynes finally lifts his head slowly. "I dunno," he whispers. "It hurts."

A circle of worried Globetrotters forms around their fallen teammate. Abe Saperstein bends over Haynes's head. Pressley is still kneeling. Haynes manages to sit up, both hands still on the floor. Pressley grabs one of his arms.

But Haynes is not ready to try to stand yet. "Wait a while," he says.

The Lakers retreat to their bench. Mikan rises slowly off his knees and stands for a second staring at Haynes, as if he can't believe that such an insignificant body could have knocked him to the floor. Then he follows his teammates.

"ok," Haynes finally says, "let me stand up."

Babe Pressley and Ermer Robinson help Haynes to his feet. He takes a few short, careful steps.

A chorus of creaking seats fills the stadium. It is not the ghoulishness of rubberneckers eager to be eye-witnesses to horror that brings additional fans to their feet. They are all as fragile and breakable as Haynes, and they are rising as if they are also in pain, as if they are also in need of several careful steps to verify that they are still in one piece.

Abe Saperstein follows him as he walks. "You want to come out?"

"No," Haynes answers quickly.

Saperstein takes hold of one of Haynes's arms, as if to steady him. Since Haynes is already steady on his feet, the gesture is more an expression of Saperstein's worry than it is support for Haynes.

"If I sit on the bench," Haynes tells Saperstein, "I'll get cold."

He twists himself gingerly.

"I'm good and warm," he says. "Let it stay as such."

He twists himself again, and Saperstein runs his eyes up and down Haynes's body, searching for the site of his injury.

"What is it, your back?"

Haynes nods and continues to twist himself slowly.

"You better come out," Saperstein says.

Haynes shakes his head. "On the bench, I'll stiffen up."

"I think you should come out," Saperstein repeats.

"No!" Haynes insists. "If I keep playing, I can stay warm."

He is determined to remain in the game, and he breaks away from Saperstein's support and trots a tight circle to test himself.[1] As he does so, the applause begins as tentative clapping that is soon mingled with whistles and cheering. The cheering is at first a simple expression of the audience's relief. An ominous and smoky mood of separation has hung over the two teams, not just because they are so different in history and character but because, like it or not, they seem to mirror and simplify antagonisms that are in the immediate Chicago streets, where white hoodlums beat blacks with baseball bats, and a thousand miles away in Washington DC, where President Truman's Jefferson-Jackson Day speech calling for racial reconciliation is received with jeers and catcalls.

There could not have been a more violent impact than the midair collision between a boyish David and a mighty Goliath.[2] It could easily have exploded into violence and rampage. Globetrotters and Lakers could have begun swinging at each other. As they had done in Syracuse a year earlier, fans could have come streaming onto the floor, determined to fight on one side or the other. Those same fans could have begun swinging at each other in a racial melee as muddled and smoky as battlefield troops in hand-to-hand combat. But the Lakers have withdrawn quietly to their bench. Meanwhile, the Globetrotters watch Haynes carefully as he trots another circle, and Ermer Robinson's pointed finger of blame at George Mikan is forgotten. Mikan is not to blame any more than Haynes is. It was an accidental collision, born of the passions of the game, not personal rancor. The moment has passed. Nothing in what remains of the game can possibly be as provocative as what has just occurred. And the cheering, which continues to rise, is in celebration now of the fact that the game will continue as high drama, not low street-fight.

Haynes trots one more experimental circle. The officials watch him carefully. He nods to Abe Saperstein and Babe Pressley. He is ready.

Lakers' ball out of bounds.

Herm Schaefer stands at midcourt trying to inbound the ball. But Haynes is immediately in front of him, waving his hands and leaping again and again in an effort to block the in-bound pass. Each leap triggers even louder cheering from the crowd, and for a moment Schaefer seems stunned by Haynes's pressing defense. Only seconds ago he was flat on the floor, knocked silly. Now he is bouncing and leaping like a pesky rabbit. In desperation, Schaefer tries to loop an overhead pass to Jim Pollard, but Haynes deflects the ball and then pounces on it.

The fact that he doesn't break immediately for the Globetrotters' basket with his low dribble is the only evidence that he might have been injured in the collision with Mikan. Instead, he moves slowly up the floor with the high comic dribble of earlier in the game. He is the dribbling trickster again, indestructible, full of high jinks and clever sliding stops and starts and pivots, and there is not one person in Chicago Stadium who is not on his or her feet, whooping and howling for joy in a resounding testimonial to rabbity resilience and persistence.

Bucky and Babe, Roosie and Goose, Johnny and Abe, the Kangaroo Kid, Ma Piersall, Monkey Joe, Olson's Terrible Swedes, Chick
and Pop—it sounded like the cast of heroes and villains in a children's book instead of the characters in the epic story of the integration of professional basketball. Still, by February 1948, as the clock
wound down in Chicago Stadium, the story was unfinished. Most of
the bigotries and white rationalizations that Bucky Lew had braved
were still embraced. Blacks weren't team players, the bigots con-
tended, and they weren't smart enough to learn complicated plays.
Their ropy, disjointed bodies weren't right for the game. They were
dancers and comic Sambos, not driven competitors who would bring
white fans to witness their victories. The only thing they could possibly bring to the game of serious basketball was violence.

There were enough subscribers to those cruel prejudices to keep
blacks out of the professional game. It was not surprising, then,
that as the Lakers and Globetrotters battled in Chicago Stadium,
the lowly Eastern League of Pennsylvania was one of the few integrated professional leagues in the country.[3] With teams in such
obscure burgs as Hazelton and Pottsville and Lancaster and Sun-
bury, the league was a humble basketball stage for the continuation
of the basketball drama, but the *Baltimore Afro-American* wrote that
the five black players in the league were giving "creditable accounts
of themselves."[4] The fact that league attendance was up proved, the
Afro-American insisted, that the bigots were wrong and that the integration of professional basketball could occur "without any strain."

There was one other encouraging piece of news, the *Afro-
American* believed. The little town of Ahoskie, in northeastern
North Carolina, had made national news the previous summer when
an African American resident had won the Kiwanis raffle of a brand-
new Cadillac, then been denied his rightful prize. But now basketball teams of both races were practicing side by side in Ahoskie, and
nobody seemed unhappy. What had created the sudden "interracial
amity," the newspaper explained, was an emergency. Ahoskie's all-
white high school basketball team had found itself without a court
while its new gym was under construction. At that point the all-
black Van High School had graciously offered to share its gym with
the Ahoskie team. "Now white players practice on one end of the
court," the *Afro-American* wrote, "and colored on the other."[5]

As a measure of progress since the town's shameful Kiwanis raffle, it seemed worth celebrating. But as a measure of the progress in "interracial amity" in athletics in the years since Bucky Lew, it was insignificant. And there was no denying that by February 1948, the story was crying for something dramatic and spectacular that would dumbfound the bigots, and neither an obscure league in Pennsylvania nor a small gym in the North Carolina boondocks was the proper theater for the presentation of the next act in a basketball drama that had been unfolding for fifty years.

Haynes suddenly abandons his high dribble and bends his trunk to get low to the floor, as if he is preparing to hurl a flat stone across a lake, and he skips a bounce pass off his dribble into Willie King, who is cutting for the basket.

As soon as he gets the ball, King stops, his defender slides by him, and he shoots the ball off his shoulder.

Field goal, King.

Lakers 56, Globetrotters 57.

Lakers' ball.

Jim Pollard works his way down the right sidelines against two Globetrotters defenders, who have him pinched no matter which direction he tries go. Not yet at half-court, and in what appears to be a desperate retreat, Pollard backs up on his dribble and tries to outflank the two Globetrotters by dribbling a banana course toward the far sideline. Once he gets there and crosses the ten-second line, he is blocked again, this time up against the left sidelines with no possible retreat or evasion. In desperation, he picks up his dribble and loops a pass forward to Herm Schaefer. For a moment, Schaefer seems to have a clear path to the basket, but before he can put down his dribble his path is blocked by two Globetrotters.

In the deep corner, Jack Dwan is wide open and calling for the ball, holding both arms out as if to embrace the world, and Schaefer's flat bullet pass thumps into his chest and drops to the floor before he can close his arms and pick up the ball.

It is enough of a delay in the execution of his set shot that Ermer Robinson, racing to the spot, can leap into the air and deflect it just as it leaves Dwan's outstretched fingers. At the peak of its flight, the ball seems to die in the air like a shot bird and begins dropping to the floor, far short of the basket. Mikan struggles to push Goose Tatum aside so that he can get to the falling shot, but Goose is stuck firmly in place with his feet spread and his long arms out to restrain Mikan like railroad barricades.

Jim Pollard, rushing up the floor after his pass out of the trap, jumps and reaches to catch the ball, but he can only flick at it with his fingertips. Still, he manages to deflect the ball back into the air, where it caroms off the backboard straight into the hands of Ducky Moore, who fumbles it and drops it to the floor.

Someone kicks the ball, and it skitters across the court like a puck. Ermer Robinson finally has it. He spots Haynes at half-court. With the windmill motion of a softball pitcher, he whips an underhand pass to Haynes, who has only Swede Carlson to beat for a layup.

But he doesn't even try, and it is the second indication that beneath his springbok zip he has been broken in some way by his collision with Mikan. Instead, he takes an abbreviated step into a one-hand shot that is obviously tight and painful, with none of the darting ease that is the mark of every Haynes move.

Field goal by Mar-keeeeeez Hayyyyyyynes.

Lakers 56, Globetrotters 59.

Haynes backpedals slowly across half-court. Weakened by the realization that he is seriously hurt, the crowd delivers a feeble cheer that is as tight as his shot and reflects a fear that Haynes may have to leave the game. It won't leave the Globetrotters without shooters, because Robinson is just as deadly a shooter. And it won't leave them without strength or size, because they are all bigger and stronger than he is. But he is the only one who carries within him a seamless melding of comedy and athleticism. Every serious basketball move he makes is graced with an exhilarating lightness, and he is their spiritual center. Without that center, the Globetrotters are doomed. Their 3-point lead means nothing.

The determination in Jim Pollard's blade face is apparent as he receives the inbound pass from Herm Schaefer and dribbles up the floor against the double-team defense of Goose Tatum and Ermer Robinson. His determination is part habit, acquired after a thousand games in which the ball has wound up in his hands as time runs out and game forces—coaches and teammates, even opponents—conspire to make him the central character in the last clock ticks of the drama. There is also something to be said during these final minutes for the pervasive influence of Mikan's competitive intensity, vibrating in him like a tuning fork that sets the pitch for everybody on the floor.[6] But Pollard's determination is neither acquired nor an answer to anybody else's grit. It is the expression of a gift he has had since boyhood, which is that his athletic body will dictate what to do, especially in emergencies, and the best course of action is for him to give himself up to it.

He is also determined not to let himself get trapped against the sidelines again, and he wheels repeatedly on his dribble to shake Goose Tatum and Ermer Robinson. In the bull's-eye of the mid-court jump circle, he reverses his dribble direction suddenly and heads for the right sideline. Trying to change directions quickly, Goose stumbles backward and slides along the floor on his rear end, his feet up and his arms spread. Only Robinson remains for Pollard to beat. On the Globetrotters' bench, Babe Pressley stands suddenly to shout advice, "Watch him! Watch him!" trying to warn Robinson that another direction reversal is coming.

It comes so quickly that Robinson is left half a step behind Pollard as he takes two more long dribble strides to the left. At full stride, a flashbulb pops again and catches him as if he is dropping into the splits.

He plants his lead foot and brings his feet together. He jumps exactly at the same moment he grasps the ball bouncing up from his dribble. For a second as he rises, the impression is that the ball is a rocket that is he holding on to for dear life as it carries him higher and higher.

He delivers the jump shot from long range by snapping his body in midair. When he alights, Ermer Robinson has caught up and slid himself into position to keep Pollard from any rebound.

But Pollard makes no effort to go for the rebound, because he already knows there won't be one.

Score by Jim Pollard.

Lakers 58, Globetrotters 59.

Four minutes.

20

The Father, the Son, the Holy Ghost

Globetrotters' ball.

They try to run up the heels of the Lakers after Pollard's jump shot, but the Lakers retreat quickly and frustrate every effort of the Globetrotters to make a dribbling slash at the basket for a layup.

When the ball finally comes to Ermer Robinson, he is standing near the sideline, thirty feet from the basket. As soon as he draws aim for a long set shot, cheering in the third tier cracks like distant thunder and floats down to the floor. The cheering is encouragement for him to shoot, because he has already made several dramatic set shots from nearly as far out. But now he is beyond his comfortable shooting range, and the deliberate and overdrawn motions with which he pretends to be taking dead aim on the basket are only meant to entice Jim Pollard into a shot-blocking leap, beneath which Robinson can then sneak for a drive to the basket.

Pollard doesn't bite and instead concedes Robinson the long shot. But the ball misses the rim entirely and only catches the far edge of the backboard and glances straight into George Mikan's hands.

Mikan turns and dribbles down the floor immediately, as if he is also swept up by the power of the thunderous cheering. It is a second before it dawns on his teammates and the Globetrotters that he is setting off down the middle of the floor on a solo flight straight for the far basket, and heaven help whoever gets in his way.

Cameramen sitting beneath the basket at the far end of the floor fix their cameras on him, and white flashes split the thunderous cheering like heat lightning. He is a basketball demon now, drawn like a gigantic, articulated bug toward those flashes of light, bearing straight down on them as they freeze him again and again in a repeat performance of a classic picture that has appeared in news stories and magazine profiles and basketball programs all over the country. It is a picture of George Mikan on the loose. Of the thousands of photographs that capture him in basketball action, this is the one picture that goes to the heart of who he is, his eyes pinched, his glasses crooked, shards of sweaty hair in his face, his mouth open and twisted revealing his clenched teeth, one elbow flying, the fingers of his dribbling hand so stiff on the ball he might as well be trying to dribble with the branch of a tree, his socks flopping, caught in full stride coming straight at the camera, his legs wobbly and gangling and crisscrossed, the only thing keeping him on a steady course his fierce will.[1]

Goose Tatum catches up to him and tries to reach in and poke the ball away, but he collides with the lurching Mikan. Again, the shriek of the whistle is lost in the bedlam, and Mikan continues on his course toward the basket before the official slides on his knees into the center of the action to stop the play.

Foul on Tatum. His fifth.

Sam Wheeler replaced Goose Tatum, who went straight to the far end of the bench and sat down, sullen and withdrawn. He draped a warm-up jacket over his knees and stared at the center of the floor, lost in thought that seemed a million miles from Chicago Stadium.

It was classic Goose Tatum, this sudden transformation from court clown to mope. In 1941, after Goose joined the Globetrotters, traveling from one big city to another, he remained the Arkansas homeboy and bought a cream-colored Cadillac to cruise the streets of Chicago. On those rare occasions he invited teammates to go cruising with him, he hardly talked as they moved slowly along the streets.[2] His sulking nature was so far removed from the lightheartedness of his court antics it was hard to believe he was the same person. And at times, Goose could turn downright nasty. On a trip to Mexico City, drinking beer at a long bar, Goose had gotten angry at a teammate and threw the bar spittoon at him, spraying tobacco juice everywhere. Even during play, the nastiness would occasionally bubble up from the cauldron of meanness inside him, and if his teammates stopped to watch one of his comic reems, he would snarl at them, "Don't stand and watch me! You're gettin' paid!" Whenever they hit a new town on the road, the other players searched out a good restaurant that would accept them, but Goose disappeared to prowl what his teammates described as the low-life section of town, filled with "meatballs and greasers."[3]

Despite the moan from worried Globetrotters' fans, Goose's removal from the game did not signal doom for the team. Goose's natural athletic talent was all funneled into court comedy. Even his back-to-the-basket hook-shot prayer, which Abe Saperstein had insisted he learn for its comedic impact, had no tactical importance. Goose's main offensive contribution to the game had been three baskets, two of them harmless sleepers.[4] Meanwhile, neither he nor Pressley had been able to stop Mikan. With both of them gone now, and the burly Ted Strong switched to guard Mikan, the Globetrotters' prospects were, if anything, improved.

The Lakers substitutes are all on their feet. Only Johnny Kundla remains seated, his legs crossed, his arms crossed, one hand cradling his chin, nearly as detached and distant as Goose Tatum as he watches George Mikan make his traditional stiff-armed offering of the ball to the basket before he dips for the free throw . . . and misses.

The din slides into another deep moan over the missed free throw. It is the seventh one he has missed, and the moan seems to identify the free-throw ritual he observes before each shot as the *reason* why he is missing. The ritual is too elaborate, too full of holy rite with poses and dips and carefully measured pauses.[5] If just one piece of the elaborate ritual is slightly offbeat or wrong, it will lead to disaster. Why doesn't he just step up and shoot it? Why does he turn free-throw shooting into an act of communion from his Catholic boyhood?

Ted Strong rebounds the missed free throw.

Globetrotters' ball.

The score is still: Lakers 58, Globetrotters 59.

The deafening roar presses the cigarette smoke into a layer of scud at the ceiling. As if he is sliding down the steep face of the crowd's roar like surf, Marques Haynes drives the middle straight at the high stone jetty of Mikan and Pollard guarding the basket. Just before he smashes into them, he skids to a stop. He throws his one hand out in a fake shot at the same time he backhands a pass out to Ermer Robinson, unguarded just beyond the free-throw line.

Robinson doesn't need the crowd's sudden whoop of surprise at how wide open he is to encourage him to shoot. But the shot bangs the front of the rim and trickles into Mikan's hands. Surrounded by clawing Globetrotters, Mikan clears room for himself by swirling his shoulders. Then he offers the ball to Pollard, who has to lock his grip on it before Mikan will relinquish it in order to speed off down the floor.

Two minutes.

Lakers' ball.

They are in no hurry, confident still as they spread themselves wide on the floor and pass the ball on the perimeter, looking for an opportunity to feed Mikan, who jockeys for position against the burly Ted Strong. As soon as he has Strong pinned behind him, he raises one arm to call for the ball, but Strong quickly slides to Mikan's side, and the two of them bump and shoulder each other in a crude tango. Just as Mikan turns to glare at the official closest to him, pleading the case that he is being bludgeoned, the pass slams into his chest and bounces in front of him.

The loose ball is like a magnet, drawing everybody on the floor to it, collapsing them in a ragged patch of bodies. Mikan is the first to grab it. He rips it off the floor and tries to raise it over his head. Sam Wheeler, his arms entangled with Mikan's, rises momentarily along with the ball, then drops away into the snake tangle of players.

In the din, the only indication of a foul is the sight of one official skipping around the tangle as he tries to stop the action by clawing the air with a breast stroke and humping himself as he blows into his whistle like a dog trying to bring up a grassball.

Foul on Sam Wheeler.

Performed in the sudden courtesy of silence that falls, George Mikan's free-throw attempt seems even more ritualized and sacred than it already is. While the official waits and the players arrange themselves on the lane, he crosses himself slowly . . . in the name of the Father . . . in the name of the Son . . . in the name of the Holy Ghost . . . amen.

The official bounces the ball to him and backs out of the lane. Mikan takes a deep breath that widens the silence in Chicago Stadium. A distant and solitary shout of encouragement echoes as if in a cloister. He waits until the echo dies. Then he lifts the ball so slowly with both hands that it looks like he is again making a sacrificial offering to the basket. He holds the aiming for what seems like an eternity. The beer bottles in a vendor's ice chest clink against each other. More echoes. A distant, nervous "yeeowwww" raises laughter like wind chimes tinkling. More waiting, waiting, waiting. When he finally dips and swings the ball, swirls of cigarette smoke are drifting over the backboard in the silence, and it is as if he is swinging a censer to consecrate the basket.

The ball in flight is way too flat. He has already missed three in a row, and now something appears to have gone wrong again. The dip, the pause, the prayer he must have been silently offering while the ice chest rang like vesper bells—whatever it was, it has led to this, a free throw with no more arch to it than the horizon. And the shot appears to have no chance. It can't even be saved from flat failure by Mikan's efforts to freeze his arms in full extension, like a magician trying to work magic on the flight of the ball, trying to coax it into the basket by hocus-pocus.

It ticks against the front rim in passing, goes dead against the back rim with a thunk and sinks into the net.

Lakers 59, Globetrotters 59.

Ninety seconds.

Globetrotters' ball. Time-out.

In the silence observed for the churchly performance of Mikan's free throw, the fans had held back their screaming anxiety like a ticklish sneeze they didn't dare release until the two teams huddled in front of their benches. Then, from numerous pockets throughout the three tiers of fans, isolated chants urging victory for the Lakers or Globetrotters broke out. The chants gained strength as surrounding fans picked them up and carried them into the din of a hundred other such chants. All of it created a high howling that rose and fell like the wind blasts of a cyclone.

The two teams gathered in front of their benches, strangely removed from the furor surrounding them. Everybody on the Globetrotters' bench, including Goose Tatum, joined their huddle. Bent at the hips, his stub legs as stiff as posts, Abe Saperstein had to shout to be heard. His plan was to work the ball in for a close shot that would seal the victory. No one disagreed with the plan, even though it made little sense. Except for Goose's sleepers and the fast-break opportunities, they hadn't been able to go inside on the Lakers all night. George Mikan and Jim Pollard, the human stone jetty that Marques Haynes had just skidded into, were too formidable.[6]

It was Babe Pressley who interrupted Saperstein. Raising his voice only a little, he delivered clipped, precise directions that no one could hear but each assumed was a reminder of the plan they had executed in hundreds of situations just like this one, the clock ticking down, the ball in the Globetrotters' hands, waiting for an opportunity for the last shot. As he spoke, Marques Haynes lifted his eyes to meet Ermer Robinson's, and they nodded at each other. What to do had become second nature to them. They didn't need to hear Pressley's reminder, if indeed that was even what he was doing. How they would move, and where, and by what signals—it was all as gut level as getting up at night at Ma Piersall's and finding their way in the pitch dark to the common bathroom at the end of the corridor.[7]

In the Lakers' huddle, no one interrupted Johnny Kundla's directions. Time-outs were the one circumstance where the usually patient Kundla demanded attention. None of them would ever forget the episode that had driven that lesson home.

It had happened during a game in which George Mikan's play had been uncharacteristically erratic. He had bobbled passes, missed open cutters, and broken numerous plays to take foolish shots. It seemed poetic justice that his erratic play had led to a dislocated finger that required an injury time-out. During the time-out, as Kundla had quietly lectured Mikan about his play and yanked at the finger to reset it, Mikan had repeatedly interrupted his coach.

Finally, Kundla had raised his voice and stunned everybody. "Shut up, George, and listen to me!"

"ok, coach," Mikan answered. "But all I'm trying to tell you is, you're pulling on the wrong finger."[8]

Beneath the laughter that had broken out among the players, there was a deeper appreciation for what Johnny Kundla expected during a time-out. And now, even though his directions were also swallowed by the noise, they gave him their undivided attention: "Play them loose," he said, "don't foul them . . . make them take an outside shot."

When both teams broke from their huddles, the numerous chants had all been abandoned in favor of one simple plea that had begun somewhere in the third tier and then slowly joined into a deep drumbeat that thumped with a steady rhythm: "Freeze—the—ball! Freeze—the—ball! Freeze—the—ball!"[9]

The plea shook the entire stadium the way the custom-built organ could make it shudder at full volume. The chant was driven in part by Globetrotters' fans who recognized logically that their best chance for victory lay in having the last shot. But there was also something irrational and mad in the chant, something as wild and frenzied as the incitements of a mob. "Freeze—the—ball!" Send the game into overtime. Postpone the dreaded possibility of defeat! It had been a magnificent game. In the seesaw battle, both teams had lost leads, then regained them. Neither had quit, neither should have to suffer the disappointment of losing. In the hysteria of the moment, the Madhouse on Madison had truly become a madhouse in which holding the ball for the last shot would mean a continuation of the tie, a continuation of the happy state of perfect equilibrium. "Freeze—the—ball!" Freeze time! A tie forever!

The madhouse cheering gave Johnny Kundla goose bumps again, the way he had felt them as that callow kid from Star Junction who had been awestruck to find himself the focus of cheering as a star player at the University of Minnesota. It was just as awe-inspiring for tiny Abe Saperstein, to find himself now at the center of a mob gone half-mad for *his* team, which he had begun in the dank, monastic seclusion of a basement hideaway on—where else?— Hermitage Street in Chicago. Seclusion, anonymity, elevation from rude beginnings—it was the story line for all of the principal players on that Chicago Stadium stage. They were all escapees who had become as big as museum figures made out of the wax of their simple pasts—George Mikan out of a simple Joliet tavern, the Kangaroo Kid humbly tooting his trumpet for the Salvation Army, Goose Tatum's past so mysterious nobody knew what it was, Marques Haynes escaping his simple Oklahoma roots, and finally the quiet and reclusive Ermer Robinson, who had risen from a basketball court beside "No Man's Land" in San Diego.

21

The Shot

Ermer Robinson inbounds the ball to Marques Haynes, who dribbles up the court in a half-bent posture that is somewhere between the erect parody of his childish dribble and the low, sliding scuttle of his keep-away game. He moves slowly into the frontcourt with a creep-dribble that suggests he is still suffering from the effects of his crash to the floor after his collision with George Mikan.

The Globetrotters are spread out ahead of Haynes on their half of the floor.

Thirty feet from the basket, Herm Schaefer tightens his defense and stops Haynes from advancing the ball.

Haynes glances up at the clock while maintaining a slow dribble. One minute.

He retreats and circles slowly with his dribble. There is nothing coy in his retreat and his circling. It isn't meant to entice Schaefer or any of the Lakers into a chase game. It is done to kill time and to give himself room to concentrate on how much time is left on the clock.

He glances at the clock again.

Forty-five seconds.

It is clear to the fans now that the Globetrotters are going to go for a last-second desperation shot, and the "Freeze—the—ball!" chant passes from the boom-boom-boom rhythm of a cannon salvo into a continuous roar. Everyone is standing. And set loose from the obligations of the chant, the fans howl wildly as the seconds tick down. The noise is earsplitting, beyond anything that seems reasonable for a last-second shot, however cliffhanging and melodramatic the circumstance. This is the battle cry from an army of troops. This is the Niagara Falls of noise, raising a cigarette mist in the stadium. This is the whole restless earth cracking and rumbling.[1]

The only explanation for such a cataract of noise is that it isn't simply bedlam over basketball. This is the members of what Robert Abbott and his *Chicago Defender* preferred to call "the Race," on their feet now in Chicago Stadium and letting loose their hope that one victory here, though endless others haven't, might lead to change. This is that hope, buried for years, suddenly blowing itself out like a geyser over a shot that promises to resolve more than just the seesaw swings of the score. This is an emotional explosion over a shot that has a chance to be one more piece of incontrovertible evidence in an argument that has lasted for decades, from Bucky Lew to Harry S. Truman trying to promote his civil rights plan and calling for an end to a society based on privileges and entitlements.

And this is the noise of a few white nerves jangling over the realization that *if* the shot is good, *if* the Globetrotters win, *if* the mighty Lakers lose, all of the arguments supporting that privileged order of things will be stood on their head, and a whole new stone tablet of rationalizations and specious arguments will have to be carved by those desperate to hang on to their privileges.

Finally, this is the noise of thousands more fans howling with the realization that despite the mayhem in the streets, there is nothing to fear here, despite the basketball collisions and seesaw tensions, nothing in the game of basketball, not even the Globetrotters' hilarious reems and their antic comedy, could be more entertaining and thrilling than this.

With twenty seconds on the clock, the Globetrotters clear out the left side of the floor.[2] Haynes dribbles a wide arc toward the left sideline, in an effort to get around Herm Schaefer, who slides with him.

Johnny Kundla comes to his feet with his hands cupped to form a mouth megaphone so that he can shout as the two men pass in front of the bench, "Don't foul him! Don't foul him!"[3]

With a sudden jet-burst of speed, Haynes changes direction and angles for the free-throw line and the basket, but Jim Pollard and George Mikan are both waiting for him, poised to leap and block the shot.

Meanwhile, Herm Schaefer, who has been outmaneuvered badly, reaches around from behind Haynes and manages to stab at the ball and knock it out of bounds.

Globetrotters' ball.

Ten seconds.

Out of bounds! It presents an opportunity for another time-out, for either the Globetrotters to set up a play or the Lakers to gather themselves before stopping them. But the Globetrotters already know what they want to do, and although the Lakers don't know what that is, they see no point in letting the Globetrotters take their own sweet time to do it, and both teams move into position quickly for the inbounds.

As they arrange themselves, there is a slight but recognizable tailing off in the cheering, like the echoes between cracks of thunder. However slight it is, it seems like the stadium has been suddenly hushed because the ball, which once had life and bounce and was the heart of the game, has died. Now the game itself is dead, and the slight drop in the noise marks a moment of unbearable suspense over whether its heart will ever start beating again and bring the game back to life, whether with just seconds remaining the game will ever be resumed, whether any of the questions hanging in the balance will ever be resolved, or whether the suspense and uncertainty and irresolution will last forever.

Holding the dead ball to his chest, the official waits as the two teams position themselves. Then he quickly bounces the ball twice with both hands, as if to bring it back to life. He hands the resurrected ball to Ted Strong, who lifts it over his head and passes to Marques Haynes under the basket.

Herm Schaefer immediately blankets Haynes, and they are an odd combination, like a bowling ball and a stick fixed to each other. Haynes begins dribbling away from the baseline, beating a hasty dribble retreat from the basket. Each dribble takes him farther away from a chance to score. He passes beyond the outer edge of the free-throw circle still in hasty retreat, not even looking for the basket or a shot, headed into an improbability zone, toward half-court and a hundred-to-one shot territory.[4]

He seems to be heading straight for the bull's-eye jump circle at center court. It is as if the Globetrotters' plan is to give the game epic balance by having it end at the very spot where it began, the score just as deadlocked at the end as it was in the beginning. If nothing else, it will be an ending that will dramatize the equality of the two teams. After all, whether or not anybody is willing to admit it, whether any journalist, black or white, is able to write about it except by implication, for the Globetrotters this is a battle for equality as much as anything. In that battle, the points don't matter except as a measure of equality. So, let Haynes dribble out the clock, let the game end deadlocked. Whatever happens in the overtime will be less important than the fact that the two teams ended regulation time in perfect equilibrium.

The mystery of what the Globetrotters intend to do changes the pitch of the cheering in Chicago Stadium to a high keening.

Five seconds.

Haynes lifts his head and spots Robinson, who is coming at full speed from half-court. In the instant their eyes meet, Haynes narrows one eye. It could be mistaken for a wince from the pain he feels in his back every time he turns his shoulders or bends to dribble. But it is too subtle for that, just a slight, quick narrowing of one eye that seals the agreement for a plan that is as clear to both of them as if they are following ruts cut in the floor with diagramming knives.[5]

Robinson stops suddenly, and Haynes pushes a bounce pass to him and then squares himself to screen Jim Pollard.

Two seconds.

There isn't time enough for Pollard to fight around the screen to get at Robinson, so he pushes against Haynes, who has to struggle to hold his position.

One second.

Robinson drops his left foot slightly and sets himself, the ball tucked to his chest like a keepsake he doesn't want to give up. He fixes his eyes on the basket. Then he flexes his knees and begins the shot.

It is the same strange shot he had begun experimenting with over a decade earlier on an asphalt basketball court in San Diego. It is the same "flashy" shot that he took five hundred times a day as he refined it at San Diego High School, and it is the same shot that he has already missed three times in a row in Chicago Stadium, none of them from this far out.

He is ten feet beyond the top of the free-throw circle, at least thirty feet from the basket. He is going to have to throw his entire body at the basket just to get the ball there. The desperation lunge will eliminate any chance for refinement, all touch and delicacy will be lost.

But the shot is smooth and unhurried. The Kangaroo Kid, who has a reputation for seldom fouling while playing leaping, tenacious defense, jumps with one hand stuck high in the air as if he is about to curl in a rebound, and the ball passes just beyond the reach of his outstretched fingertips.[6]

The silence of the crowd is as sudden as the quiet following an explosion. Despite the drifting smoke, there is a brief moment of clarity in Chicago Stadium. The ball rises into the silence and clarity like a hot-air balloon. Then a strident horn sounds and shatters the clarity, melts it into a watery blur.

His hands still cupped to form a megaphone, Johnny Kundla does not even watch the flight of the ball but turns to the official standing in front of the scorer's table. The official is still tracking the ball and makes no sign concerning the shot, despite Lakers players already leaving the bench to plead with him that the shot is too late.

In the stands, Coach Ray Meyer watches the ball rise and then brings his eyes back to Ermer Robinson, who is frozen in a follow-through, his right arm extended, his wrist rolled down, his fingers flared.[7] Much later, Meyer will describe the shot as having come from "another time zone," but as he watches Robinson hold the shot pose, Meyer recognizes from his own basketball experience that it is a case of the shooter savoring the moment, because everything associated with the shot, from the feel of the ball as it rolls off his fingertips to the smooth flow of every part of his body into the shot, has been perfect.

"My God!" Meyer shouts to his wife before he knows what the fate of the shot is, "it's good!"

His back still to the shot, Haynes is so determined to keep Jim Pollard at bay that he doesn't look up and pick up the flight of the ball until it begins to descend and materializes out of the glare of the lights. From Haynes's dribble retreat to his eye signals to Robinson, this is a shot that the two have performed with only slight variations over and over again in road games.[8] It is part of the Globetrotters' choreography to end a quarter or a half or even a game with a dramatic long bomb that will bring down the house as surely as one of Goose's Prayers. But this shot is from much farther out than planned, and all Haynes has to cling to as he watches the ball in flight is the desperate hope that it is good.

At the end of the scorer's table, Fay Young throws all of his pregame warnings about objectivity and calm to the wind and struggles to his feet.[9] He has to lean far forward to follow the path of the ball, but he has a perfect line on the shot, and it seems to be following a course to the basket as true as a planet. The only question is range, and given the number of shots that evening that have bunged the front rim or smashed against the backboard, it seems an exercise in foolish fantasy, no matter what is at stake, to expect that this shot will find the target. It will be another desperate and improbable dream smashed.

22

Sweetwater

"I'll be damned!" Fay Young shouted at the top of his voice when the shot settled softly into the net.[1]

In the pandemonium, not even the intern to whom Young had given his pregame lecture on athletic objectivity could hear him.

The ball stuck in the net for a split second, as if the basket wanted to hold on to the historic moment before it let the ball drop to the floor.

Final score: Lakers 59, Globetrotters 61.

No game mayhem or political exuberance in the Madhouse on Madison was ever wilder than this. Screaming fans in the first tier streamed from the seat rows in rivulets that merged into rivers in the aisles and poured down onto the court, where they surged and boiled like whirlpools.

At the scorer's table, the two official scorers argued over whether the shot had beaten the clock.[2]

In a separate whirlpool on the floor, Johnny Kundla and the Lakers surrounded the official who had tracked the shot from midcourt.[3]

"It shouldn't count!" they shouted at him. "He shot it after the gun!"

But the official was emphatic: the shot was good!

The Globetrotters lifted Ermer Robinson on their shoulders and carried him to their locker room, led by a jubilant Abe Saperstein, who used his briefcase like a splitting wedge to crack a path through the fans. Once the Globetrotters reached the safety of their small locker room, it was Saperstein, smiling from ear to ear, whom they lifted on their shoulders. A flashbulb popped to capture the moment: Goose Tatum's head buried in Saperstein's armpit, Saperstein's head jammed against the low ceiling of the locker room, Ermer Robinson standing immediately at Saperstein's feet, for once in his life that timid smile of his breaking into a toothy grin, the rest of the Globetrotters packed into the locker room, even those too far away to touch him, reaching for Saperstein as if the victory was his miracle and not theirs.[4]

The only Globetrotters player who couldn't fully enjoy the victory was Marques Haynes. That night in Ma Piersall's, his body cooled finally from the exhaustion of having played the entire game, he went to bed early but couldn't sleep. A pounding pain in his back kept him wide-awake all night. Not even the ministrations of his roommate, Sam Wheeler, who lay beside him on the bare springs rubbing his back, could relieve the pain. By morning, he knew something was seriously wrong, and he took a cab to Chicago's Grant Hospital. X rays determined that he had fractured his fourth lumbar vertebrae after the collision with George Mikan. The doctors cemented him in a cast from his armpits to his hips and sent him on his way.[5]

"Mikan Cooks Tatum's Goose," the *Daily Sun and Times* reported on Friday. It hardly seemed worth mentioning that the Globetrotters had actually won. What mattered, according to the *Daily Sun and Times*, was that Goose Tatum, who had scored only three baskets, two of them on lazy sleepers, had "quickly become cold hash under Mikan's relentless exhibition."[6] The biased reporting was in part a case of diehard loyalty to George Mikan, the local boy who had become the King of Basketball. But the story also characterized Goose as a "devilish pivot trickster," which made it sound as if a character from African American fables had been outwitted by a white giant.

In subsequent accounts of the game, the Globetrotters' victory was obscured by conflicting reports concerning the exact distance of Ermer Robinson's dramatic shot, whether he had shot it with two hands or one, and whether it had beat the clock.[7]

Meanwhile, the Globetrotters had no time to enjoy their victory. Without Marques Haynes, the next night they were in Richmond, Indiana, and in succeeding nights in Kentucky, Ohio, Pennsylvania, then up and down the East Coast.[8]

By March 4 they had racked up their three thousandth victory in twenty-one seasons.[9] Before March ended, they were back in the blue smoke of Chicago Stadium, this time in front of sixteen thousand screaming black and white fans who were still talking about Ermer Robinson's last-second shot against the Lakers and who "yelled with glee . . . as they went through their clown tactics" and then thumped the famous New York Celtics.[10] They finished the 1947–48 season with 152 victories and only 5 defeats. The *Chicago Defender* wrote that among nearly a million people who saw them that year, they had a legion of South Side Chicago fans who delighted in their crowd-pleasing antics and their "unbelievable" talent.[11] They were, the *Defender* felt, the greatest basketball team in the world.

Despite the loss, the Lakers' juggernaut continued on its victorious course through the NBL that season. Minnesota journalists, who hadn't had a winner to celebrate since the Golden Gophers national football champions of 1941, wrote that the Lakers had given Minnesota and especially Minneapolis a new sports life.[12] Owners Max Winter and Ben Berger demonstrated their appreciation by giving cars to the Kangaroo Kid and Johnny Kundla. Among the gifts for George Mikan was $100 worth of dance lessons, as if to ensure the continuation of the light-footedness that Ray Meyer had taught him at DePaul.[13] It did just what the owners hoped, and in April 1948 Mikan led the Minneapolis Lakers to the first of what would be six league championships before they moved to Los Angeles. They also entered the World Professional Basketball Tournament in Chicago Stadium, determined to prove that they, not the Globetrotters, were the best team in the world. After they beat one hapless team in the opening round of the tournament by 50 points, a fan shouted at them, "Don't you ever show mercy?"[14] No, they didn't, and they went on to win the tournament by beating the New York Rens, with Pop Gates and a gentle giant named Nat Clifton, nicknamed "Sweetwater" because of his fondness for soda pop. But the victory was meaningless, the *Chicago Defender* believed, because the Rens "lacked the fire and dash" of the Globetrotters, who passed up the tournament to tour Hawaii.[15]

Meanwhile, the struggle to integrate the professional game continued, and Abe Saperstein found himself at the center of the battle. Some owners in the NBL and its upstart rival, the Basketball Association of America (BAA), which had been organized in 1946, saw financial incentives now for the integration of professional basketball. But those same owners worried that drafting blacks would weaken the Globetrotters and make an angry Saperstein back out of arrangements for money-making doubleheaders featuring his crowd-pleasing basketball tricksters and professional teams.[16] Those doubleheaders were helping to keep both leagues afloat, and it left some owners feeling they were financially damned if they integrated their teams and damned if they didn't. It prompted the *New York Amsterdam News* to write that the BAA had a color line as strict as big league baseball once had.[17] But the *Chicago Defender* tried to take a positive approach. "Our national sports leaders are learning a great truth," they wrote. "The American public will not only accept Negro participants in sports contests, but will make heroes out of Negroes who excel."[18] While southern segregationists sulked in their dark corners, the *Defender* pointed out, countless white Americans were already cheering for Jackie Robinson. "Baseball proved there is plenty of gold across the color line," they insisted.

Six months after the Globetrotters' victory over the Lakers, the Chicago Stags of the BAA signed six black players for the 1948–49 season.[19] And when the New York Knicks fell seven games behind the Washington Caps in the BAA, New York papers reported that the Knicks were "looking for a good Negro basketball player . . . of the skyscraper variety" to turn things around.[20] Then the powerful Washington Bears, with a roster of former New York Rens players, were brought into the NBL as the Dayton Rens and led by player-coach Pop Gates, who scored 44 points in one game. The Rens finished the 1948–49 season as the only all-black team in the history of American major league professional sports.[21]

In 1949, almost exactly a year after that first game and again during the "Mud Month," the Lakers and the Globetrotters met once more in Chicago Stadium, this time before an even larger crowd of 20,046 screaming fans. Herm Schaefer, the Crisco Kid, predicted to Abe Saperstein that the vengeful Lakers would win this time by 100 points.[22] But with Swede Carlson and Jim Pollard both out with injuries, the Globetrotters won again, this time by a seemingly comfortable 4 points.[23] The Globetrotters even clowned, and Marques Haynes taunted the Lakers like Brer Rabbit with his dribbling artistry.[24]

That second Globetrotters' victory, captured in Movietone News footage that ran in movie theaters all over the country, showcased black basketball talent even more than the first victory had. Unfortunately, during the summer of 1949 the NBL and the BAA finally buried their differences and merged to become the National Basketball Association (NBA). A straw vote among the team owners in the new league rejected the idea of signing black players, and the courage of the men who had followed Bucky Lew as the true pioneers of professional basketball—like Pop and Roosie and Duke and Sonny—seemed to have led nowhere.[25]

By the summer of 1950 the new league was struggling to attract fans, and suddenly owners and managers were financially smart enough and democratic enough to try to save the league. Ned Irish of the New York Knicks kept looking for a good black player "of the skyscraper variety." At an NBA board of directors meeting on the eightieth floor of the Empire State Building, he pounded the table and insisted that without a black skyscraper, he couldn't win games or draw fans. Then he walked out of the room.[26] Eventually, the owners revoted, the straw vote of a year earlier was reversed, and the first three blacks signed by the NBA—Earl Lloyd, Chuck Cooper, and Sweetwater Clifton—became integration icons who would obscure the contributions of the real pioneers. Immediately after the landmark meeting, one of the owners insisted angrily that professional basketball had just been ruined.[27]

The two straight Globetrotters' victories should have settled once and for all the issue of who was the better team, but there were financial incentives for Max Winter and Abe Saperstein to keep the series going. In the third game, in the Minneapolis Municipal Auditorium packed with 10,122 fans, the Lakers won easily.[28] They even put on a dribbling exhibition, confounding the racists who still thought that basketball minstrelsy should be left to African Americans.

During the fourth game in 1950, in Chicago Stadium again, with television broadcasting the game now and the Lakers winning handily, Johnny Kundla had to stop the Kangaroo Kid in the middle of a full-court drive for a certain score.

"What's the matter?" Pollard demanded to know in the huddle.

"We've got to take a TV time-out!" Kundla explained.

For the Kangaroo Kid, it was an unpardonable interference with the juggernaut, and he took himself out of the game and refused to go back in.[29]

Still, the series continued until January 1958, when the Lakers beat the Globetrotters for the sixth straight time.[30] After the game, an unhappy Abe Saperstein called off the series and disappeared for two hours, presumably to brood over the threat to his barnstorming empire by the NBA, which was now signing the best African American players "of the skyscraper variety."

VI

OVER TIME

23

Shaq

Bucky Lew, whose ancestors had been fifers and drummers in the American Revolution, died in 1963. The Savoy Ballroom in Chicago, where song and dance and basketball had converged during the Jazz Age to give rise to the Globetrotters, was demolished in the 1970s. Without the attraction of luxury boxes and restaurant esplanades offering garlic French fries and exotic hot dogs, the Madhouse on Madison became a relic of the past, and wrecking balls working like giant pestles ground it into a fine dust. It meant that the setting for the Globetrotters-Lakers game had been struck like a stage set, and it turned the Globetrotters' dramatic victory into something as fanciful and distant as classical theater.[1]

Max Winter, whose friendship with Abe Saperstein had led to the idea for the game, became a fixture at Lakers' appearances in Minneapolis, greeting friends at the entrance to Municipal Auditorium as he counted fans on an attendance clicker. Despite the first two losses to the Globetrotters, Winter's friendship with Saperstein endured, and at halftime of one of the games in the series, he presented Saperstein with a wristwatch as a token of their friendship. However, his relationship with Ben Berger dissolved, and after the two quarreled repeatedly, Winter left the organization in 1958. Until he died in 1996, Max Winter would call that February 1948 contest "[t]he most memorable basketball game of all time."[2]

Maurice White, the wealthy Chicago manufacturer who had wanted to build a basketball empire, died penniless.[3] Meanwhile, Abe Saperstein, whose father had argued that sports should be business, not pleasure, saw his basketball empire grow steadily after the 1948 game. A month after the Globetrotters' victory, Saperstein's friends paid tribute to him at halftime of a game at Chicago Stadium against the New York Celtics. However, after the ceremony the *Chicago Defender* recalled that it was those same friends who had laughed at Saperstein when he had predicted he would have the "best known cage aggregation" in America.[4] As that prediction became reality, Saperstein moved his sister, Fay, from the bedroom on Hermitage Street, where she had typed letters for him, to an office in the Empire State Building. Still, the Globetrotters remained largely a one-man organization, and in March 1966, bearing his accordion briefcase stuffed with papers and letters, he set off alone for Australia to book future games. Unprepared for the cold, he caught walking pneumonia and was forced to return to the United States. Hospitalized shortly after for prostate surgery, he suffered a heart attack during the surgery and died.[5]

The athletic feats of the Kangaroo Kid became the stuff of Minnesota athletic legend. Like Superman, Jim Pollard could leap tall buildings in a single bound. Playing baseball in the summer in the small town of Jordan, Minnesota, his monster home runs were too long to be measured, and after one bounced into the boxcar of a passing freight train, observers joked that he had hit a home run in Minnesota that landed in Missouri.[6]

In May 1978 Jim Pollard was elected to the Basketball Hall of Fame. After the ceremony, he stood for a photograph beside George Mikan, who had been enshrined almost twenty years earlier.[7] The two men held Pollard's plaque for press pictures, both of them smiling from ear to ear, Pollard's humble days of trumpeting with the Salvation Army as far behind him as Mikan's in a Joliet tavern. Neither one betrayed signs of the difficult accommodations they had each made to learn to play together or the disappointment of their losses to the Globetrotters.

The team pictures of the Minneapolis Lakers and Jim Pollard taken through the years stand as evidence of how dramatically the game was changing. Arranged in the pictures by height, the players that first year made a gradual slope up to Pollard and George Mikan at the end of the line. But by the time he retired from professional basketball in 1955, Pollard stood in the middle of the pack, half the team taller than he was, almost a runt among the skyscrapers who were taking over the game.[8] But when he died in 1993 in Stockton,

California, at the age of seventy, he stood as a giant in talent and basketball history.

Johnny Kundla would remain the unassuming kid from Star Junction despite a growing fame that he was never quite comfortable with. "Whoever heard of little me?" he told reporters in New York in 1952.[9] The real stars of the Lakers were George Mikan and Jim Pollard. Kundla's deference helped preserve his anonymity, and St. Louis sportswriters talked about how the Lakers were known from Keokuk to Broadway, but nobody knew who coached them. In Philadelphia, they observed that few basketball fans could "tell you right off who is the coach of Minneapolis."[10] Whoever he was, they wrote, he had the horses. He was *supposed.* to win, and he got little credit for Lakers' successes that first year. Still, every year during the playoffs, his ulcers kicked up as if he were taking a landing craft onto a bloody beach in the South Pacific again. "I'm not worried about scores," he said in an effort to explain his nervousness, "just keeping us a happy family."[11] That characteristic deference hid the truth that he was one of the first of a new breed of "players' coaches," smart enough about the game to understand which of its nearly infinite tactical possibilities were the right ones for the artistry of his players. Others called his ability to take proven stars and get them to play together a coaching masterpiece.[12]

Johnny Kundla bought a modest home on Zenith Avenue in north Minneapolis, and after his retirement from basketball he and his wife, Marie, raised four sons. In the first years after his retirement, Johnny and Marie liked nothing better than to spend a cold winter night on one of the neighborhood ice rinks, warming themselves at a potbellied stove that seemed a universe away from the limelight and pressures of professional basketball.[13]

In January 1995 he was elected to the Basketball Hall of Fame.[14] With the start of the third millennium, at eighty-four years old, and still in the same home on Zenith Street in Minneapolis, warnings of millennial cataclysms and news of multimillion-dollar salaries in professional basketball did nothing to diminish his clear recollections of that game in February 1948. With a grim irony, he captured the truth of how an all-white team from Minnesota and an all-black team from Chicago were most alike.[15] Over the eight-game series, the two teams had thrilled well over a hundred thousand fans and given them the best basketball the world had ever seen. "And none of us," Kundla remembered, "*none of us* ever got an extra penny."

"It's hard to believe," Kundla said and flashed his trademark grin as he tried to understand such basketball innocence, "how dumb we all were."

George Mikan blamed himself for the loss to the Globetrotters. The pregame publicity for the "duel of the century" between him and Goose Tatum had all gone to his head, he said.[16] He had been anxious to outdo Tatum and lead the Lakers to victory. "I tried to beat the Globetrotters all by myself," he wrote.

Not long after the game, Ray Meyer, who had taught George Mikan how to dance and play basketball, sat with his wife watching Mikan perform in an NBA All-Star game. With the score tied and only seconds on the clock, Mikan's team took a time-out. Using the same basketball insights he had employed to call Ermer Robinson's shot, Meyer turned to his wife again. "The ball's going to Mikan," he predicted. "He'll either score or get fouled."[17]

He did both, with the predictable tenacity that Meyer had been the first to recognize. It was tenacity that became the engine for the Minneapolis Lakers and made defenders hammer and pound on him. They broke both his legs, both feet, one wrist, his nose, his thumb, and three fingers, and what they couldn't break they slashed for a total of 166 stitches during his eight-year career.[18]

After the second Minneapolis championship, Chicago columnists wrote that he would soon leave the Lakers and return to Chicago to play, but he had learned to love Minneapolis, and he had become their icon, a lovable basketball Paul Bunyan. Lakers' letterhead featured a picture of Mikan turning for a left-hand drop-step hook shot, his right elbow pointed like a spear.[19]

He was the leader of the first class elected to the Basketball Hall of Fame in 1957. Sportswriters voted him the greatest basketball player of the first half of the century.[20] But over time his name would gradually be forgotten, and some writers would apologize for that loss by explaining that, unlike baseball, basketball was a game without a written history, too fast and furious to encourage anything but coffee-table picture books that captured only the ballet of the game.

In February 1997, at a halftime ceremony of an All-Star game in Cleveland, the NBA honored their fifty greatest stars of all time. Suffering the ravages of diabetes, George Mikan had to be helped to the stage so that he could stand with Bill Russell, Wilt Chamberlain, Kareem Abdul Jabbar, Oscar Robertson, Magic Johnson, Larry Bird, Julius Erving, and Michael Jordan.[21] In 1999 doctors amputated his right leg below the knee. Two years later at the Target Center in Minneapolis, he appeared in a wheelchair for the unveiling of a life-size statue depicting him stepping for a left-hand hook shot.[22] When he took the microphone, he thanked Ray Meyer, "who took a six-ten gangling kid and turned him into a statue."

Finally, at a ceremony in April 2002, the Los Angeles Lakers paid tribute to their origins by raising a banner with the five Minneapolis championships to the roof of Staples Sports Center. In the long-overdue celebration of the franchise's Minneapolis origins, nobody seemed to notice or care that it had really been six championships.[23] The only representatives from the game in 1948 were Johnny Kundla, who stood grinning and grinning and grinning, and Mikan in a wheelchair, looking gaunt, the toes of his left leg also amputated now, and on kidney dialysis three times a week.[24]

In a retro uniform the colors of the Swedish flag, with MPLS printed on the front, Shaquille O'Neal got down on his knees so that a battery of photographers could take his picture beside Mikan. In an instant, the separations of race and fifty years of basketball disappeared. Side by side, they were two of the most celebrated giants in the history of the game. Still, from his wheelchair, Mikan had to reach up to put his hand on O'Neal's shoulder.

24

Rigo

Goose Tatum's death was as shrouded in mystery as his life. He had been planning to fly to Dallas to make an appearance at a Goose Tatum benefit game. But he died before the benefit, on January 18, 1967, in El Paso, Texas, at only forty-five years old.[1] The few Globetrotters who traveled to El Paso to attend the funeral discovered that the only ceremony was at graveside, at Fort Bliss National Cemetery, where he was buried with simple military honors—a folded flag, a rifle volley, and taps.[2] There were numerous explanations for his premature death. One rumor was that he was suffering something grisly and terminal, and he had sought treatment in hospitals in Wichita, Detroit, and finally Texas. Another rumor was that he had been grief stricken because his son had been tragically killed while changing a flat tire somewhere in Texas. Others recalled a frantic halftime phone call during a game in Chicago, when he had had to warn his Kansas City "lady friend" that her jealous Gary, Indiana, counterpart had come to Chicago with a gun. He had "lady friends" everywhere, they said, and the complications of trying to juggle those affairs had finally caught up with him.[3]

There was a familiar theme in all the rumors: he remained a baffling incongruity, mean and sullen and surrounded by conflict off the court, but on court he was a sensational comic who delighted the fans with his windmill shot and his flatfoot antics. Despite his genius, there would be those who faulted him and the Globetrotters for playing the part of black fools for the amusement of white fans.[4] But in 2002 the Globetrotters organization retired his jersey and rightly hailed him as a "Clown Prince."[5] They were celebrating the truth that when Goose bawled in protest after being whistled for an obvious foul, he was all of us, black and white, protesting our innocence; when he sashayed up and down the court in a woman's fur wrap or strutted in a bowler hat, he was all of us wishing we were rich; when he snatched a camera from the audience and then mugged and preened for his self-portrait, he was all of us trying to be more glorious than we are; when he hid the ball from pompous officials, tucking it beneath his jersey and then impishly waddling around, he was all of us rankled by authority and mocking it.

Marques Haynes spent two months in a plaster body cast, then months more in a crude brace that was supposed to keep his back immobilized so that it could heal. The immobilization meant that he was finished with basketball that season. Others, misled by his fragile, sticklike shape, feared that his body had snapped like a twig in the collision with Mikan and that his promising career as a basketball player was over. The following summer, as the Globetrotters prepared for the 1948–49 season, they left him out of the prepublished program and prepared to go on the road without him.[6]

But by November he was back with the Globetrotters when they opened their season in Chicago Stadium. All eyes were on him, the *Chicago Defender* wrote, to see whether he had fully recovered from the severe injury he had suffered the previous February during the "great victory over the Lakers for the unofficial world's championship."[7]

That next season he was as skittish and rabbity as ever, circling and darting around stooge defenders who couldn't strip him of the ball even when they got sucked in by his dribbling audacity and tried. In 1950 Saperstein took his Globetrotters on a barnstorming tour, playing against teams of college All-Stars coached by Ray Meyer. For the African American players on the tour, it meant enduring segregated hotels and rude restaurants, but sportswriters dubbed it the "World Series of Basketball," and the Globetrotters won more than half of the games.[8] It was more triumph that made the NBA sit up and take notice.

In every town, while the All-Stars and the Globetrotters went out and partied, Ray Meyer and Marques Haynes stayed behind to talk basketball. Meyer, who thought that Haynes and Ermer Robinson were both good enough to play in the NBA, enjoyed the opportunity to talk basketball strategy into the late hours with Haynes. And they had both grown tired of restaurants where they sat ignored by waitresses who would only serve them glasses of water.[9]

"The country was so segregated then," Haynes would recall later, "so ill-minded."

In 1953 Abe Saperstein began to receive overtures from NBA franchises eager to sign Marques Haynes. Subsequent negotiations included efforts by Saperstein to sell Haynes to the Philadelphia Warriors.[10] His electrifying play would have had a positive effect on the entire league, still struggling at the gate, but New York sportswriters, who seemed to know Haynes's mind as well as he did, predicted that he wouldn't show in New York.[11] He didn't, and after he quarreled with Abe Saperstein over his Globetrotters' contract, he recruited Goose Tatum and formed the Harlem Magicians, convinced that the only real prosperity in basketball at that time, whether barnstorming with Saperstein or drafted into the NBA, lay in ownership.

That same faculty for enterprise and independence eventually led him into a career in private business in Dallas, Texas.[12] But no matter what he did out of basketball, he would be remembered, despite thousands of successors who would come skidding and sliding in his footsteps, as the world's finest dribbler and ball handler.

Ermer Robinson went on to become the only Globetrotters player who appeared in all eight games of the series with the Lakers. On the road with the Globetrotters, he was too earnest about basketball and life to participate in what others called the team's "monkeyshine." His role was to score often, usually with his one-hand shot, and help secure a lead that would permit others more theatrical than he was to do the clowning.[13] It meant that over time, as his last-second shot became less talked about, his stellar play went largely unnoticed and his reputation declined. But those who had been in Chicago Stadium that night never forgot him or his dramatic shot.

As the Globetrotters' organization grew and they began barnstorming by air, his teammates nicknamed him "Shaky" because he threw up on airplanes and hated to fly.[14] While other Globetrotters took the opportunity of a day or two off from barnstorming to fly home for a brief rendezvous with families, Robinson came home only if a stop in San Diego was included in a whirlwind tour up and down the West Coast.

He ended his playing career with the Globetrotters in 1959, then worked for the organization managing team tours to South America. In the spring of 1961 Abe Saperstein, angry over the denial of what he felt was a promised NBA franchise in Los Angeles, formed the rival American Basketball League. The league was as doomed as Maurice White's basketball pipedream, and it folded after two years, but not without Ermer Robinson serving as one of the country's first African American coaches of professional basketball, with the Oakland Oaks.[15]

In 1979, back in San Diego, Robinson was diagnosed with laryngeal cancer, and for three-and-a-half years he was in and out of the hospital.[16]

In 1982 his Garlic Center friend and San Diego High teammate Rigo Rodriguez returned to San Diego after a long career in the military. Rodriguez had earned his doctorate and had become a professor at San Diego State, but his first thought back in San Diego was to renew old friendships. He was particularly interested in finding any of his old friends from Garlic Center.[17]

Robinson's brothers delivered the news that Robinson was in the Veterans Administration Hospital in La Jolla. It was clear that Robinson was gravely ill, and Rodriguez drove up to La Jolla as soon as he could.

At the nurse's station on Robinson's floor, he asked, "What room is Ermer Robinson in?"

"Who?"

"Ermer Robinson."

The nurse checked the charts. "That him," she said and pointed to a patient walking slowly down the hall, "over there."

Rodriguez caught up to him and introduced himself. Robinson's hair was white, his skin in folds, his face gaunt. He was only months away from death, which came on December 29, 1982. But now he managed a tenuous smile as he peered at a visitor he was clearly supposed to recognize.

"It's *me*," Rodriguez smiled and repeated.

Still, there was no recognition. Whatever memories Robinson had of the asphalt court next to "No Man's Land" where he had perfected his one-hand shot, or sharing a cowflop pastry at San Diego High with Rodriguez and his friends, or that private kitchen dinner that the two had settled for in Chino, or even Robinson's greatest moment of glory in Chicago Stadium in February 1948—all of it was buried deep beneath the intervening years of barnstorming and life, and now a deadly disease.

"Ermer," Rodriguez said, raising his voice now. "It's me . . . *Rigo*! We played basketball together as kids."

One day in mid-October 1957, after forty-five years with the *Chicago Defender*, Fay Young sat down to write his weekly column, "Fay Says." It had been nine years since Ermer Robinson's dramatic shot, and in the interim Young had suffered numerous bouts of ill health and been repeatedly rushed to the hospital. He had endured five major operations to keep him alive, and only that August he had been rushed to the hospital again.[18] It was as if the excitement and heart-stopping frenzy of that February night in 1948 had never left him.

"Those fabulous Globetrotters are at it again," he began his column, then went on to describe the team's roster for the upcoming 1957–58 season. It would be Ermer Robinson's twelfth season with the team, he explained, and they were "the greatest aggregation of basketball players in the world," mixing expert play with entertaining razzle-dazzle.[19]

On Friday, October 23, he delivered the column to the *Defender*'s offices on Indiana Street. For an hour, he chatted about the Globetrotters with Russ Cowans, another *Defender* writer. Before he left, he asked Cowans to get him tickets to an upcoming prizefight. But on Sunday morning he came back to the offices and left a note on Cowans's door. "You don't need to get tickets for me for the fight," the note said. "I'll be out of town."[20]

It was as if he saw his own death as clearly as he saw the need for integration in athletics, and by that afternoon he was dead. His final column celebrated the Globetrotters' organization, which had given him one of the greatest thrills of his journalistic life. And among all the things he left behind, including a *Defender* office draped in black bunting to mourn his passing, perhaps the most notable were his stories of the February 1948 Globetrotters' victory. His account of the game gave the sports world the best written record of high basketball drama.

But not even Young's account of the Globetrotters' victory caught the full significance of the story. That February night he had stayed at the scorer's table pecking away at his typewriter long after the lights over the court had been dimmed and the stale smoke seemed to be draped from the ceiling like Spanish moss.[21] "Never will we forget that last 10th of a second," he wrote, "the instant the ball left Ermer Robinson's hand, the gun barked the end of the game. Of course, we knew the ball was in play—so did the Lakers."[22] He later confessed that the thrill of the last-second shot had caused him to lose the "religion" of his pipe-smoking composure, but as he fashioned his story line in that blue light, he seemed more determined to lay to rest any controversy over the last shot than to recognize what the Globetrotters' victory over the Lakers might have meant.

In the days and weeks following the game, two-dozen newspapers and periodicals throughout the country, including *Time* magazine, decided that the Globetrotters were good enough to justify stories about their basketball skills instead of their minstrelsy.[23] But none of the stories spoke directly to the issue of what the game meant in the history of basketball and race.

What *did* it mean? Cynics argued that what happened in the Madhouse on Madison was just another African American triumph that would be ignored, while their defeats and humiliations elsewhere would continue. It was pessimism inspired in part by events in Chicago Stadium the very night after the Globetrotters' victory. Beneath fresh clouds of blue smoke, two black boxers—the veteran Ezzard Charles and handsome, young Sam Baroudi—squared off in a light-heavyweight match, and Charles knocked Baroudi unconscious. Rather than risk being turned away from a nearby hospital, where he wasn't on the staff, the physician attending Baroudi decided to take the young fighter halfway across Chicago for treatment. It was an hour before Baroudi could be treated, and his eventual death brought bitter charges that Chicago's hospitals were racist.[24] Then, later that spring, the homes of African Americans trying to integrate the west side of Chicago were bombed. Over the course of three weeks in April, there were seven bombings and no arrests. On Calumet Avenue, a family of six narrowly escaped death after angry white neighbors set fire to their porch. Set against those continuing tragedies, the Globetrotters' victory seemed to mean little, if anything.

Two Hollywood movies made about the Globetrotters in the years immediately after the game were sprinkled with fantasies that featured Ermer Robinson, Marques Haynes, Goose Tatum, and their teammates delivering the world from racial evil.[25] It was all in keeping with a host of movies during the period, from *High Noon* to *Shane*, that featured the dramatic triumph of good over evil. But racism did not disappear from the American landscape or basketball, and our national dialogue about race would continue to be as strained as ever. Researchers citing "fast-twitch" and "slow-twitch" muscle fibers as explanations for the modern-day African American domination in athletics were angrily dismissed as pseudo-scientists and racists.[26] Meanwhile, Mississippi senator Trent Lott would celebrate the good ol' days of politics, which included lynchings and poll taxes. And as an ironic demonstration of how racial insensitivity would remain a part of our national character, Shaquille O'Neal mocked the language of Yao Ming, the NBA's newest superstar.[27]

The truth of what the game in February 1948 meant could be found somewhere in between the cynics who said it meant nothing and the Hollywood dream machine. Basketball was described as the most American of all our games, because it was borrowed from no other country.[28] The game itself, then, was a mirror, reflecting an American character that incongruously prized both individual improvisation and teamwork. Yet in 1948 the game was also a mirror of our cultural character and our racism. The 17,823 fans in the Madhouse on Madison that night, and the millions more who read about the game afterward, could not help but recognize in the standoff between the two teams, perhaps more dramatically and intensely focused than anywhere else, the country's divided racial character. That divide was as profound as what separated Minneapolis in the "land of sky blue waters" from what was once called "the black city" because of its industrial soot. And if nothing else, the photograph that accompanied the story in *Time* magazine, picturing George Mikan stretching to smother Goose Tatum's trick hook shot, was our national family portrait. It reflected our racial standoff just as much as those grim portraits of huge families all standing around a bearded and seated patriarch reflected the paternalism of an earlier era.

For those interested enough to look beneath the surfaces of the portrait, the game was also a showdown—with all the drama of that screen shootout a few years later between Shane and Wilson in Grafton's saloon—featuring reality versus racist illusion.[29] The illusion was that the Globetrotters were only minstrel Sambos who could laugh and entertain with wizardry but were otherwise too cursed by their fast-twitch heritage and jungle genes to run plays or be any good. After that dramatic February victory, only diehard racists would be able to insist that the Globetrotters were nothing but devilish tricksters and dancing clowns. What lay beneath the trickiness and dancing was a spectacular athleticism. And only the same bigots who argued that blacks were too shiftless or muscle-bound for basketball would be able to deny that athleticism.

Finally, the game meant something else. Even without the Globetrotters' victory, even conceding that Robinson's shot had been lucky, even if it hadn't beaten the clock, the game itself mattered. On a magnificent and dramatic stage in the heartland of America, two teams that mirrored the country's racial divide in February 1948 had met each other against the explosive backdrop of firebombings, coaches with six-guns tucked in their belts, and a national argument over poll taxes and lynching. The two teams had battled each other down to the last shot. Yet that supercharged atmosphere of smoke and frenzy had produced nothing but the collisions and tensions of fierce basketball. For years separatists had been warning that integration, especially in sports, would lead to violence and mayhem. What violence there was, orchestrated in part by the very same people who issued the warnings, left its nervous mark on interracial games. Yet for one night at least, the fans in Chicago Stadium had put those worries aside and let themselves be swept up by the drama of a basketball game that had all the emotional peaks and valleys of a hair-raising story. It proved that a good game, with seesaw fortunes and then an almost unbearable suspense before a breathtaking ending, could sweep everything else aside. It was proof of the power of *the game*. No matter who played it, no matter where, no matter what enveloping menaces, the game of basketball, which had begun as tank warfare, had become a stage for heart-stopping balletic moves by every player. All that mattered was that they all be athletic. Only those same diehard racists would fail to see that the game itself, with those serial moments of thrilling basketball ballet, had made race meaningless. And after 17,823 white and black fans had nearly blown the roof off Chicago

Stadium, who could fail to see that those fans were just what basketball needed?

In October 1998 Marques Haynes became the first Globetrotters player elected to the Basketball Hall of Fame.[30] It had been half a century since he and George Mikan had collided in midair in the Madhouse on Madison with a crash almost biblical in its force. Now, it seemed like a colossal irony that the Globetrotters brave David and the Lakers mighty Goliath were the last two players from the game still around to give witness to the struggle and what it had meant.

"It's God's will," Haynes would say, as if the game and its players, and those who survived to tell the tale, were all part of a divine plan.[31] "It's the only way to look at it. It's God's will. And you don't question that."

Notes

1. THE RACE

1. "99-in-Row Trotters Face Stadium Test," *Chicago Herald-American*, February 18, 1948; "Fiery Meteor Blast Seen in 6 States," *Chicago Herald-American*, February 20, 1948; "Trotters Meet Lakers on Stag Card Tonight," *Chicago Tribune*, February 19, 1948; "17,823 See Trotters Shade Mikan," *Daily Sun and Times*, February 20, 1948; "Winning Basket in Air at Game's End," *Chicago Herald-Tribune*, February 20, 1948; "Snow Begins Falling in Chicago," *Daily Sun and Times*, February 11, 1948; "Suddenly It's Spring," *Daily Sun and Times*, February 18, 1948; "New Cold Wave Grips Midwest," *Daily Sun and Times*, February 20, 1948; "Trotters Spill Lakers in Last Second," *Minneapolis Morning Tribune*, February 20, 1948; Roland Lazenby, *The Lakers: A Basketball Journey* (New York: St. Martin's Press, 1993), 79–81; "The Story of the Harlem Globetrotters, 1948–49 Edition," yearly program, courtesy of the Harlem Globetrotters; Marques Haynes, interview by author, tape recording, Dallas, Texas, January 18, 2002; Lee Knorek, from notes of telephone interview by author, August 27, 2001; John "Bud" Palmer, from notes of telephone interview by author, August 27, 2001; Ray Meyer, from notes of telephone interview by author, March 27, 2002; Larry Hawkins, from notes of telephone interview by author, April 1, 2002; Fay Saperstein, interview by author, tape recording, San Mateo, California, September 25, 2001; John Kundla, interviews by author, tape recordings, Minneapolis, October 10, October 12, 2001; John Kundla, from notes of telephone interview by author, October 30, 2001.

2. Fay Young, "Through the Years," *Chicago Defender*, March 6, 1948.

3. E. Franklin Frazier, *The Negro in the United States* (rev. ed., New York: Macmillan, 1957), 510, 561; Todd Burroughs, *Turn of the Century Births: The Chicago Defender*, BlackPressUSA.com.

4. Enoch Waters, *American Diary: A Personal History of the Black Press* (Chicago: Path Press, 1987), 194.

5. Fay Young, "Wednesday, Thursday," *Chicago Defender*, January 26, 1929; A. C. "Doc" Young, "The Black Sportswriter," *Ebony*, October 1970, 62–65.

6. Jim Reisler, *Black Writers/Black Baseball: An Anthology of Articles from Black Sportswriters Who Covered the Negro Leagues* (Jefferson NC: McFarland, 1994), 33.

7. Jon Entine, *Taboo: Why Black Athletes Dominate Sports, and Why We Are Afraid to Talk About It* (New York: BBS Public Affairs, 2000), 4, 121–22, 152, 174, 223, 247–48; Gwendolen Captain, "Enter Ladies and Gentlemen of Color: Gender, Sport, and the Ideal of African American Manhood and Womanhood during the Late Nineteenth and Early Twentieth Centuries," *Journal of Sport History* 18, no. 1 (spring 1991): 81–102; Kenan Malik, "Why Black Will Beat White at the Olympics," kenanmalik.com; Martin Kane, "Black Is Best," *Sports Illustrated*, January 18, 1971, 73–83; Frazier, *The Negro in the United States*, 667, 669. For a discussion of desegregation and the likelihood of violence, see "The Effects of Segregation and the Consequences of Desegregation: A Social Science Statement," Appendix to Appellants' Brief, *Brown v. Board of Education*, Supreme Court of the United States, October 1952.

2. MA PIERSALL

1. "Hoodlums Mob Man on Street," *Chicago Defender*, January 3, 1948; "Hoodlums Attack Calumet Ave. Home," *Chicago Defender*, February 28, 1948; "Fired as Coach, Blames Ouster on Klan Fight," *Chicago Tribune*, February 21, 1948; "Coach Packs a Gun," *Minneapolis Star*, February 18, 1948.

2. For the text of Truman's speech, see "President Truman's Speech" in the *New York Times*, February 20, 1948. For additional details, see also David McCullough, *Truman* (New York: Touchstone, 1992), 576, 579–80, 588–89, 593, 613, 892–93; "Truman in an Impromptu Speech," *New York Times*, February 20, 1948; "Mississippi Democrats," *Daily Sun and Times*, February 12, 1948; "Southerners Boycott $100 'Keynote' Dinner," *Chicago Tribune*, February 20, 1948.

3. "South in Revolt Over Truman Rights Program," *Chicago Defender*, March 27, 1948; "Governors Balk Over Civil Plea," *Chicago Defender*, February 14, 1948.

4. "Southerners Boycott."

5. "Minority Rule," *Chicago Defender*, February 21, 1948.

6. "Confidentially Yours," *New York Amsterdam News*, December 20, 1947; "Jackie Signs Again with the Dodgers," *Chicago Defender*,

February 14, 1948; "Rickey Claims That 15 Clubs Voted to Bar Negroes from the Majors," *New York Times*, February 18, 1948; "Wrigley Denies Majors Took Anti-Negro Stand," *Chicago Herald-American*, February 19, 1948; "Rickey Clears Rival Owners," *Daily Sun and Times*, February 19, 1948.

7. Kenneth L. Shropshire, *In Black and White: Race and Sports in America* (New York: New York University Press, 1996), 29–32; "Another Victory," *Chicago Defender*, March 13, 1948; "Color Line in Tennis," *Chicago Herald-American*, February 13, 1948; "A.B.C. Will Meet On Negro Question," *New York Times*, February 20, 1949; "PGA's Poor Sportsmanship," *Baltimore Afro-American*, January 24, 1948; "Boxing's Bad Boys," sportal.co.uk, January 23, 2002; "Our Stand on Fox-Lamotta Affair," *New York Amsterdam News*, December 7, 1947.

8. "The New Year," *Chicago Defender*, January 3, 1948.

9. "Rolling Along," *Chicago Defender*, March 13, 1948.

10. "Big Time for Basketball," *Daily Sun and Times*, February 15, 1948.

11. "Story of the Harlem Globetrotters."

12. "99-in-Row Trotters."

13. "Northern Pump Floormen Upset Trotters," *Minneapolis Star*, December 16, 1942.

14. George Mikan, *Mr. Basketball* (New York: Greenburg, 1951), 51; Stew Thornley, *Basketball's Original Dynasty: The History of the Lakers* (Minneapolis: Nodin Press, 1989), 21; Kundla, interviews, October 10, October 12, 2001; Tom King, from notes of telephone interview by author, March 1, 2002.

15. For a sample "Uniform Players Contract," see Richard F. Triptow, *The Dynasty That Never Was* (Chicago: Richard F. Triptow, 1996), 62–64; Kundla, interviews, October 10, October 12, 2001.

16. "Harlems Combine for Lakers Clash," *Minneapolis Star*, February 19, 1948; "Lakers, Harlem in Pro 'Dream,'" *Minneapolis Morning Tribune*, February 19, 1948; "Trotters Wallop All Stars," *Pittsburgh Courier*, January 24, 1948; "The Trotters Keep Rolling Along," *Pittsburgh Courier*, January 31, 1948; "2 Globetrotters 5s Play on Same Card," *New York Amsterdam News*, December 6, 1947; Haynes, interview, January 18, 2002.

17. "White Quints Lose to Wilberforce State Five," *Chicago Defender*, February 14, 1948.

18. Robert W. Peterson, *Cages to Jump Shots: Pro Basketball's Early Years* (Lincoln: University of Nebraska Press, 2002), 204–5; "NBA Legends: William 'Pop' Gates," NBA.com.

19. Haynes, interview, January 18, 2002.

20. "2 Actresses Sue Hotel in Chicago," *Baltimore Afro-American*, January 10, 1948.

21. "Decision Awaited" and "Minority Group Property Rights Hang in Balance," *Pittsburgh Courier*, January 24, 1948; Frazier, *The Negro in the United States*, 261.

22. Mikan, *Mr. Basketball*, 51; "George Mikan vs. 'Goose' Tatum," advertisement, *Chicago Tribune*, February 19, 1948; "Trotters Meet Lakers"; "All Time Basketball Record," *Chicago Defender*, January 3, 1948; "George Mikan Hopes to Cook Trotters' Goose," *Daily Sun and Times*, February 19, 1948; "Story of the Harlem Globetrotters."

23. "17,823 See Trotters"; "N.Y. Next for Stags Thursday," *Daily Sun and Times*, February 16, 1948; "Globetrotters Here on Feb. 19; Play Lakers," *Chicago Defender*, February 14, 1948; "99-in-Row Trotters"; "Lakers and Trotters," *Minneapolis Star*, February 18, 1948; "No Laughing Matter," *Time*, March 1, 1948, 51–52; "Lakers, Harlem in Pro 'Dream.'"

3. THE KANGAROO KID

1. Radio script of interview with Jim Pollard and George Mikan, WLOL Radio, Minneapolis, March 13, 1948, courtesy of John Kundla.

2. Meyer, interview.

3. George Mikan and Joseph Oberle (contributor), *Unstoppable: The Story of George Mikan, the First NBA Superstar* (Indianapolis: Masters Press, 1997), 135.

4. Mikan and Oberle, *Unstoppable*, 3–66; Dan Barreiro, "Before Wilt, Kareem and Shaq, There Was Mikan," thesunlink.com, December 23, 1999; "High Guy," originally published in *Liberty Magazine*, circa 1946, reprinted at Basketball Jones, finest.net/bjones/highguy; "Hall of Famers: Ray Meyer," hoophall.com; Ross Bernstein: *Hardwood Heroes: Celebrating a Century of Minnesota Basketball* (Minneapolis: Nodin Press, 2001), 24–25; Triptow, *Dynasty That Never Was*, 41.

5. "The Laker Story," videotape of original film, produced by Leslie Winik, 1952, courtesy of Whitey Skoog.

6. Arilee Pollard, interview by author, tape recording, Lodi, California, November 18, 2001; Gene Rock, from notes of telephone interview by author, December 6, 2001; Jack Rocker, from notes of telephone interview by author, September 25, 2001; Bill Durkee, from notes of telephone interview by author, October 8, 2001; Stanley W. Carlson, *The Minneapolis Lakers, World Champions of Professional Basketball, 1948–49-50: A Pictorial Album* (Minneapolis: Stanley W. Carlson/Olympic Press, 1950).

4. BABE

1. Bill Hoover, "Wilbur King," unpublished profile, in the author's possession.

2. Haynes, interview, January 18, 2002.

3. Haynes, interview, January 18, 2002.

4. "Harlem Globetrotters: 6 Decades of Magic," produced by Fries Home Video/Fries Entertainment, 1988; "Globetrotters vs. Lakers at Chicago Stadium," Fox Movietone News, March 1949; "Chicago Stories: Chicago's Harlem Globetrotters," produced by Jay Smith, WTTW-TV, 2002; "The Harlem Globetrotters," produced by Alfred Palca, Columbia Pictures, 1951; "Go, Man, Go," produced by Alfred Palca, United Artists, 1954; "Story of the Harlem Globetrotters."

5. Haynes, interview, January 18, 2002; King, interview; "The Harlem Globetrotters," *Basketball Illustrated*, 1949 edition, 13; Frank Deford, "Still Sweet: Globetrotters Continue to Provide Plenty of Good Times," cnnsi.com, March 14, 2001; "They Girdle the Globe," *Clair Bee's Basketball Annual*, 1949, 45–47.

6. Kundla, interview, October 10, 2001.

7. Kundla, interview, October 10, 2001; Haynes, interview, January 18, 2002.

8. Kundla, interview, October 10, 2001; Neil Isaacs, *Vintage* NBA: *The Pioneer Era, 1946–1956* (Indianapolis: Masters Press, 1996), 52.

9. James Watkins, from notes of telephone interview by author, April 3, 2002; Bob Karstens, from notes of telephone interview by author, November 20, 2001; Haynes, interview, January 18, 2002.

5. GOOSE

1. Zora Neale Hurston, *The Sanctified Church* (New York: Marlowe, 1981), 69–78; *Go Gator and Muddy the Water: Writings by Zora*

Neale Hurston, edited by Pamela Bordelon (New York: W. W. Norton, 1999), 78–83.

2. "Harlem Globetrotters Legends: Reece 'Goose' Tatum," Harlemglobetrotters.com.

3. *Negro Leagues Baseball: Reece "Goose" Tatum, the Indianapolis Clowns, and the Kansas City Monarchs* (1946), Academy Film Archives, Academy of Motion Picture Arts and Sciences, Los Angeles.

4. James A. Riley, *The Biographical Encyclopedia of the Negro Baseball League* (New York: Carroll and Graf, 1994), 760; Haynes, interview, January 18, 2002; Bob Luksta, from notes of telephone interview by author, March 19, 2002.

5. Karstens, interview.

6. "Globetrotter Circus Heading for Midwest," *New York Amsterdam News*, February 17, 1948; "N.Y. Next for Stags Thursday"; "16,000 to See Pro Cage Bill," *Daily Sun and Times*, February 19, 1948.

7. Haynes, interview, January 18, 2002; Watkins, interview, April 3, 2002; King, interview; Saperstein, interview, September 25, 2001; Dick Burdette, from notes of telephone interview by author, March 11, 2002; Isaacs, *Vintage NBA*, 94, 103; Chuck Menville, *The Harlem Globetrotters: Fifty Years of Fun and Games* (New York: David McCay, 1978), 30–32, 39–40; "Harlem Globetrotters Legends: Reece 'Goose' Tatum"; Nelson George, *Elevating the Game: Black Men and Basketball* (New York: HarperCollins, 1992), 51–56; "Story of the Harlem Globetrotters"; Aaron Meyers, "Sports: Harlem Globetrotters," Africana.com; "The Harlem Globetrotters: The First Showmen of Basketball," www.tomdawg.de (accessed October 7, 2001; site now discontinued).

8. Haynes, interview, January 18, 2002; J. Michael Kenyon, e-mail message to author, August 30, 2001.

6. ERMER

1. Rigo Rodriguez, interviews by author, tape recordings, San Diego, California, June 25, August 5, 2002.

2. "Hillers Humble Hoover," *San Diego Union*, January 14, 1942; "Poly Rally Subdues San Diego," *San Diego Union*, February 24, 1942; "San Diego Cagers End Season," *The Russ: Senior A Edition*, February 4, 1942, 9.

3. Rodriguez, interviews.

4. "Hoover Five Plays Poly," *San Diego Union*, January 14, 1942; "Quote Me," *The Russ: Senior A Edition*, February 4, 1942, 8.

5. "Hillers Humble Hoover."

6. "News In Brief," *The Russ: Senior A Edition*, February 4, 1942, 2.

7. Rodriguez, interviews; George Capatanos, interview by author, tape recording, San Diego, California, June 25, 2002; Edward San Clemente, interview by author, tape recording, San Diego, California, June 27, 2002; William Tsunoda, interview by author, tape recording, San Diego, California, August 5, 2002; Donald R. King, *Caver Conquest: An Athletic History of San Diego High School* (San Diego CA: SDHS Foundation, 1994), 132–40; Richard Pourade, *The History of San Diego* (San Diego CA: A Copley Book, 1977), 8–9, 32–33, 36–37; "The Grey Castle," *San Diego High Yearbook*, February 1942. Additional stories on San Diego High basketball, 1941–42: *San Diego Union*, December 8, 11–13, 17–21, 28, 1941; January 7, 13–14, 16, 21, 23–24, 26, 28, 30–31, February 13–16, 1942; "City of Chino: Our City," cityofchino.org; "Chicago Stories."

8. Frazier, *The Negro in the United States*, 459, 481–85, 491, 667.

9. "1939 Class Prophecy," *The San Miguel*, Memorial Junior High, 4.

10. Watkins, interview, April 3, 2002; Fred Scolari, from notes of telephone interview by author, October 5, 2001; Rodriguez, interviews; "They Girdle the Globe," 46; "Globetrotters Open on Saturday, Nov. 6," *Chicago Defender*, October 30, 1948; "Ermer Robinson Succumbs," *San Diego Union*, January 1, 1983.

7. THE FASTEST RUNNER

1. Lawrence M. Brings, ed., *Minneapolis: A Story of Progress in Pictures* (Minneapolis: T. S. Denison, 1954), 60.

2. "Minnesota, the Empire State of the New North-West" (Board of Immigration for the State of Minnesota, 1878), 65.

3. June Holmquist, ed., *They Chose Minnesota: A Survey of the State's Ethnic Groups* (St. Paul: Minnesota State Historical Society, 1981), 78, 81.

4. Sinclair Lewis's 1947 best-selling novel *Kingsblood Royal* (New York: Modern Library, 2001) tells the story of the prejudices and racism endured by an African American in the fictional small town of Grand Republic, Minnesota.

5. Bernstein, *Hardwood Heroes.*

6. Brings, *Minneapolis*; "The Laker Story."

7. Advertisement, *Chicago Tribune*, February 19, 1948.

8. Carl Sandburg, "Chicago," in *Poems of the Midwest* (Cleveland: World Publishing, 1946), 27–28.

9. Irving Cutler, "Jews Make Chicago a Home," *Chicago Sun-Times*, October 19, 1999.

10. Donald L. Miller, *City of the Century: The Epic of Chicago and the Making of America* (New York: Simon and Schuster, 1996), 468–82.

11. Cutler, "Jews Make Chicago a Home."

12. James T. Farrell, "The Fastest Runner on Sixty-first Street," in *The American Tradition in Literature*, vol. 2 (New York: W. W. Norton, 1956), 1234–46.

13. Farrell, "The Fastest Runner," 1245.

14. Frazier, *The Negro in the United States*, 257.

15. Joseph Boskin, *Sambo: The Rise & Demise of an American Jester* (New York: Oxford University Press, 1986), 167.

16. Jim Brown, from notes of interviews by author, Arcata, California, January 29, 1960; Chico, California, February 28, 1960.

8. BLACKIE

1. Bernstein, *Hardwood Heroes*, 66.

2. Bernstein, *Hardwood Heroes*, 14; "Berger Memories," geocities.com/Heartland/Plains/1329; "Official Basketball Magazine: Lakers," 1947, 2, courtesy of Bill Durkee; Sid Hartman with Patrick Reusse, *Sid! The Sports Legend and the Inside Scoops and the Close Personal Friends* (Stillwater MN: Voyageur Press, 1997), 67–69; Kundla, interviews, October 10, October 12, October 30, 2001; Arilee Pollard, interview.

3. Hartman, *Sid!*, 31, 47–49.

4. Hartman, *Sid!*, 67; Bernstein, *Hardwood Heroes*, 14; Thornley, *Basketball's Original Dynasty*, 9.

5. Bernstein, *Hardwood Heroes*, 15.

6. Bill Hoover, letter to author, September 30, 2001; Hoover, "Wilbur King."

7. Thornley, *Basketball's Original Dynasty*, 17–18; Kundla, interview, October 10, 2001; Ron Fimrite, "Big George," *Sports Illustrated*, November 6, 1989, 128–40.

8. "Official Basketball Magazine: Lakers"; Isaacs, *Vintage NBA*, 197; Sid Hartman, "Helping with Lakers," *Minneapolis Star Tribune*, October 29, 1989; Sid Hartman, "My Memories of Max Winter," *Minneapolis Star Tribune*, July 28, 1996; Hartman, *Sid!*, 69–70; Bernstein, *Hardwood Heroes*, 15; Thornley, *Basketball's Original Dynasty*, 9.

9. Kundla, interview, October 10, 2001; Hartman, *Sid!*, 70; Thornley, *Basketball's Original Dynasty*, 9.

10. "Kundla Named Minneapolis Pro Cage Coach," *Minneapolis Morning Tribune*, July 16, 1947; Kundla, interview, October 10, 2001.

11. Fimrite, "Big George"; Thornley, *Basketball's Original Dynasty*, 17–18; Kundla, interview, October 10, 2001; Ken Exel, from notes of telephone interview by author, November 6, 2001.

12. "Official Program: AAU Basketball Championship of America," March 1947.

13. "Overheard," *San Francisco Chronicle*, August 21, 1947.

14. Harold Olson, Chicago Basketball Club, letter to Jim Pollard, August 26, 1947; Arilee Pollard, interview; Durkee, interview; Bill Durkee, letter to author, November 3, 2001.

15. Durkee, interview.

16. Durkee, interview; Rocker, interview; "Official Basketball Magazine: Lakers."

17. Thornley, *Basketball's Original Dynasty*, 18; "Pro Cagers Sign Pollard—Report," *Oakland Post-Enquirer*, August 27, 1947.

18. "Slim Jim," *Minneapolis Morning Tribune*, September 24, 1947.

19. Arilee Pollard, interview.

20. Durkee, interview; Rocker, interview; Arilee Pollard, interview; "More Bittner Aces Offered Pro Contracts," *Oakland Post-Enquirer*, September 2, 1947; "Pollard Sees Pro Title for Minneapolis Entry," *Minneapolis Morning Tribune*, September 24, 1947.

9. THE KING OF BASKETBALL

1. "We've Got Champ," *Minneapolis Sunday Tribune*, April 18, 1948; Bernstein, *Hardwood Heroes*, 15–16; Kundla, interview, October 10, 2001; Durkee, interview; Rocker, interview; Exel, interview, November 6, 2001.

2. Stan Carlson, ed., "Laker Bits and Banter," in *Laker Basketball, World Champions* (Minneapolis: Olympic Press, 1950); "Height?

Lakers Have One 'Big' Guy," *Minneapolis Morning Tribune*, August 2, 1947; Thornley, *Basketball's Original Dynasty*, 18.

3. Arilee Pollard, interview; Bernstein, *Hardwood Heroes*, 16; Thornley, *Basketball's Original Dynasty*, 18.

4. Kundla, interview, October 10, 2001.

5. Kundla, interview, October 10, 2001.

6. Roger Meyer, "Minneapolis Lakers: 1947–48, Game-by-Game Review," undated, in the author's possession.

7. Durkee, interview; Kundla, interview, October 10, 2001; Arilee Pollard, interview; Isaacs, *Vintage* NBA, 52.

8. Triptow, *Dynasty That Never Was*, 113.

9. Mikan, *Unstoppable*, 67–79; Triptow, *Dynasty That Never Was*, 65–81; "The NBL (1937–49)," www.tomdawg.de (accessed September 25, 2001; site now discontinued); "Mikan Sued by Gears," *New York Times*, January 18, 1947; "Mikan Suit Called Test for Pros," *New York Times*, January 21, 1947; Roger Meyer, "Chicago Gears: National Basketball League, 1946–1947," undated, in the author's possession. Additional news stories on this period of Mikan's career can be found in the *Chicago Tribune*, December 18, 1946; January 5, 17, 31, 1947; December 22, 1998.

10. Mikan, *Unstoppable*, 78–81; "Saint Loop Folds," *Minneapolis Star*, November 13, 1947; Roger Meyer, "Professional Basketball League of America, 1947," undated, in the author's possession; Thornley, *Basketball's Original Dynasty*, 18; "The NBL (1937–49)"; Triptow, *Dynasty That Never Was*, 122–25.

11. Bernstein, *Hardwood Heroes*, 16–17; "Saint Loop Folds"; Mikan, *Unstoppable*, 83–85; Hartman, "Helping with Lakers"; Sid Hartman, "Game Was Different in NBA's Early Years," *Minneapolis Star Tribune*, February 13, 1994; Hartman, "My Memories of Max Winter"; Hartman, *Sid!*, 71.

12. Kundla, interview, October 10, 2001.

10. THE CRISCO KID

1. Jeanne Pollard, interview by author, tape recording, Lodi, California, November 18, 2001.

2. Exel, interview, November 6, 2001; "NBA Legends: Jim Pollard," NBA.com.

3. Kundla, interview, October 10, 2001; Durkee, interview; Meyer, interview.

4. Mikan, *Unstoppable*, 87; Kundla, interview, October 10, 2001.

5. Kundla, interviews, October 10, October 12, 2001; Exel, interview, November 6, 2001; Mikan, *Unstoppable*, 87–88; Bernstein, *Hardwood Heroes*, 17.

6. Kundla, interview, October 10, 2001.

7. Kundla, interview, October 10, 2001; Arilee Pollard, interview; Durkee, interview; Rocker, interview; Exel, interview, November 6, 2001.

8. "Pollard Back to Old Stride," *Minneapolis Star*, December 8, 1947.

9. Bernstein, *Hardwood Heroes*, 19; Durkee, interview; Exel, interview, November 6, 2001; Thornley, *Basketball's Original Dynasty*, 20.

10. Kundla, interview, October 10, 2001.

11. Mikan, *Unstoppable*, 88; Mikan, *Mr. Basketball*, 51; Rodger Nelson, *The Zollner Piston Story* (Fort Wayne IN: Allen County Public Library Foundation, 1995), 114; Kundla, interview, October 10, 2001; Carl Bennett, from notes of telephone interviews by author, January 8, February 7, 2002; Exel, interview, November 6, 2001; Carlson, *Minneapolis Lakers*.

12. Program, "The Minneapolis Star and the Minneapolis Lakers Basketball Clinic," December 27, 1947; the author was in attendance at the clinic.

13. Kundla, interview, October 10, 2001.

14. "Lakers Hot?" *Minneapolis Star*, December 16, 1947; Carlson, *Minneapolis Lakers*; Meyer, "Professional Basketball League of America."

15. Kundla, interview, October 10, 2001; Durkee, interview; Rocker, interview; Meyer, "Minneapolis Lakers, 1947–48."

11. OLSON'S TERRIBLE SWEDES

1. J. Michael Kenyon, e-mail message to author, December 3, 2001; Jon Entine, "Hoop Dream Hebrews," *Jewish World Review*, June 21, 2001, jewishworldreview.com; Peterson, *Cages*, 11–12, 64–68, 95–98, 101–7; Mike Bogen, "An Era of Beautiful Basketball," February 8, 2001, masslive.com/Hooptown.usa; Mike Bogen, "Basketball Icons Recall Color Barrier," February 15, 2001, masslive.com/Hooptown.usa.

2. George, *Elevating the Game*, 33–40; John Hareas, "Remembering the Rens," NBA.com; "Confidentially Yours," *New York Amsterdam News*, December 20, 1947; "NBA Legends: William 'Pop' Gates"; Michael Hudson, "Black Legends," October 19, 2000, BlackAthlete.com; Bijan C. Bayne, *Sky Kings: Black Pioneers of Professional Basketball* (New York: Franklin Watts, 1997), 17–21.

3. "Globetrotters Helped End Color Bar: Bernard Price Obituary," *Chicago Tribune*, February 1, 2002; Scott A. Newman, "Jazz Age Chicago: Savoy Ballroom," Chicago.urban-history.org; J. Michael Kenyon, e-mail message to author, March 23, 2002; "Hall of Famers: Abe Saperstein," hoophall.com; Menville, *Harlem Globetrotters*, 7–13; Bayne, *Sky Kings*, 22; "Harlem Globetrotters: The First Showmen"; Aaron Myers, "Harlem Globetrotters," Africana.com; Jay T. Smith, "Rewriting History: The Birth of the Globetrotters," NetworkChicago.com.

4. George, *Elevating the Game*, 48; "Globe-Trotters Bring Big Crowd," *St. Peter Herald*, December 19, 1934; "Globetrotters Remember Their Stops in Detroit," *Detroit News*, February 2, 2001; Bijan C. Bayne, "True Ambassadors," April 19, 2001, groups.yahoo.com/group/APBR; "Story of the Harlem Globetrotters"; Stew Thornley, "The Minneapolis Lakers vs. Harlem Globetrotters," stewthornley.net; "Harlem Globetrotters The First Showmen."

5. Dave Quinn, John Duxbury, Steven Brainerd, William F. Himmelman, Steve Dimitry, and Robert Bradley, "World Professional Basketball Tournament 1939–48," Association for Professional Basketball Research (APBR), APBR.org; Kenyon, e-mail message, March 23, 2002.

6. "Still Sweet: Globetrotters Continue to Provide Plenty of Good Times," cnnsi.com, February 14, 2001; "Harlem Globetrotters: 6 Decades of Magic"; "Chicago Stories"; "Harlem Globetrotters," Columbia Pictures; "Go, Man, Go"; "Globetrotters vs. Lakers at Chicago Stadium."

7. "Story of the Harlem Globetrotters."

8. Mikan, *Mr. Basketball*, 51; Mikan, *Unstoppable*, 89–91; Haynes, interview, January 18, 2002.

9. Peterson, *Cages*, 105–7; Bill Jones, from notes of telephone interviews by author, January 7, May 8, 2002; James Watkins, from notes of telephone interviews by author, April 3, June 10, 2002; "Harlem Globetrotters: The First Showmen."

10. Kundla, interview, October 10, 2001; Wally Salovich, from notes of telephone interview by author, July 10, 2002.

11. Warren Perkins, from notes of telephone interview by author, July 8, 2002.

12. Jones, interviews, January 7, May 8, 2002; Karstens, interview; Watkins, interviews, April 3, June 10, 2002; Bob Luksta, from notes of telephone interview by author, February 27, 2002; "Story of the Harlem Globetrotters"; "They Girdle the Globe," 46–47; "The Harlem Globetrotters," *Basketball Illustrated*.

13. Haynes, interview, January 18, 2002; "They Girdle the Globe," 45–47; "Globetrotters Open"; "2 Globetrotter 5s."

14. Haynes, interview, January 18, 2002; "Starting in 1927–28, Famous Quintet Has Won 2,886," *Chicago Defender*, January 3, 1948.

15. Haynes, interview, January 18, 2002; Karstens, interview; Luksta, interview, February 27, 2002.

16. "Starting in 1927"; "99-in-Row Trotters"; Watkins, interviews, April 3, June 10, 2002; Karstens, interview; Luksta, interview, February 27, 2002; King, interview; J. Michael Kenyon, e-mail message to author, August 31, 2001.

17. "Globetrotters vs. Lakers at Chicago Stadium."

18. Lawrence W. Levine, *Black Culture and Black Consciousness: African-American Folk Thought from Slavery to Freedom* (New York: Oxford University Press, 1977), 102–21, 370–75, 383–84; Boskin, *Sambo*, 103.

12. SAMBO

1. Levine, *Black Culture*, 322.

2. Entine, "Hoop Dreams Hebrew"; Entine, *Taboo*, 162.

3. Philip Deloria, "I Am of the Body: Thoughts on My Grandfather, Culture and Sports," *South Atlantic Quarterly* (spring 1996): 321–38.

4. Entine, *Taboo*, 21.

5. Boskin, *Sambo*, 10.

6. Deloria, "I Am of the Body," 321–38; Hurston, *Sanctified*, 54–55; Entine, *Taboo*, 4, 73, 121–22, 152, 174, 247; Captain, "Enter Ladies and Gentlemen"; Frazier, *The Negro in the United States*, 667, 669; Boskin, *Sambo*, 94, 167; Kane, "Black Is Best"; Shropshire, *In Black and White*, 31–35.

7. Boskin, *Sambo*, 75; Hurston, *Sanctified*, 49–51, 103–7.

8. Levine, *Black Culture*, 434–35; Boskin, *Sambo*, 97.

9. "Effects of Segregation"; Levine, *Black Culture*, 317, 321.

10. Boskin, *Sambo*, 12, 117; Bayne, "True Ambassadors."

11. Haynes, interview, January 18, 2002; Kundla, interview, October 10, 2001.

12. Mikan, *Mr. Basketball*, 51.

13. "Basketball," *Baltimore Afro-American*, January 10, February 14, 1948.

14. "Globetrotters Win 52 in Row," *Baltimore Afro-American*, January 10, 1948; "Trotters Keep Rolling Along"; "The Goose Hangs High," *Pittsburgh Courier*, January 17, 1948; "Chicagoans Put On Clever Cage Circus," *New York Amsterdam News*, March 6, 1948; "Confidentially Yours," *New York Amsterdam News*, December 27, 1947; "Globetrotter Circus"; "Starting in 1927–28"; "Harlem Globetrotters," *Pittsburgh Courier*, January 10, 1948; "In White Plains," *New York Amsterdam News*, February 27, 1948; Haynes, interview, January 18, 2002; King, interview; Watkins, interview, April 3, 2002.

13. JOHNNY AND ABE

1. "Remembering the 'Big Barn' on W. Madison and Its Big Barton Pipe Organ," www.catoe.org/barton; Scott A. Newman, "Jazz Age Chicago: Chicago Stadium," 2001, Chicago.urban-history.org; Don Hayner and Tom McNamee, *Chicago Stadium*, www.geocities.com/Colosseum; Kundla, interview, October 12, 2001; Scolari, interview; King, interview; Ron Etherton, from notes of interview by author, Belmont, California, July 2, 2002; Watkins, interview, April 3, 2002; Knorek, interview; Palmer, interview.

2. "Parades, Protests and Politics in Chicago: The 1932 Republican National Convention," www.chicagohs.org/history/politics/1932.

3. Kundla, interviews, October 10, October 12, October 30, 2001.

4. Kundla, interviews, October 10, October 12, October 30, 2001.

5. Kundla, interviews, October 10, October 12, October 30, 2001.

6. Kundla, interviews, October 10, October 12, October 30, 2001.

7. Kundla, interviews, October 10, October 12, October 30, 2001.

8. "Sportologue," *Minnesota Daily*, February 5, 1937.

9. Kundla, interviews, October 10, October 12, October 30, 2001.

10. Kundla, interview, October 10, 2001.

11. Kundla, interviews, October 10, October 12, October 30, 2001.

12. Kundla, interview, October 12, 2001.

13. Saperstein, interview, September 25, 2001; Haynes, interview, January 18, 2002; "Story of the Harlem Globetrotters"; "Hall of Famers: Abe Saperstein."

14. Haynes, interview, January 18, 2002.

15. Saperstein, interview, September 25, 2001; Paul Berman, ed., *Blacks and Jews, Alliances and Arguments* (New York: Delacorte Press, 1994), 47.

16. Saperstein, interview, September 25, 2001.

17. Saperstein, interview, September 25, 2001.

18. King, interview; Saperstein, interview, September 25, 2001.

19. "Sports Honor Roll," *New York Amsterdam News*, December 27, 1947; "Merit," *Chicago Defender*, May 15, 1948.

20. Watkins, interview, April 3, 2002; Burdette, interview.

21. Saperstein, interview, September 25, 2001.

22. George, *Elevating the Game*, 48.

23. Haynes, interview, January 18, 2002.

24. Haynes, interview, January 18, 2002; King, interview.

25. Kundla, interviews, October 10, October 12, October 30, 2001; "Mikan, Gola, Beard Lead Picks for All-time NIT Team," March 15, 1997, Nando.net (accessed September 16, 2001).

26. King, interview; Haynes, interview, January 18, 2002.

27. Haynes, interview, January 18, 2002.

14. BUCKY

1. Newman, "Jazz Age Chicago: Chicago Stadium"; "Parades, Protests, and Politics."

2. George Avakian, "Chicago Style Jazz: The Original 1927–35 Jazz Classics," Liner Notes, Columbia Records CL 632.

3. Mike Bogen, "Basketball Hall to Unveil African-American Exhibits," masslive.com/Hooptown.usa, February 1, 2001; Mike Bogen, "1st Black Pro Hoop Player's Recognition Near," masslive.com/Hooptown.usa, February 1, 2001; Bayne, *Sky Kings*, 15; Peterson, *Cages*, 131; "Black History Month: A Salute to Barzillai Lew (1743–

1821)," Groups.yahoo.com/group/APBR/message/8383; "A Family's Journey in American History," *Boston Globe*, February 23, 1999; "Pioneer Years: Paving the Way," hoophall.com; "Family Trees with Roots That Run Deep," *Washington Post*, July 18, 1998; "Bucky Lew Made Basketball History," *Haverhill Eagle-Tribune*, February 22, 2001.

4. Shropshire, *In Black and White*, 27.

5. Entine, *Taboo*, 209.

6. Donald Spivey, "End Jim Crow in Sports: The Protest at New York University, 1940–41," *Journal of Sport History* 15, no. 3 (winter 1988): 282–303.

7. Peterson, *Cages*, 124–39, 200–202; "The National Basketball League," infoplease.com (accessed September 25, 2001); "The NBL (1937–1949)"; "The National Basketball League," HickokSports.com; "The NBL: Opportunity Arrives," hoophall. com; Bennett, interview, January 8, 2002.

8. Jones, interview, January 7, 2002.

9. Nelson, *Zollner Piston Story*, 119–20; Bennett, interview, January 8, 2002; Jones, interview, January 7, 2002; Peterson, *Cages*, 130–31.

10. Watkins, interview, April 3, 2002; Peterson, *Cages*, 130–31.

11. Douglas Stark, "Paving the Way," *Basketball Digest*, February 2001, 75–77; Michael Funke, "The Chicago Studebakers: How the UAW Helped Integrate Pro Basketball and Reunite Four Players Who Made History," *Solidarity*, July 1992, 16–19; Michael Funke, from notes of telephone interview by author, February 5, 2003.

12. Jones, interview, January 7, 2002.

13. Stark, "Paving the Way," 75–77.

14. Thornley, *Basketball's Original Dynasty*, 18; Carlson, *Minneapolis Lakers*; Kundla, interview, October 12, 2001.

15. Kundla, interview, October 12, 2001.

16. Program: "Minneapolis Star and the Minneapolis Lakers Basketball Clinic."

15. POP

1. "Pop Gates: Basketball Star Who Helped Integrate Professional Game," *New York Times*, December 5, 1999; "Sports Biography: Gates, 'Pop' (William)," HickokSports.com; "NBA Legends:

William 'Pop' Gates"; Susan Rayl, "Renaissance Man," hoophall. com; "Pop Gates Earned His Grits," *New York Times*, February 19, 1989; Hareas, "Remembering the Rens"; George, *Elevating the Game*, 36, 39–40; Bayne, *Sky Kings*, 19–21; Isaacs, *Vintage* NBA, 77; Davage Minor, from notes of telephone interview by author, November 5, 1996.

2. Mikan, *Unstoppable*, 134; Kundla, interview, October 12, 2001; Exel, interview, November 6, 2001; Al Grenert, from notes of telephone interview by author, October 23, 2001; Scolari, interview; Whitey Macknowsky, from notes of telephone interview by author, October 26, 2001.

3. Chick Meehan, from notes of telephone interview by author, October 5, 2002; Ron Gersbacher, from notes of telephone interview by author, June 3, 2002; Al Kirk, letter to author, May 24, 2002.

4. Exel, interview, November 6, 2001; Grenert, interview.

5. "Players Fight as Hawks Drop Syracuse Tilt," *Rock Island Argus*, February 25, 1947; "Blackhawks Have Victory String Snapped at Seven," *Moline Daily Dispatch*, February 25, 1947; "Meehan Didn't Know Who Hit Him in Eye," *Syracuse Herald-Journal*, February 25, 1947; "Meehan Hurt in Slugfest at Armory," *Syracuse Herald-Journal*, February 25, 1947; "Nats' Hectic 53–47 Win Over Moline: Gates Attacks Meehan, Causes Tense Episode," *Syracuse Post-Standard*, February 25, 1947; Meehan, interview; Exel, interview, November 6, 2001; Grenert, interview.

6. Meehan, interview; Exel, interview, November 6, 2001; Grenert, interview.

7. "Meehan Hurt."

8. Exel, interview, November 6, 2001; "Players Fight."

9. Meehan, interview; "Meehan Didn't Know."

10. Dick Triptow, from notes of telephone interview by author, February 8, 2002.

11. "Pop Gates"; Johnny Ezersky, from notes of telephone interview by author, August 21, 2001; Scolari, interview; Macknowsky, interview.

12. Pop Gates, letter to Chick Meehan, March 11, 1947, copy of letter in the author's possession.

13. "Pop Gates."

14. Rayl, "Renaissance Man."

15. "Pop Gates"; George, *Elevating the Game*, 67; Entine, *Taboo*, 211; Macknowsky, interview; Exel, interview, November 6, 2001; Scolari, interview.

16. "Meehan Didn't Know."

17. "Collegians," *New York Amsterdam News*, February 15, 1930.

18. Karstens, interview.

19. Marques Haynes, interview by author, tape recording, Dallas, Texas, January 20, 2002.

16. MARQUES

1. Haynes, interview, January 18, 2002.

2. "Hall of Famers: Marques Haynes," hoophall.com; Menville, *Harlem Globetrotters*, 37; George, *Elevating the Game*, 53–55; "Marques Haynes," CBSsportsline.com (accessed September 25, 2001).

3. "Go, Man, Go"; "Alfred Palca and the Blacklist," *New York Times*, August 20, 1997; "Chicago Stories"; "Harlem Globetrotters: 6 Decades of Magic."

4. Thornley, "Minneapolis Lakers vs. Harlem Globetrotters"; Karstens, interview; Meyers, "Sports."

5. "Basketball Fans Will Eye Marquez [*sic*] Haynes," *Chicago Defender*, October 23, 1948.

6. Etherton, interview; Scolari, interview, October 5, 2001; Newman, "Jazz Age Chicago: Chicago Stadium"; Hayner and McNamee, *Chicago Stadium*.

7. J. E. Lighter, *Random House Historical Dictionary of American Slang*, vol. 1, *A–G* (New York: Random House, 1994), "play it cool," 474.

8. George, *Elevating the Game*, 61–63.

9. Kundla, interviews, October 12, October 30, 2001.

10. Haynes, interview, January 18, 2002; Saperstein, interview, September 25, 2001.

17. TED

1. Kundla, interviews, October 10, October 12, October 30, 2001.

2. Haynes, interview, January 18, 2002.

3. Walter E. Meanwell, *The Science of Basketball for Men* (Madison WI: Democrat Printing Company, 1924), 94–111; John Christgau, *The Origins of the Jump Shot: Eight Men Who Shook the World*

of Basketball (Lincoln: University of Nebraska Press, 1999), 12–15; Meyer, interview.

4. Rocker, interview; Durkee, interview.

5. Program: "Minneapolis Star and the Minneapolis Lakers Clinic."

6. Haynes, interview, January 18, 2002; Karstens, interview; Menville, *Harlem Globetrotters*, 21–22; "Story of the Harlem Globetrotters"; "4000 Fans Cheer Globetrotters," *New York Amsterdam News*, March 6, 1948.

18. THE WEE ICE MON

1. "Sports Biographies: Hogan," HickokSports.com.

2. Box scores of the game from the *Minneapolis Morning Tribune*, *Minneapolis Star*, and *Chicago Herald-American* list a technical foul on George Mikan. John Kundla, George Mikan, and Marques Haynes have no recollection of the technical. If a free throw was awarded to the Globetrotters, it was missed.

3. Haynes, interview, January 18, 2002.

4. Saperstein, interview, September 25, 2001.

5. "Story of the Harlem Globetrotters"; Charles Geckley, photo, *Daily Sun and Times*, February 20, 1948.

19. DAVID AND GOLIATH

1. Haynes, interview, January 18, 2002.

2. Saperstein, interview, September 25, 2001.

3. "Eastern Pro League Retains Tan Cagers," *Baltimore Afro-American*, February 14, 1948.

4. "Eastern Pro League Retains Tan Cagers," *Baltimore Afro-American*, February 14, 1948.

5. "They Practice Together and Nobody Utters Howl," *Baltimore Afro-American*, February 14, 1948.

6. Meyer, interview; Kundla, interviews, October 10, October 12, October 30, 2001; Lazenby, *Lakers*, 85; Mikan, *Unstoppable*, 32–33, 227.

20. THE FATHER, THE SON, THE HOLY GHOST

1. "16,000 to See Pro Cage Bill."

2. Watkins, interview, April 3, 2002; Luksta, interviews, February 27, March 19, 2002.

3. Watkins, interview, April 3, 2002; Haynes, interview, January 20, 2002.

4. "Mikan Cooks Tatum's Goose," *Daily Sun and Times*, February 20, 1948.

5. "Globetrotters vs. Lakers at Chicago Stadium."

6. Haynes, interview, January 18, 2002.

7. Haynes, interview, January 18, 2002.

8. Kundla, interview, October 12, 2001.

9. Haynes, interview, January 18, 2002; "Last Second Win by Globetrotters," *Chicago Defender*, February 28, 1948; Young, "Through the Years."

21. THE SHOT

1. Haynes, interview, January 18, 2002; Kundla, interviews, October 10, October 12, 2001; Watkins, interview, April 3, 2002; Saperstein, interview, September 25, 2001; Meyer, interview; "Last Second Win"; Allen Camelli, *Basketball: Great Teams, Great Men, Great Moments* (New York: Bantam Pathfinder, 1972), 31–32; Mikan, *Unstoppable*, 90–91.

2. Haynes, interview, January 18, 2002.

3. Kundla, interviews, October 10, October 12, 2001.

4. Haynes, interview, January 18, 2002.

5. Haynes, interview, January 18, 2002; "Diagram of Robinson's Shot," Marques Haynes, January 18, 2002, in the author's possession; Camelli, *Basketball*, 31–32.

6. "Pollard Cleanest Player in NBA," from 1953–54 Lakers program, courtesy of Arilee Pollard.

7. Meyer, interview.

8. Haynes, interview, January 18, 2002.

9. Young, "Through the Years."

22. SWEETWATER

1. Young, "Through the Years."

2. Watkins, interview, April 3, 2002; Saperstein, interview, September 25, 2001; Meyer, interview; Kundla, interview, October 12, 2001; Haynes, interview, January 18, 2002; King, interview; "Lakers Seek Return Tilt," *Minneapolis Star*, February 20, 1948; "Last Second Win"; "Winning Basket in Air."

3. Kundla, interview, October 12, 2001; "Lakers Seek Return Tilt."

4. "Story of the Harlem Globetrotters"; "Last Second Win."

5. Haynes, interview, January 18, 2002; "Basketball Fans."

6. "Mikan Cooks Tatum's Goose."

7. "Lakers Seek Return Tilt"; "Trotters Spill Lakers"; Menville, *Harlem Globetrotters*, 42–43.

8. "Globetrotter Circus"; Haynes, interview, January 18, 2002.

9. "Globetrotters Return Here Sunday," *Chicago Defender*, March 20, 1948.

10. "Globetrotters Beat Celtics before 16,416," *Chicago Defender*, March 27, 1948.

11. "Harlem Globetrotters Open Season," *Chicago Defender*, November 6, 1948; "Trotters Toy with Toledo," *Chicago Defender*, November 13, 1948; "Story of the Harlem Globetrotters."

12. "We've Got Champ."

13. Meyer, "Minneapolis Lakers 1947–48."

14. Mikan, *Mr. Basketball*, 52.

15. "Rens Blow Free Throws and National Pro Cage Title," *Chicago Defender*, April 17, 1948.

16. Bogen, "Basketball Icons"; "Chicago Stories"; Hartman, "My Memories of Max Winter"; Peterson, *Cages*, 170–71; Kenyon, e-mail messages, August 30, August 31, 2001; Nelson, *Zollner Piston Story*, 173; George, *Elevating the Game*, 96; Bennett, interview, January 8, 2002.

17. "Confidentially Yours," *New York Amsterdam News*, March 6, 1948; Hareas, "Remembering the Rens."

18. "Another Victory"; "As Thousands Cheer," *Chicago Defender*, May 8, 1948.

19. George, *Elevating the Game*, 67.

20. "Knickerbockers Seeking Negro," *Chicago Defender*, December 19, 1948.

21. "NBA Legends: William 'Pop' Gates"; Stark, "Paving the Way," 77.

22. Mikan, *Mr. Basketball*, 55.

23. Haynes, interview, January 18, 2002; Kundla, interview, October 12, 2001; John Duxbury, Dave Quinn, Jim Rasco, Robt. Bradley, "Results of Harlem Globetrotters–Minneapolis Lakers Games," August 7, 2001, APBR.org.

24. "Globetrotters vs. Lakers at Chicago Stadium"; Kundla, interview, October 12, 2001; Haynes, interview, January 18, 2002.

25. Bogen, "Basketball Icons"; "Chicago Stories"; Peterson, *Cages*, 170–71; Kenyon, e-mail messages, August 30, August 31, 2001; Nelson, *Zollner Piston Story*, 173–74; Bennett, interview, January 8, 2002.

26. Bennett, interview, January 8, 2002; Nelson, *Zollner Piston Story*, 161; George, *Elevating the Game*, 95–102.

27. Bennett, interview, January 8, 2002. Additional details on the integration of the NBA can found in Ron Thomas, *They Cleared the Lane: The NBA's Black Pioneers* (Lincoln: University of Nebraska Press, 2002); Bayne: *Sky Kings*.

28. Kundla, interview, October 12, 2001; Duxbury et al., "Results."

29. Kundla, interview, October 12, 2001.

30. Kundla, interview, October 12, 2001; Mikan, *Unstoppable*, 121; Duxbury et al., "Results."

23. SHAQ

1. Bijan C. Bayne, "More Info on Pioneer Harry 'Bucky' Lew," groups.yahoo.com/group/APBR, February 11, 2000; "Bucky Lew"; Newman, "Jazz Age Chicago: Savoy Ballroom," Chicago.urbanhistory.org.

2. Kundla, interview, October 12, 2001; Ken Exel, from notes of telephone interview by author, March 1, 2002; Saperstein, interview, September 25, 2001; Hartman, "My Memories of Max Winter."

3. Triptow, *Dynasty That Never Was*, 162.

4. "To Honor 'Honest' Abe Saperstein at Stadium, March 21," *Chicago Defender*, March 20, 1948.

5. Fay Saperstein, interview by author, tape recording, San Mateo, California, May 15, 2002; "Hall of Famers: Abe Saperstein"; "Chicago Stories."

6. Kris Hjelmeland, "A Baseball Stadium Full of Memories," May 3, 2000, Jordanbrewers.com.

7. Photograph courtesy of Arilee Pollard.

8. Arilee Pollard, interview; Carlson, *Minneapolis Lakers*.

9. "Kundla Lets Mikan and Co. Do Talking," *New York Post*, April 23, 1952.

10. "Lakers Coach John Kundla Called 'Brains' Behind Mikan's Success in Pro Basketball," *Philadelphia Bulletin*, November 5, 1952; "Kundla Is Coach Nobody Knows," *Sporting News*, January 30, 1952.

11. "John Kundla," *Minneapolis Star*, September 16, 1953.

12. "Johnny Kundla, 35, Has Won 4 Titles in 5 Years with Lakers," *Honolulu Star-Bulletin*, April 30, 1952; "The Powerhouse," *New York Sunday News*, February 11, 1951.

13. Kundla, interview, October 12, 2001.

14. "Hall of Famers: John Kundla," hoophall.com.

15. Kundla, interview, October 12, 2001.

16. Mikan, *Mr. Basketball*, 51.

17. Meyer, interview.

18. Bert Randolph Sugar, *The 100 Greatest Athletes of All Time* (New York: Carol Publishing Group, 1995).

19. Lakers letterhead courtesy of Whitey Skoog.

20. "NBA Legends: George Mikan," NBA.com.

21. "NBA Legends Upstage All-Stars," February 9, 1997, Canoe.com.

22. Kundla, interview, October 12, 2001; "Lakers Neglect Roots," *Los Angeles Times*, October 29, 2001.

23. The six championships were: NBL 1947–48; BAA 1948–49; NBA 1949–50, 1951–52, 1952–53, 1953–54.

24. "Lakers Honor Heritage," *Minneapolis Star Tribune*, April 12, 2002; "A Banner Night for All the Lakers," *Los Angeles Times*, April 12, 2002.

24. RIGO

1. "Goose Tatum Dies," United Press International, January 18, 1967; Dick Burdette, letter to author, March 11, 2002; Haynes, interview, January 20, 2002; Burdette, interview.

2. Burdette, interview.

3. Haynes, interview, January 18, 2002; Burdette, interview; Watkins, interview, April 3, 2002; Luksta, interviews, February 27, March 19, 2002.

4. George, *Elevating the Game*, 48–50.

5. "Harlem Globetrotters Legends: Reece 'Goose' Tatum."

6. Haynes, interviews, January 18, January 20, 2002; "Story of the Harlem Globetrotters."

7. "Basketball Fans."

8. Official Program, "21st Annual *Chicago Daily News* Relays," March 16, 1957.

9. Meyer, interview; Haynes, interview, January 18, 2002.

10. "Globetrotters Go for Legitimacy," November 16, 2000, cnnsi.com; Haynes, interview, January 18, 2002.

11. Haynes, interview, January 18, 2002; Marques Haynes, from notes of telephone interview by author, February 22, 2002.

12. Haynes, interview, January 18, 2002.

13. Duxbury, et al., "Results"; Haynes, interview, January 18, 2002; "Ermer Robinson Succumbs."

14. Watkins, interviews, April 13, June 10, 2002.

15. Robt. Bradley, with Steve Dimitry, Roger Meyer, and Dick Pfander, "History of the American Basketball League," apbr.org; "Ermer Robinson Succumbs."

16. "Ermer Robinson Succumbs."

17. Rigo Rodriguez, interviews by author, tape recordings, San Diego, California, June 25, August 5, 2002; Rigo Rodriguez, from notes of telephone interview by author, July 9, 2002.

18. Fay Young, "Trotters on Parade," *Chicago Defender*, November 2, 1957; "Fay's Defender Pauses for Him," *Chicago Defender*, November 2, 1957; "Frank 'Fay' Young," *Chicago Defender*, November 9, 1957.

19. Young, "Trotters on Parade."

20. "Frank 'Fay' Young."

21. Haynes, interview, January 18, 2002.

22. Young, "Through the Years."

23. "No Laughing Matter," 51–52.

24. "Negro Patient Ban Blasted at Inquest," *Chicago Defender*, February 21, 1948; "Dead Aim," *Time*, March 1, 1948, 51.

25. "Harlem Globetrotters," Columbia Pictures; "Go, Man, Go"; "Alfred Palca and the Blacklist."

26. Kane, "Black Is Best"; Harry Edwards, "The Myth of the Racially Superior Athlete," *Intellectual Digest* 2 (March 1972): 58; Malik, "Why Black Will Beat White"; Richard Lapchick, "Pseudo-Scientific Prattle about Athletics," *New York Times*, April 29, 1989.

27. Irwin Tang, "Shaq's Ethnic Slurs Deeply Offend One Yao Fan," AsianWeek.com, January 3–9, 2003.

28. *The American People's Encyclopedia: Anu to Bayonne Decree* (New York: Grolier, 1964), 514–15.

29. *Shane*, Paramount Pictures, 1953.

30. "Hall of Famers: Marques Haynes."

31. Haynes, interview, January 20, 2002.

Sources and Acknowledgments

Six newspapers were critical sources for the play-by-play details upon which my reconstruction of the game of February 1948 is based: the *Minneapolis Star, Minneapolis Morning Tribune, Chicago Tribune,* Chicago *Daily Sun and Times, Chicago Herald-American,* and *Chicago Defender.* Numerous photos from the game appeared in those papers as well as in *Time* magazine and in "The Story of the Harlem Globetrotters," their program for the 1948–49 season. I drew upon those pictures as sources for my action vignettes. I am also grateful for the personal recollections of bits and pieces of the game given to me by Johnny Kundla, Marques Haynes, Ray Meyer, James "Nugie" Watkins, Larry Hawkins, Fay Saperstein, Bud Palmer, and Lee Knorek.

There is no surviving radio account or film footage of the game. But the sources above, supplemented by game stats provided by the Association for Professional Basketball Research (APBR), were instrumental in helping me to determine, by a process of deduction and elimination, who scored what and when. My re-creations of game action are drawn from my own observations and recollections of the two teams and their players, refreshed by the motion picture sources I cite in my notes. The news footage provided to me by Peter Bregman of Fox Movietone News was especially helpful. Although the Movietone film footage is of the second Lakers-Globetrotters game, the principal players are on the same stage, performing many of the same balletic moves of the first drama.

Only researchers more dedicated and gifted than I am could have dug out some of the remote basketball history I relied upon, and I am grateful to Robert Bradley, John Grasso, Al Kirk, Bob Kuska, Roger Meyer, Bijan C. Bayne, John Duxbury, Dave Quinn, Jim Rasco, Steve Brainerd, William Himmelman, Steve Dimitry, and especially J. Michael Kenyon and William Hoover—all of them members of the APBR—for providing me with background on specific players and the history of professional basketball and its various early leagues.

Johnny Kundla is the mother lode for information and recollections of the Minneapolis Lakers, and especially their first season in Minneapolis. Others who helped were: Ken Exel, Bill Durkee, Jack Rocker, Bob Polk, Alan Lubke, and Wally Salovich. Arilee Pollard's home in Lodi, California, is an archivist's dream, filled with mementos and treasures of her husband's brilliant pro career as well as NBL, BAA, and NBA history. I am grateful to Arilee and her daughter, Jeanne, for helping me sort through her personal archives for relevant information.

I still have the notes I took one night over forty years ago in Arcata and Chico, California, while listening to my roommate and San Francisco State teammate Jim Brown talk about growing up on Chicago's South Side. I am as grateful today as I was then for his dramatic stories.

Govoner Vaughn of the present-day Harlem Globetrotters organization passed along several documents important to my reconstruction of the game and the Globetrotters team of 1947–48. James "Nugie" Watkins, Bob Karstens, and Bob Luksta were generous with their recollections of travel with the Globetrotters, and the journalist Dick Burdette shared his own research into the Globetrotters organization and players of a later era. Bill Jones and Fay Saperstein also gave me important anecdotes and memories.

I regret that I never enjoyed firsthand the excitement of a political gathering or an athletic contest in Chicago Stadium. I hope that my story of the 1948 game doesn't betray that hole in my life. *Chicago Stadium*, by Don Haynes and Tom McNamee, helped me imagine the mayhem and excitement of being in the Madhouse on Madison. Former Purdue track star Ron Etherton gave me a personal account of the stadium's unusual acoustics and the shattering level of noise.

One of the historical losses in the media's tendency to depict the NBA as the cradle of professional basketball is that the two older leagues out of which the NBA grew—the NBL and the BAA—are often ignored. Former players Dick Triptow, Whitey Macknowsky, Freddie Scolari, Tom King, Al Grenert, Johnny Ezersky, Warren Perkins, Bud Palmer, Lee Knorek, and George Nelmark helped me relive pieces of that history. Carl Bennett gave me extensive recollections of his days with the Fort Wayne Zollner Pistons and eventually the BAA and the NBA.

Rigo Rodriguez, George Capatanos, Ed San Clemente, and William Tsunoda told me stories of San Diego High and Ermer Robinson. Rigo and William were kind enough to take an afternoon off to give me a guided tour of Garlic Center.

I am grateful to Red Bettendorf for his willingness to read portions of the manuscript with his splendid critical eye.

Others who helped with leads and important bits and pieces were: Seymour Smith, Phil Sokody, Bill Jones, "Jumpin'" John Burton, Gene "Lefty" Rock, Ron Berridge, Judy Zugelder, Les McCreery, Bill "Tosh" Tosheff, Todd Caso, Ron Gersbacher, the Rock Island Public Library, the Moline Public Library, the Allen County Library, and Mary Rogers of the Rock Island Historical Society.

Finally, in the fall of 1947 I met a young black World War II veteran named Carl Fraction, who my father was counseling at the Minneapolis Veterans Administration. We became brief friends during a pheasant-hunting expedition to our family farm in southern Minnesota. As we walked the corn rows, it was Carl who set me straight on how good the Globetrotters were. Wherever you are, Carl, thanks.